I0605808

Escape, Survive – or Die

By the same author and in print with Pen & Sword Books:

With the East Surreys in Tunisia, Sicily and Italy 1942–1945: Fighting for Every River and Mountain (2012)

The Decisive Campaigns of the Desert Air Force 1942–1945 (2014)

Air Battle for Burma: Allied Pilots' Fight for Supremacy (2016)

Airmen's Incredible Escapes: Accounts of Survival in the Second World War (2020)

Escape, Survive – or Die

Inspiring Stories of Survival During WWII

Bryn Evans

Pen & Sword
MILITARY

First published in Great Britain in 2025 by
Pen & Sword Military
An imprint of Pen & Sword Books Limited
Yorkshire – Philadelphia

ISBN 978 1 03610 088 9

A CIP catalogue record for this book is
available from the British Library.

Typeset by Mac Style
Printed in the UK by CPI Group (UK) Ltd, Croydon, CR0 4YY.

The Publisher's authorised representative in the EU for product
safety is Authorised Rep Compliance Ltd., Ground Floor,
71 Lower Baggot Street, Dublin D02 P593, Ireland.
www.arccompliance.com

For a complete list of Pen & Sword titles please contact

PEN & SWORD BOOKS LIMITED
47 Church Street, Barnsley, South Yorkshire, S70 2AS, England
E-mail: enquiries@pen-and-sword.co.uk
Website: www.pen-and-sword.co.uk
or
PEN AND SWORD BOOKS
1950 Lawrence Road, Havertown, PA 19083, USA
E-mail: uspen-and-sword@casematepublishers.com
Website: www.penandswordbooks.com

For Jean,

as always my muse without whose love and inspiration
this book and all my writing would not have been possible.

'I was…the kid across the street,
The medical student at graduation. The mechanic in the corner garage…
The gardener who cut your lawn,
The clerk who sent your phone bill.

I was an Army private…a Naval commander,
an Air Force bombardier.
No man knows me…no name marks my tomb,
for I am every serviceman,
I am the unknown soldier.'

War Memorial at Bargara, Queensland, Australia.

Contents

Acknowledgements

By 2021 the pandemic was affecting nearly everyone in some way, if not physically then mentally to some degree. There seemed to be no end in sight to constraints and lockdowns. In Australia, leaving the country required formal government approval which was granted only for essential work or compassionate grounds. We felt marooned. With my wife Jean's exhortation, I duly submitted an application to the Australian Government, substantiated by an invitation from my publishing manager at Pen & Sword, Brigadier Henry Wilson, to meet with him in London to discuss my next proposed book, *Escape, Survive – or Die.* While Jean's application to travel to the UK to visit elderly relatives on compassionate grounds was rejected, surprisingly I received approval to travel.

So *Escape, Survive – or Die* was conceived. In essence, this book is dedicated to the men and women in this collection of stories, who endured extraordinary struggles to survive. Throughout the book I have tried to acknowledge all sources and contributors, on the shoulders of whom this collection of stories rests. It is their book and I must make special mention and appreciation to some of the most prominent.

The amazing story of Bill and Augusta Hersey in their escape and survival in the chaotic and bloody evacuation at Dunkirk owes everything to their eyewitness accounts and to two most accomplished historians, David Scott Daniell in *The History of the East Surrey Regiment* – Volume IV, and Richard Collier in *The Sands of Dunkirk.* Bill and Augusta had a love and bond which were unbreakable.

For the Bomber Command raids on Berlin, Nuremberg and Stuttgart in Chapters 2 and 3, I am indebted to the accounts of various aircrew, notably Flying Officer Albert Hollings and Flight Sergeant Keith Campbell, backed by the work of the doyen of Bomber Command historians, Martin Middlebrook.

Lieutenant Douglas Davidson was one of those men who was never going to accept being a prisoner of war (PoW). His numerous escapes, defying the risk of execution when caught, and which were ultimately unstoppable, were provided by his son Ian Davidson.

The intensity of the nerve-racking, knife-edge life of a bomber pilot is brought into stark illumination by the diary and memoir writing of Squadron Leader

Bill McRae. For a number of years Bill was a delightful friend and a mentor to me for my writing.

The sea-drenched accounts of the cat-and-mouse searches and destruction of U-boats are drawn from two men who were there and survived: Peter Craig, a gunner on HMS *Woodcock*, and Alan Burn, the Gunnery Officer on HMS *Starling* in the Battle of the Atlantic.

In one of the stories of warfare in the freezing temperatures and seas of the Arctic Circle, Lesley Sommerville sent me the account of her husband, Flying Officer Robert Sommerville, who was one of six survivors of what is thought to be the most northerly air-sea rescue of ditched airmen in the Arctic Ocean.

For a combatant's account of the Malaya Campaign I am indebted to Major Bill Gingell for his lucid summary and the assistance of Alan Mornement, the Surrey History Centre, David Scott Daniell's *The History of the East Surrey Regiment* – Volume IV and the mysterious letter bequeathed to my wife Jean by her father Harry Skilton, a veteran of the East Surreys.

In 'Escape from Corregidor' the eyewitness accounts of the miraculous escapes from the Japanese invasion of the Philippines of General MacArthur, his closest staff and Lieutenant John Chamberlin and his colleagues in the US code-breaking team are drawn from many sources but especially from two: records at The General MacArthur Museum in Brisbane, Australia and Diane Capewell, the daughter of John Chamberlin.

At Milne Bay in New Guinea in August 1942, Australian troops inflicted the first land defeat on the Imperial Japanese Army. Allan Gardner was one of those soldiers and thank you to his daughter Rhyll Hansen who provided his front-line soldier's account of the battle's mayhem; also to Ken Broadhead for the official report of Major General Clowes.

The survival stories in the fall of Singapore and subsequent ordeals in Japanese PoW camps, of troops and civilians as slave labour came from those who were there and found a way to be still alive in September 1945. I must record a sincere thank you to Debra Brittingham and Carol Payne for the most poignant story of their parents' survival, and to David Clemens, Ivan Sebastian and David Keeling for their eyewitness material.

As with all my books, I have been blessed with the support of my publishing manager, Brigadier Henry Wilson, the staff at Pen and Sword Books, and my editor Richard Doherty, whose encyclopedic knowledge of the Second World War is always invaluable.

For my own part, I could not have done the hard yards, the daily research and writing to bring this book to fruition, without the love, support and encouragement of my wife Jean, with her resilience and love of life.

It is eighty years since Germany's surrender in May, and Japan's in August 1945, brought an end to the Second World War. This book and, in particular, the final chapter – 'Liberation – and the ultimate triumph' – acknowledges and salutes the spirit, endurance and sacrifice of men and women of the 'Greatest Generation' in overcoming tyranny and defending freedom.

Bryn Evans
December 2024

Foreword

The Struggle to Survive

The inspiration and essence of this book came from a combination of the impacts of the Covid pandemic and images from the Russian invasion of Ukraine, subsequently reinforced by the war in Gaza. During the constraints of the pandemic, there were periods of being confined to quarantine at home, only allowed out for essential work or shopping for groceries, banned from travel, local or international, living with shortages of essential foods and other items, and the uncertainty of how long it could last, or whether one would survive. It led me to think of how millions of civilians in the Second World War suffered far worse conditions for far longer, and whose lives were cut short in much greater numbers.

During the Second World War countless millions of men and women, both in the armed forces and civilian life, found themselves in life-or-death situations with the odds stacked against them. Inevitably, in the vast majority of cases their experiences and the outcomes will never come to light but when they do we can only feel inspired. There are probably millions of untold stories of remarkable survival, and in every case the experience is unique to the individual. Perhaps in nearly every case the circumstances and adversity were unexpected. The eyewitness personal accounts in this book are just a few of so many ordinary men and women in extraordinary struggles to survive.

* * *

From September 1939 the so-called 'phoney war' in Europe stretched into the early months of 1940 before coming to an abrupt end. In late May 1940 Bill Hersey was an infantry soldier in the British Expeditionary Force (BEF) in France when the surprise invasion by the Germans forced the BEF into retreat. Yet, in the eight months that Hersey had been deployed in France and Belgium with the 1st Battalion East Surrey Regiment, he had found time for a whirlwind romance with a French girl, Augusta, and in April they had married. Now not only must Hersey fight with his Surrey comrades to find a way back to Britain, could he also find a way for his new bride to escape with him?

Hersey pushed himself in front of his company commander, 'Sir, is there anything you can do for my wife?' Without any hesitation, Hersey was told to bring his wife with him in the immediate withdrawal. Within minutes he sped away on his bicycle to find Augusta. Over rain-slicked cobble roads, Hersey was oblivious to the risk of falling off. He would not join the retreat without Augusta. Once he was on the rue Clinquet he soon reached the café where Augusta worked and lived with her family. It was a little before midnight and it was all closed up. He knocked on the door again and again violently. There was no time; the battalion would be leaving without them.

* * *

By late 1943 the Allies' Arctic convoys, carrying military and other supplies through the Barents Sea to Murmansk in Russia, were proving crucial for the Soviet Union to counter and turn back the German invasion of their country. Losing merchant ships in the convoys to U-boats was a constant risk but there was a more lethal threat. Lurking in the Norwegian fjords were the Kriegsmarine's modern and powerful battleships, *Tirpitz* and *Scharnhorst*.

In December 1943 *Tirpitz* and *Scharnhorst* lay at harbour, protected by torpedo nets in the Altafjord close to North Cape. However, *Tirpitz* had been under major repairs for several months after being attacked by British midget submarines and was not yet seaworthy. *Scharnhorst* waited for orders in the Langfjord, another arm of the Altenfjord.

Unbeknown to the Kriegsmarine, Norwegian spies were monitoring the German ships in the Altafjord and sending reports by radio to Allied Intelligence.

In the town of Alta, two civilian employees of the local council, Karl Rasmussen, the paymaster, and Torstein Räby, a roads office employee, were also agents spying for Britain. There were two more agents in the branch fjords, Harry Petterson in Käfjord, and Jen P. Digre in Langfjord. On Christmas Day 1943 at 19.00 hours, Digre called Pettersen who then called Rasmussen with the coded message, 'Grandmother has left on her Christmas holiday'. Räby immediately telegraphed British Intelligence.

Scharnhorst and its five destroyers had sailed for the open sea. Could the Royal Navy intercept *Scharnhorst*, and prevent it decimating the latest convoy on its way to Murmansk? Would the Norwegian spies be detected by the Gestapo and pay the ultimate price?

* * *

Like many who enlisted in the Royal Navy in the Second World War, Peter Craig had no idea what he was getting into. Craig became a gunner on HMS *Woodcock*, in the Royal Navy's long war in the Battle of the Atlantic against Germany's

U-boats. A Scot, he was born on 4 November 1922 in Uddingston, Lanarkshire, near Glasgow.

Craig first tried to enlist in the Royal Navy at age eighteen, then again at nineteen, but was rejected on both occasions because he was employed in construction, a reserved occupation. He was influenced by his elder brother,who was in the Royal Navy. Finally, at age twenty, Craig was successful and, after training, was posted in October 1943 to HMS *Woodcock,* an anti-submarine sloop deployed in the Royal Navy's 2nd Support Group, known as the 'Johnnie Walker Group', hunting U-boats in the Atlantic. Craig thought it was just the right thing to do. 'It was just the fashion when the war started. All the young fellows thought they'd be brave.'

On his first operational voyage and engagement with German U-boats, Peter Craig on HMS *Woodcock* realised that the North Atlantic and its ferocious weather were as dangerous as the enemy below the waves.

I had just turned twenty-one and thought it was the end of me. The seas pounded us so hard they forced our forward guns into their full elevation. They were jammed and unusable. To make it worse our ammunition lockers, although made of steel and welded to the deck, were torn loose by wave after wave, and washed overboard. We were at the mercy of the sea and the enemy.

* * *

Until recently Diane Capewell never knew her father. Only a chance discovery by her daughter's friend brought to light that he was an American, John Chamberlin. He, too, had never known his father, and his mother died when he was only eight. At age sixteen John Chamberlin joined the US Navy.

In early 1942, as the Japanese invasion surged across the Philippines archipelago, at the entrance to Manila Bay the US Navy's submarine USS *Seadragon* cast off its moorings and slipped away from the pier on the island of Corregidor. Into the night the USS *Seadragon* dived quickly into the darkened sea. Despite being dangerously overloaded with evacuating passengers, including many US Naval staff in flight from the Japanese, *Seadragon* was forced to dive to an extreme depth to evade attack from Japanese depth charges and enemy aircraft.

On board was US Navy Lieutenant John V.E. Chamberlin, a pivotal member of the US codebreaking unit. It was critical, and of the highest strategic importance, that Chamberlin and his colleagues escape from the Philippines to re-establish their team elsewhere. Their work to break the Japanese diplomatic cypher (PURPLE) would enable the reading of Japanese military planning and associated force deployments. Such intelligence would be crucial for the US and its Allies to resist and then turn back the Japanese onslaught.

* * *

In February 1942, after a lightning advance north to south down the Malay peninsula, the Japanese Army surged across the causeway into Singapore and forced the British commander and the colonial government to surrender. In the ensuing chaos and devastation of the Japanese attack, a British gunner, Stan Durston, and his local Singaporean wife were taken prisoner and separated.

Besides the many casualties suffered by British and Allied forces, the Japanese executed thousands of Singapore civilians, especially any suspected of having worked for, or been associated with the British authorities.

Durston was imprisoned in the Changi PoW camp, and his wife of only a few months was incarcerated in a women's prison at Sime Road. Without any contact with each other, or knowledge of each other's condition or even survival, could they both survive years of the most brutal imprisonment?

* * *

The above are just a few extracts of this book's diverse eyewitness stories. They cover individuals fighting in jungles, deserts, on and below the seas, in mountains, valleys and plains, prison camps, in battles in the sky, or as fugitives hunted in enemy territory. In almost every corner of the world, in conditions of extreme adversity, our forebears, military and civilian, confronted an unavoidable choice – escape, survive or die.

These stories show us the resilience and stoicism that we need to face the ultimate challenge. The most powerful force of democratic countries is the determination and self-sacrifice of ordinary individuals to endure and fight for their families, their country and freedom.

Survivors' personal accounts in *Escape, Survive – or Die* have the power to inspire and sustain us in the never-ending struggle for liberty just as the Ukrainian people resisting the Russian invasion are doing so gallantly today.

Prologue

A Secret Voyage, a Gamble for the Survival of the Free World

On Monday 4 August 1941 the Royal Navy's battleship HMS *Prince of Wales*, with an escort of three destroyers, set sail from Scapa Flow in the Orkney Islands to cross the North Atlantic. During the night, the four warships ran into a horrendous storm, in which *Prince of Wales*,

> was shaking and shuddering, green mountains went hissing past the steel plates outside ... I saw that we were zigzagging all the time. Then I noticed that our escort had vanished. Winston Churchill was alone on the Atlantic![1]

Britain's prime minister was undertaking possibly the most dangerous, certainly the most significant, gamble of the war to date. His demise would leave Britain bereft and rudderless.

* * *

On Sunday 3 August 1941, two very successful authors of that time, H.V. Morton and Howard Spring, had boarded an overnight sleeper train leaving London for the north of Scotland. They had been 'commandeered' by the government to go on a journey and report on a highly secret assignment, of which they had been told nothing. The next morning they alighted from the train in the mist and rain in Thurso. Situated on the north coast of the Scottish County of Caithness, Thurso is the most northern town of Britain's mainland.[2]

For nearly two years, Britain had been alone in Europe fighting a war with Germany. Its vital shipping supply lines with the British Empire and Commonwealth countries were in grave danger of being severed by German U-boats. It can be argued that the truly global nature of the Second World War began not with Germany's invasion of Poland in September 1939, but with this secret journey in August 1941.

Some historians with hindsight have argued that there was in effect a continuation of the First World War into the Second. Others view the full Second World War as beginning in December 1941 when Japan attacked the

USA at Pearl Harbor. In August 1941, an event took place which would mean that Hitler's occupation of Europe, and his invasion of Russia, would lead to a full world war. Two leaders met, and two authors wrote of a secret voyage and a meeting, which would have profound consequences for the world. The values and principles discussed and agreed in those meetings would lay the foundations for the fight for liberty and the prosperity and freedoms which so many of us enjoy to this day.

Only as the train journey was underway, speeding north towards Leicester, were the two authors, Morton and Spring, informed of the secret assignment. Prime Minister Winston Churchill was on the train with his military Chiefs of Staff, and the two authors would accompany the prime minister's party when, in the north of Scotland, they boarded Britain's newest battleship, HMS *Prince of Wales*. They would then risk attack by U-boats to sail across the North Atlantic to Newfoundland, Canada where, in Placentia Bay, they would meet with the President of the United States, Franklin D. Roosevelt, and his Chiefs of Staff. Because of the threat of being torpedoed by U-boats, or even attack by long-range Luftwaffe patrol aircraft, the highest level of secrecy had been imposed about the voyage and the meeting of the two leaders of the free world.

Prince of Wales had previously fought in both the Battle of the River Plate, in which the German battleship *Graf Spee* had been scuttled, and in the pursuit and sinking of the German battleship *Bismarck*. In the battles the ship had sustained damage that required a refit. Morton's cabin was disfigured by a bump in the floor, the result of a shell from *Bismarck*.

After leaving the train at Thurso, Churchill and his entourage, accompanied by Morton and Spring, transferred to the destroyer HMS *Oribi* which quickly carried the party into Scapa Flow, where they boarded the battle-scarred *Prince of Wales*. Escorted by three destroyers, HMSs *Harvester*, *Havelock* and *Hesperus*, the battleship soon got underway, carving through the waves at over 30 knots, as if straining on a leash to cross the Atlantic.[3]

During a heavy storm on the first night at sea, *Prince of Wales* lost contact with the three escorting destroyers which were unable to match the battleship's speed, even though it was reduced in the heavy seas. In the map room of *Prince of Wales*, where every known U-boat, warship, merchant ship and aircraft was tracked with its last known positions, nerves were heightened. Lookouts scanned the sea for a protruding periscope.

In the early hours of Tuesday, after separating from the destroyers, a U-boat was detected directly ahead of *Prince of Wales*. The Prime Minister of the United Kingdom was aboard a lone battleship, unprotected by any other warship or aircraft, heading straight towards the deadly torpedo tubes of a U-boat. Had there been a leak of this secret voyage to German intelligence?

Prince of Wales immediately altered course to avoid the threat. Despite the stormy seas, the battleship increased its speed to more than 18 knots and detoured away from the lurking danger, far faster than a U-boat could match. After a few hours, *Prince of Wales* resumed its proper course for Newfoundland. However, the threat of an undetected U-boat lay at the back of everyone's mind.[4]

After more than two days at sea, the morning of Wednesday 6 August dawned with a thick white fog. It was cold but calm and, even though visibility was down to a little more than the ship's length, *Prince of Wales* was maintaining full speed. The conditions were near perfect for any U-boat lying in wait, so the battleship kept on an zig-zag course. Then, at 11.30 a.m. nerves were soothed when three Canadian destroyers' signal lamps were seen through the fog. At a pre-arranged meeting point, they took up escort duties around *Prince of Wales.*

On Friday 8 August, *Prince of Wales* anchored in Placentia Bay, Newfoundland, close to the US Naval base of Argentia. Next day, the 9th, Churchill and his aides transferred by naval barge to meet the US President Franklin D. Roosevelt on board the cruiser USS *Augusta*. Would the two leaders forge an understanding, a bond? Although they had communicated in the past, in prior years when Churchill was Britain's First Sea Lord, and since becoming prime minister, it was no certainty they would see eye to eye. It was a long time since they had first met face to face at a dinner in London in 1918.[5] Yet, within minutes, after the usual formalities, the two men were all smiles, the President smoking a cigarette, and the Prime Minister a cigar. The meetings went well and made rapid progress, with the two leaders finding common ground in their thinking and values.[6]

On the evening of 12 August, *Prince of Wales* set sail on the return voyage, everyone buoyed by the success of the meeting, but it was with some trepidation. It had become widely known that Germany had learned of the voyage and the meeting in Newfoundland of Roosevelt and Churchill. The crew were placed on the utmost vigilance and, over the next few days, *Prince of Wales* made a number of course alterations to avoid where there were known distributions of waiting U-boats. As if the gods were on watch over the prime minister, the rest of the voyage proved uneventful and the battleship sailed back into Scapa Flow on the 18th.[7]

Over just three days, Roosevelt and Churchill had cemented a personal bond and, in discussions with their staff, and based upon their mutual principles and values, agreed upon what would become known as The Atlantic Charter.

* * *

The Atlantic Charter set out eight common principles for the USA and the UK, developed and agreed by Roosevelt and Churchill which reflected their ideals and hopes for a better world:

- No territorial gains to be sought
- No territorial changes to borders without agreement of people concerned
- Self-determination of all people
- Lowering of trade barriers
- Economic co-operation and improved social welfare
- After the final defeat of the Nazi regime, all nations to live safely within their own borders
- Freedom of the seas
- A world free of want and fear

A week or two later, in September 1941, the Atlantic Charter was endorsed by representatives of a number of countries which included the USSR and China and some in Europe which were occupied by Nazi Germany. In January 1942, twenty-two additional countries signed the Charter and supported its principles.[8]

The Atlantic Charter laid the foundation not only for Britain to escape and survive the clutches of Germany, initially with the assistance of the Lend-Lease agreement with the USA, but later with the USA leading Britain and their Allies to victory over Germany and Japan. Churchill had taken an audacious risk to make the secret voyage across the Atlantic. With the passage of time it is even more astounding, for he did so by staring down his greatest fear of the war, 'that U-boats were Britain's greatest danger'.[9]

If Churchill had not initiated this meeting with Roosevelt and risked this voyage, or not survived it, or if he and Roosevelt had not reached an agreement, the consequences do not bear speculating upon. With hindsight, the Atlantic Charter had enabled the free world to begin its escape and survival from the aggression launched by the tyrannical regimes of Germany and Japan.

In 2021 the Atlantic Charter was renewed by British Prime Minister Boris Johnson and US President Joe Biden.

Notes

1. Morton, *Atlantic Meeting*, p.56.
2. Ibid, p.22.
3. Morton, op. cit., pp.23-40.
4. Morton, op. cit., pp.56-7
5. Larson, *The Splendid and the Vile*, p.25.
6. Morton, op. cit., p.63.
7. Ibid., pp.124-47.
8. Ibid. p.151, and Loosely, *Wartime charter a handy blueprint for the Indo-Pacific.*
9. Doherty, *Churchill's Greatest Fear*, p.52.

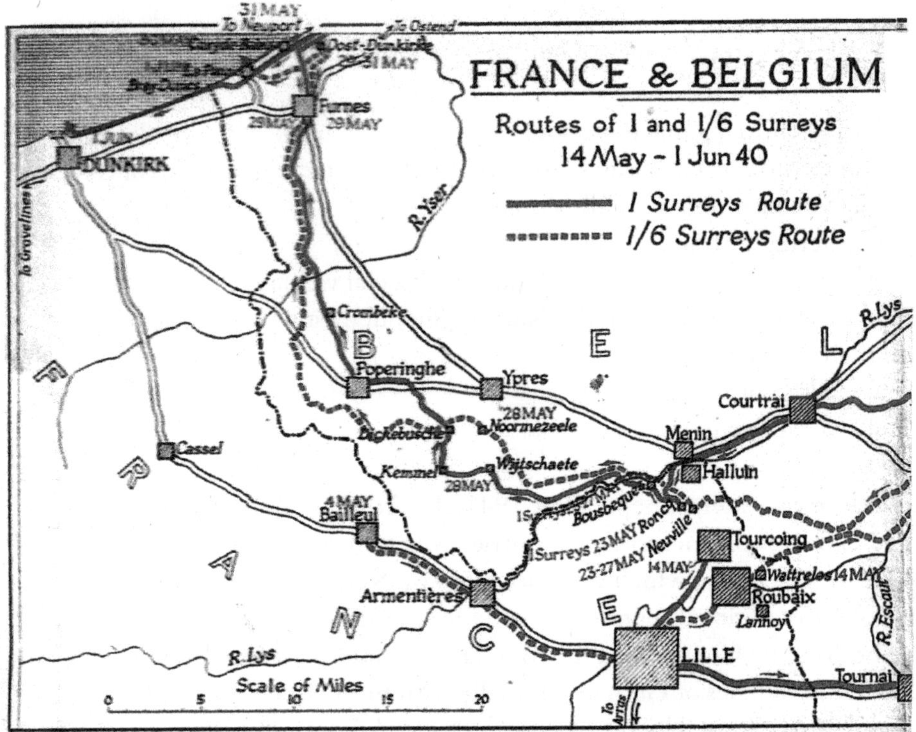

The 1st and 1/6th East Surrey Battalions in the BEF in France and Belgium, May/June 1940. (Daniell, David Scott, *History of the East Surrey Regiment*, Vol IV, map inside front cover)

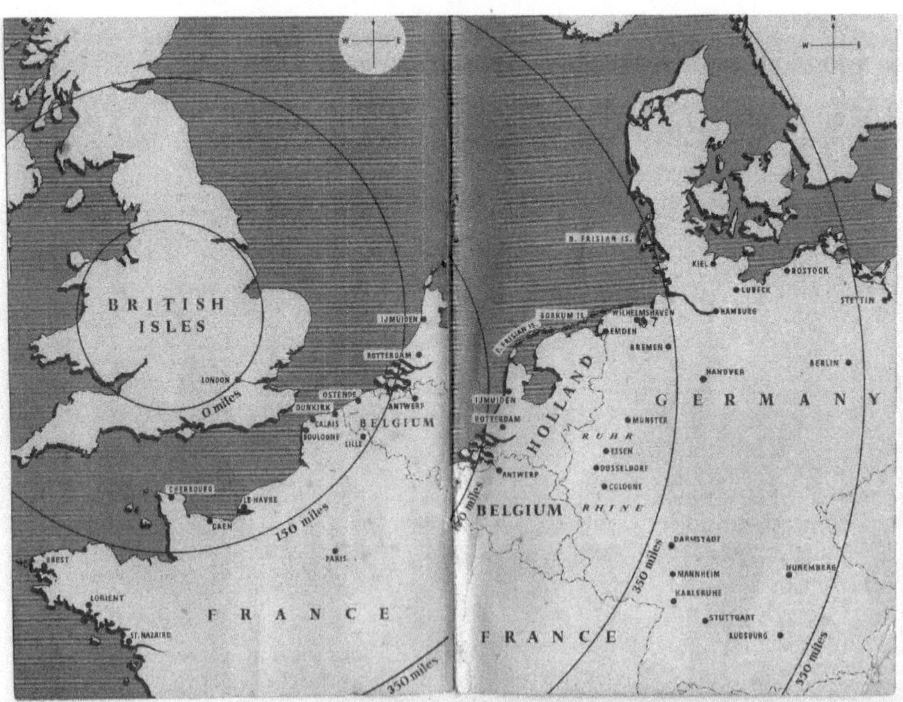

North West Europe in 1942, showing the air distances for the Bomber Command offensive. (Air Ministry and Ministry of Information, *Bomber Command Continues*, HMSO 1942)

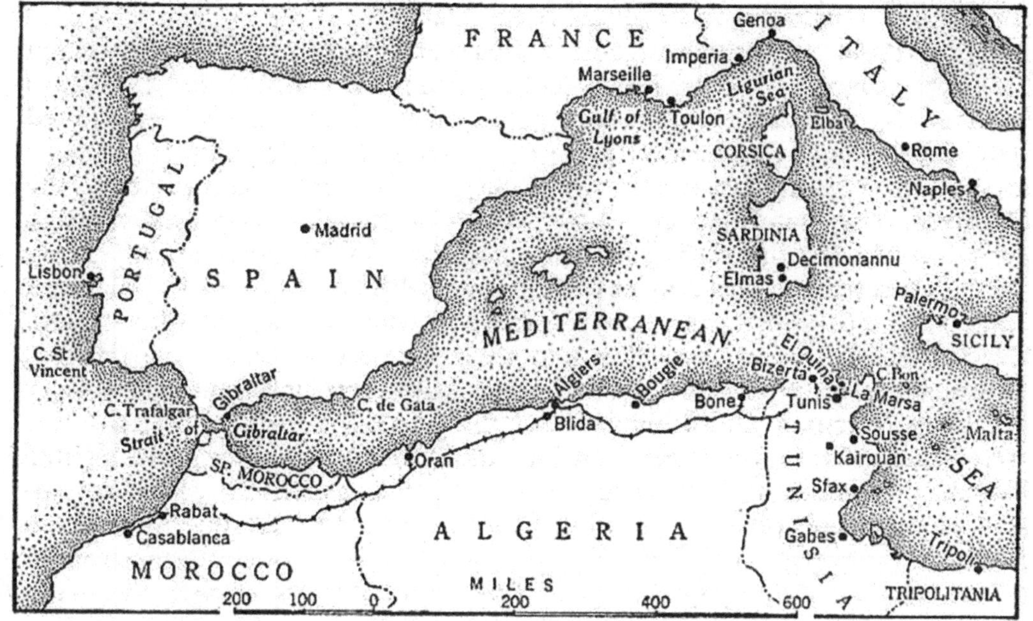

The western Mediterranean and northern Morocco, showing Malta, Tunisia and Sicily. (Herington, J., *Air War Against Germany and Italy 1939–1945*, p.412)

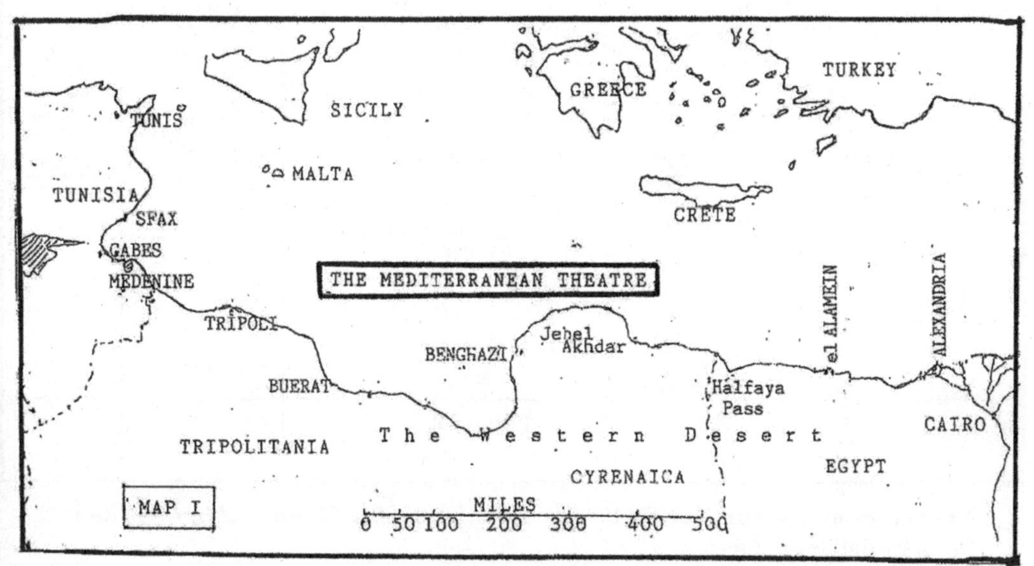

The Mediterranean Theatre in 1942. (Evans, B., *The Decisive Campaigns of the Desert Air Force 1942–1945*, p.2)

New Guinea and northern Australia 1944. (Vincent, D., *Catalina Chronicle – A History of RAAF Operations*, inside cover map)

The 2nd East Surrey and British Battalions in Malaya, December 1941 and January 1942. (Daniell, David Scott, *History of the East Surrey Regiment*, Vol IV, p.121)

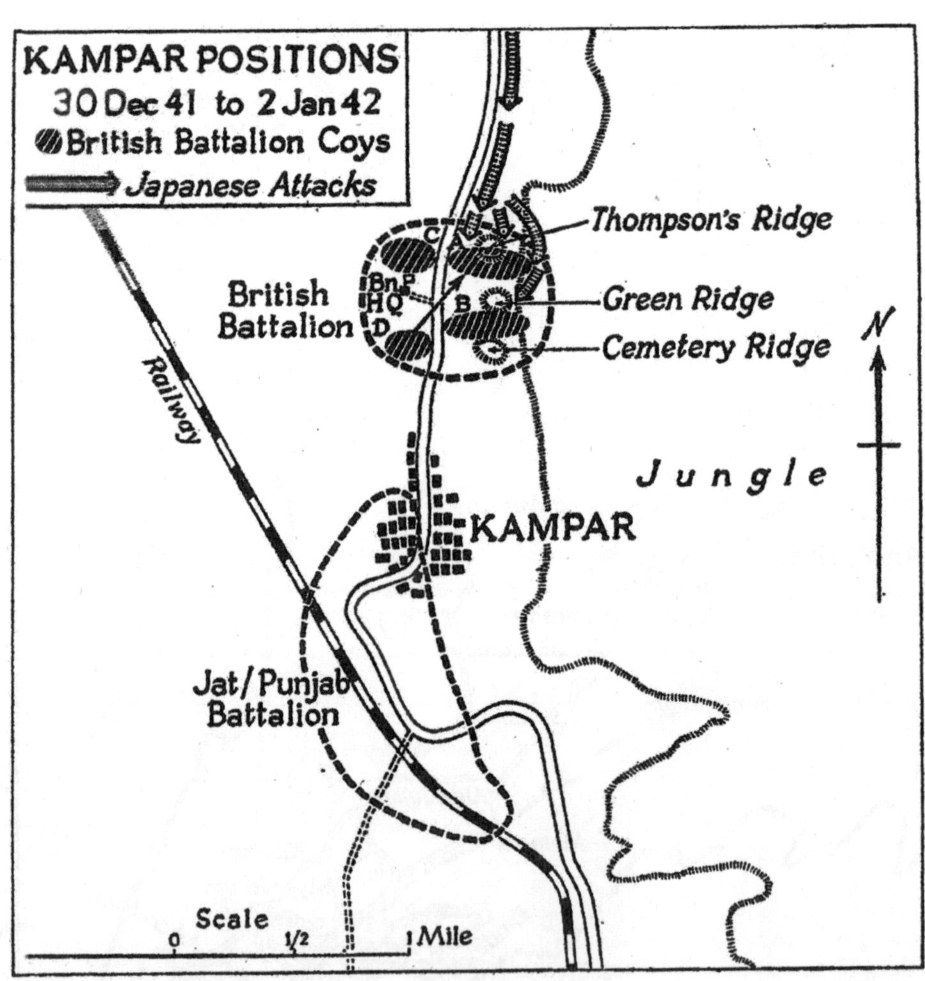

The British Battalion at the Battle of Kampar, Malaya, 30 December 1941 to 2 January 1942. (Daniell, David Scott, *History of the East Surrey Regiment*, Vol IV, p.129)

Part I

North West Europe

Chapter 1

The Miraculous Evacuation at Dunkirk – But is there Still Time for a French Romance?

In October 1939 the 1st Battalion East Surrey Regiment (Surreys) joined the British Expeditionary Force (BEF) in France.[1] In late May 1940, the Surreys were engaged in desperate rearguard battles to survive as the BEF was forced to retreat to Dunkirk. Yet in the eight months that the Surreys had been deployed in France and Belgium Private Bill Hersey had found time for a whirlwind romance with a French girl, Augusta, and, in April 1940, they even got married. Now not only must Hersey fight with his Surrey comrades to find a way back to Britain, but could he also find a way for his new bride to escape with him?

* * *

Hidden amongst the pages of *The History of the East Surrey Regiment* – Volume IV and also in Richard Collier's *The Sands of Dunkirk* is one of the most incredible survival stories of a married couple. Of the tens of thousands of escape experiences in the Dunkirk evacuation, it is also one of romance, love and unbreakable devotion.

In May 1940, the German forces drove the French Army and the BEF back across northern France and Belgium towards the Channel coast. The German Army's invasion of the Low Countries caused fear to spread through the civilian life of Belgium and northern France like a contagion. A million or more people clogged the roads seeking a safe haven 'in a honking, shouting, ear-splitting cavalcade … whole families in old rattletraps piled high with mattresses, their sole pathetic armour'.[2] French and British troops withdrawing towards Dunkirk on the coast were swamped and mixed up in this slow-moving tide of humanity. The fighters and dive-bombers of the Luftwaffe swooped on the columns, bombing and strafing without any regard for collateral damage to innocent civilians.

Following the battle on the River Escaut in Belgium, 1st East Surreys withdrew with other BEF units, marching twelve miles to Courtrai with the Germans on their heels. At Courtrai, the Surreys boarded their own transport vehicles and the trucks began a drive to take them south-west through Menin into France. When the last truck passed over various canal and river bridges on leaving Courtrai, sappers blew them up while some of the pursuing German armour fired parting shots.

On the morning of 23 May the Surreys consolidated their reduced numbers in positions at Ronecq, two miles from Tourcoing. In the battle at the River Escaut, and their subsequent withdrawal, they had paid a heavy price – 168 men lost, twenty-one dead, eighty-four wounded and sixty-three missing. However, morale was holding up and, after a day's rest, with time to wash, eat and, most of all, snatch some sleep, it improved even more. Although the move into Belgium had failed, the Surreys and the BEF were back in positions held previously and it was felt that the French would be able to stop the German divisions which had broken through to the south. Unknown to the Surreys, and perhaps senior BEF commanders, elements of the German Army had reached the Channel near Abbeville and Belgian forces in the north were retreating.

There was little time for recovery. On 25 May the Surreys moved into the front lines again, a mile or so north of Ronecq on the bank of the River Lys. For three days, with the Lancashire Fusiliers and Middlesex on either flank, they held those positions, enduring bombing, shelling and snipers, while German columns skirted the river and moved west. News came through that German forces had reached the Channel and captured the ports of Calais and Boulogne. In London on 26 May, Churchill ordered Operation DYNAMO to commence evacuation of the BEF from France.[3]

In the late evening of 27 May, some troops of the Surreys, who were billeted in a stable near Roneq in northern France, had not long been asleep when they were suddenly awoken. At an emergency company parade, a meeting for all ranks, Private Bill Hersey heard that there was to be an immediate general retreat to the Channel coast.

Once the company parade finished, Hersey pushed himself in front of his company commander, Captain Harry B.L. Smith, to say, 'Sir, is there anything you can do for my wife?' It was only six weeks since Hersey had married a French girl, Augusta, and Smith had helped in the discussions with the local church to allow the wedding to take place. Without any hesitation, Smith told Hersey to bring his wife with him in the withdrawal.

Earlier in the year, when Hersey burnt his hand badly while cooking, he had gone for help to the Café l' Epi d'Or in Tourcoing, where he had met Augusta who lived with her parents, the owners of the café, and who was a nurse at the local hospital. At once, Augusta treated his hand and for a while did so on a daily basis until it healed, and their affection and love had blossomed.

Within minutes of speaking with Captain Smith, Bill Hersey sped away on his bicycle to tell Augusta. Over rain-slicked cobble roads, Hersey was oblivious to the risk of falling off but would not join the retreat without Augusta. Once he was on the rue Clinquet, he soon reached the café a little before midnight and found it all closed up. He knocked on the door again and again violently until it opened. Augusta appeared in dressing gown and bleary eyed. He told her to quickly pack a few things; they were leaving right away.[4]

During the night of 27/28 May the exodus poured slowly westwards to the coast. More than 300,000 troops of the BEF and many more French soldiers and civilians, plus Belgian and Polish troops, in all types of transport or on foot, clogged the roads. The Surreys had orders to make for Dunkirk, some eighteen miles away, where black smoke from German bombing could be seen on the horizon.

On 28 May, the Surreys marched westward to Wytschaete before orders came to continue again west to a divisional rendezvous at Crombeke. It took a march of thirty-two miles in twenty-eight hours on a road which was congested with French transport, cavalry and civilians in some disorder making for the same destination. After the Belgian surrender, the northern flank was in German hands so that the only escape option was to make for Dunkirk. It meant the roads were filled with mixed streams of slowly moving vehicles, troops and civilians on foot. At the sides of the roads were wrecked guns and vehicles. Luftwaffe aircraft screamed down from the sky, dive-bombing and machine-gunning the dense and confused columns.[5]

Bumping along in the back of Captain Smith's truck, where space had been made for Augusta, she held her helmet tightly on her head and with her other hand clutched a rifle. The stark realization hit Augusta. She had left behind her parents and family in Tourcoing, left them to the ravages of the invading German troops. Somewhere behind in the convoy Bill Hersey sat in another truck. Neither knew how far apart they were, or whether they were each still alive. In addition to vehicle accidents and breakdowns, the streaming columns of intermingled troops of the BEF and fleeing civilians were constantly bombed and strafed by the Luftwaffe.[6]

By the early hours of 28 May word had spread – King Leopold of Belgium had surrendered his army to the Germans. Meanwhile, near the town of Dixmude, Augusta and her driver, Johnnie Johnson, needed to rest and, at a farm next to the road, came to a stop but were unable to persuade the farmer to give them some shelter. Soon after 1.00 a.m. they huddled under a pile of straw in what appeared to be an unused pigsty and, exhausted, fell asleep.

At daybreak, before climbing back into their truck to resume their flight to the coast, they found the farm's well to replenish their water bottles. It was another setback, the farmer had locked it up tight. People were stunned, fear had spread like a sudden rolling mist. Soon the Germans would be everywhere. They settled back under the pile of straw and wondered whether to look elsewhere for water before driving on.

The roads from Lille in France northwards towards the Channel coast were jammed with a million or more retreating troops and refugees. Augusta was but one tiny speck in a chaotic tide of humanity vainly seeking safety.[7]

* * *

Bill Hersey's truck driver was nearly exhausted as he turned off the clogged road and came to a stop in a farmyard. The thought that he and Augusta might never see each other again kept consuming Hersey's mind. It seemed more important than the threat of being killed by the Germans. Then he suddenly could not believe what he saw. Also parked in the farmyard was the truck of Johnnie Johnson, in which Augusta was a passenger. He leapt to the ground and ran through the farmyard shouting, 'Augusta! Augusta!'

Hersey ran towards the farmhouse and its outbuildings where, above the top of what looked to be a pigsty, he saw a helmeted head appear. At once, he recognised that it was Augusta's face. Even with his limited French his exclamation was instinctive, 'Cherie, je t'aime!' (I love you darling).

Anger rose up in Hersey that Augusta had been forced to sleep in a pigsty and he wanted to go and remonstrate with the farmer. Augusta managed to restrain him, explaining that the farmer and his family, like everyone, would be afraid of the chaos and the likely looting and pillaging of the advancing German army. Despite their predicament, Augusta laughed as if it was an exciting adventure. Yet she wondered about the fate of her parents and if she would ever see them again. At the same time in the crazy confusion of this war, Bill Hersey's love for her was what she could depend on. Augusta thought to herself, 'Your life now lies with this gentle, fair-haired soldier, your husband … .'[8]

From Crombeke, the Surreys, some in the battalion's own transport, moved to Furnes, which was three miles from the Channel, and twelve miles east of Dunkirk. They travelled light; all large guns, stores and baggage were ordered to be destroyed, except for small arms and ammunition. At Furnes, they went into the perimeter line on a canal, holding it through a long night under heavy shelling. At daylight they were relieved and sent to east Dunkirk and dug in to positions amongst sand dunes.[9]

When Bill and Augusta's truck reached the village of la Panne, they caught their first sight of Dunkirk and the sea. In the sky, however, stretching for thirty miles or more, and reaching like storm clouds thousands of feet high, was the black smoke from the burning oil tanks at St Pol. At Dunkirk, the fires also spread uncontrolled, jumping from building to building, as exhausted troops wended their way to the beaches.

> Caked with sweat and grime all those not needed for perimeter defence, wound their way through the shattered stinking port .... Above the thunder of the guns, the scream of distant bombs, came a steady crunching ....[10]

It was the boots of thousands of men grinding broken glass from the shelled and bombed ruined buildings under their feet into a fine powder.

The previous night Bill and Augusta, with a few other Surreys, found a friendly farmer who gave them some food – one slice of very dry bread to each person. Every so often on the journey they were bombed, forcing them to leave the truck and dive into wayside bushes or a ditch. Their luck held; each time they and their truck were unscathed. At la Panne they stopped near a hotel where a number of other Surreys' trucks and various vehicles were parked, all devoid of drivers and passengers.

Bill went from vehicle to vehicle looking for any available food, while Augusta and some other troops watched, thinking there was little hope. Then, with a high-pitched whine, and an almost simultaneous explosion, a shell landed not far from them. Bill jumped from the truck to seek cover, shouting to Augusta to get down. Augusta just laughed and told him she was not a dog that he could command!

Captain Harry Smith saw her reaction and could only wonder at how she stayed so happy. All Augusta knew, and told herself, was that they had reached the coast and soon they would be in England. Meanwhile, Bill's search for food proved unnecessary for he and Augusta soon joined Captain Smith and other troops who were enjoying a meal of roast beef and vegetables in the hotel. It was one of the 'food dumps' deployed for those troops charged with defending the perimeter of Dunkirk.[11]

During the night of 30/31 May, Bill was ordered to drive a truck back and forth inland to shuttle more troops down to the beach from the perimeter. Once again, as Augusta took shelter in a garage from the continual shelling landing on la Panne, she feared she may have seen the last of her husband.

After bringing in another truck full of troops, Captain Smith stopped Bill from setting off once more. He told Bill to hand over the truck to another driver and stay with his wife. Neither Bill nor Augusta ever learned of what prompted Smith's decision.[12]

* * *

Around the approaches to Dunkirk, the BEF had deployed rearguard troops who dug in along a perimeter some thirty miles in length. It ran from the mouth of the Yser river to Nieuport, through Furnes and west to Dunkirk and its sandy beaches. Inside this sliver of land either on the beach, or like the Surreys holding positions back from the perimeter, men waited and hoped for orders to go down to the shore and embark on a ship, a boat of any kind, anything afloat to take them back to their homeland.

On the night of 30/31 May the Surreys came under orders to move to Coxyde Bains, in readiness for embarkation. However, that changed with an order to drive at once to Nieuport with their own trucks which they had insisted on retaining to assist 10 Infantry Brigade on the perimeter. Keeping their own transport meant that they were an obvious choice to urgently reinforce 10 Brigade. Those who cursed the postponement of boarding ships to evacuate soon saw a silver lining.

At Nieuport the Germans had forced a gap in the perimeter defences towards the Nieuport bridge. To prevent the enemy surging through in strength, a company of 1/6th East Surreys was barely holding on at a brickworks. A plan was hatched for 1st Surreys, despite their meagre numbers, to mount a counter-attack. To save their comrades in their sister battalion, some of whom would have been family or close friends, motivation was instinctive.

All four companies of 1st Surreys, despite being reduced to only about thirty men in each, and with nothing more than small-arms weapons, advanced under enemy fire to reach the brickworks. Suffice to say they were successful, so that the two Surreys' battalions held the brickworks positions for the rest of the day. The perimeter gap was closed, holding off an imminent German breakthrough and so saving an unknown number of lives of troops waiting for ships on the beaches. Next day, 1st Surreys were ordered back to la Panne before moving to Dunkirk to embark.[13]

At first light the Herseys and other troops began to move down to the beach.

> The sands were crowded with men waiting their turn to be taken to the ships lying offshore, and the sea was full of small boats loaded down with men ferrying out to them. Derelict boats and scattered equipment littered the beaches as far as the eye could see. Over Dunkirk to the south, hung a thick pall of black smoke. Enemy aircraft dive-bombed and machine-gunned the men in the boats and on the sands.[14]

As they were advised not to provide too tempting targets to German aircraft, they walked in ones and twos through ruined streets, stepping over the dead, horses, troops and civilians, and past burning buildings. Bill had his kitbag slung over his back, while Augusta still lugged a suitcase. When they reached the beach, however, they confronted an unexpected setback – perhaps the worst so far after surviving to get to the coast.

An officer, a beachmaster, stepped in front of Augusta, 'No women allowed on the beach!' Bill gave him a withering stare and slid back the bolt on his rifle. When the officer turned and walked away, the two them re-joined the queue of troops snaking across the beach. It was not long, however, before another officer spotted Augusta and, despite a more affable sympathetic attitude, insisted that a written permit for Augusta was required from a senior beachmaster.

Bill frantically went around the nearest lines of troops, seeking such an officer. He could not stray too far from where Augusta kept their place shuffling along in the queue. In despair, Bill reluctantly realised it was nigh on impossible in the chaotic mass of would-be evacuees. He rejoined Augusta in the line of Surreys, telling those around them that they were at a loss about what to do. A voice piped up, 'Dress her up like a Surrey, she's one of us!' Quickly one man passed Augusta a spare pair of battledress trousers and a captain held out his greatcoat, so that with a helmet on she appeared no different to any other infantry soldier,

From the beach the queue began to trudge at a painfully slow pace along the temporary jetty, built over the top of a nose-to-tail line of abandoned trucks, which stretched out to sea where, beyond the breakers, it was deep enough for ships to anchor. Men cowered as one when they heard the whine and explosions of bombs and shells which rained down across the hell that was the sandy beaches of Dunkirk.

Bill looked at Augusta and in his mind questioned what he had brought her to, yet she 'looked every inch a soldier, though the men packed around her were too tired to care. Drowsy with fatigue, their eyes bloodshot, they stared patiently into the darkness, while shells and Very lights green, yellow, and red, stitched the night sky …'.

Finally, Bill and Augusta neared the end of the jetty where men climbed one by one into a small whaler, to be ferried across to a ship. Then, as if fate was conspiring to block their escape, another barrier loomed up from nowhere. As the man in front of Bill scrambled down some netting into the boat, a shout came from below, 'Only one more!' Bill's mind raced, but it seemed time stood still. He had to make a decision – fast.

Instinctively, in a split second, Bill rejected any notion of the two of them splitting up. He turned to the man behind him and told him to go ahead. When Bill was asked why not let his mate go, motioning to Augusta, he said that his mate was drunk and needed his help. As the whaler disappeared into the night to rendezvous with its ship, Bill and Augusta with the standing line of men behind them, stared into the blackness and hoped against hope that there would be another ship. The bombing and shelling seemed to be becoming more intense and the Germany Army would surely soon surge into Dunkirk.[15]

* * *

Suddenly like an apparition, another small whaler came out of the dark and tied up at the jetty. As Bill and Augusta scrambled down into the boat, they saw on a sailor's hat the ship's name HMS *Ivanhoe.* It took an hour for their boat to reach *Ivanhoe*, one of five destroyers waiting off the coast to pick up as many troops as they could take. It was late in the day of 1 June, and Bill and Augusta would not have known at the time, although they probably sensed it, that they were amongst the last groups of BEF troops to be evacuated from Dunkirk.

Their boat slowed as it reached *Ivanhoe.* It bucked and rolled in the sea swell before ropes were tied up to the destroyer. Bill and Augusta forced themselves, like all their fellow evacuees, exhausted, cold and deprived of sleep, to climb up the scrambling nets to the ship's deck. As Augusta reached the top, stepping onto the deck she stumbled, falling down and hitting her head.

On her knees, stunned, she froze trying to catch her breath and focus her eyes and brain. Bill bent down to help her and a sailor asked what was wrong with this man. Bill quickly got between the sailor's gaze and Augusta's trembling figure, saying, 'He'll be all right, just shell-shock.' He helped Augusta to her feet and, with his arm around her waist to support her, they hobbled away. Eventually, they found their way to a mess-deck packed with troops, lying where they had dropped on the floor.

All were totally exhausted, some wounded, sprawled side by side, like sardines in a can. Augusta did not care; within seconds she was asleep. Bill slid off her helmet, putting his kitbag under her head. If anyone was awake and alert enough to notice his mate's long hair, they would not have enough energy to care. For Bill and Augusta, too, it did not matter now.[16]

It was not long, however, before Augusta was awake and upright and then one of *Ivanhoe*'s crew, noticing her long hair, suggested she should go and help the casualties in the sick bay. Being a nurse, Augusta jumped at the chance. Later *Ivanhoe*'s captain, Commander Philip Hadow, came to the mess deck and told Bill to also go to the sick bay and help Augusta.

While Bill and Augusta tended to patients, disaster struck *Ivanhoe* – a bomb hit home and exploded through the forward funnel. The blast severed the main steam pipes, causing steam at 300lb pressure to burst out and spray around the boiler room, inflicting a horrific slow death on the engineering crew in there.

Simultaneously, the blast upended *Ivanhoe*'s AA machine-gun which was engaging the Luftwaffe bomber, so that it continued firing into *Ivanhoe*'s bridge and superstructure. In the sick bay, the stream of machine-gun fire was like a horizontal hailstorm, shattering every glass bottle to smithereens. As Bill and Augusta dived to the floor, a patient was decapitated, hurling his bloody skull across the room, and with the machine-gun fire destroying the sick bay's door.[17]

Ivanhoe was damaged fatally and quickly began to list. Troops came scrambling up from the ship's hold onto the deck, desperate to leave the sinking destroyer. Bodies of the dead killed by the bomb's blast were trampled underfoot. Bill and Augusta fled from the carnage in the sick bay and were once again fortunate to be unscathed. Clinging on to the wildly tilting deck, they saw a minesweeper HMS *Speedwell* coming to the rescue, rapidly closing in on *Ivanhoe* to take off survivors, those who could jump across to its lower-level deck.

As *Speedwell* came close alongside, *Ivanhoe*'s Commander Hadow used a loud-hailer to warn the minesweeper's captain that the destroyer's ammunition magazine might blow up at any moment. Men jumped from *Ivanhoe* across and down to *Speedwell*'s deck, but the sea's rolling swell meant some misjudged the gap and fell to be drowned or crushed to death between the two ships' clashing hulls. Bill and Augusta looked into each other's eyes, then with an unspoken will, hand-in-hand jumped as one. Eager hands of *Speedwell*'s sailors grabbed them as they landed. They had made it together.[18]

* * *

On the evening of 1 June, the remaining survivors of the Surreys disembarked at Dover. They had suffered total casualties of 271. Known deaths were four officers and thirty-two other ranks, with six officers and 146 other ranks wounded. Two officers and eighty-one other ranks were missing, either dead or taken prisoner, some of whom would have been wounded. In total, 338,226 troops, including 125,000 French, were evacuated from Dunkirk.[19]

It was nearly 4.00 p.m. when *Speedwell* edged into the dockside at Dover. With some 600 other survivors, who had somehow crammed onto *Speedwell*, Bill and Augusta eventually walked down the gangway. To Augusta, it appeared to be more chaos, a cacophony of noise of every kind. From an uncountable number of ships came 'a surging irresistible mass of men in soiled khaki piling down gangplank after gangplank'. On the dockside Bill and Augusta joined slow-moving queues of troops and civilians, trudging towards checkpoints, passing the waiting casualties, 'wounded of all nations lying blood-stained and exhausted on green canvas stretchers'.

For Bill and Augusta, when they finally reached a military checkpoint, things turned worse yet again. A security official accused the two of them of being spies. Only Bill's impassioned long and repetitive arguments, his Army paybook and their marriage certificate eventually brought acceptance that they were genuine. However, they were split up with no alternative option. Bill was directed onto a troop train to rejoin his battalion, while Augusta was despatched to board another train to a civilian transit camp.

While waiting for the train she fell asleep on a vacant stretcher amongst wounded German troops before she left with other displaced French civilians for London. Augusta had no belongings with her, having left behind her case of a few clothes when they jumped for their lives from the sinking *Ivanhoe.* Now she was alone, bewildered, going to where? She knew not where she might end up.[20]

To Augusta, the cheering crowds lining the rail route, and at every station, were mystifying. The BEF of some 390,000 men had surely been defeated and retreated in much reduced numbers to Britain? Suddenly, for Augusta England seemed an alien place and the character of its people beyond comprehension.

Finally, the train terminated at a station in west London and Augusta with all the refugee passengers were taken to a transit camp where she was interviewed again, and her story and marriage certificate were checked once more. After being given a meal and a bath, she was put on another train to West Byfleet in Surrey. Augusta's final destination was 23 Addison Road, Addlestone in Surrey, a cottage where Bill's parents waited for her, although they had no idea when she or Bill would arrive, or even if they had survived.

From the West Byfleet station, she set off on foot to find Addlestone and the cottage at 23 Addison Road. At last, in the afternoon, after some wrong turns, she knocked on the door of the cottage at number 23. When Bill's mother opened the door, her warm welcoming smile meant everything to Augusta. She felt lost for words, but Bill's parents said that they looked forward to their son also arriving soon. To pass the time, Bill's mother gave Augusta some sewing work to pass the time. In the calm and quiet, free from the chaotic confusion, death and destruction of war, she knew then she was home.[21]

* * *

In his book *The Sands of Dunkirk*, Richard Collier wrote a vivid and authentic account of the Dunkirk evacuation, based upon exhaustive research, and countless interviews in Britain, France and Germany of participants and those effected. For one of those interviews in the post-war years, he visited Bill and Augusta Hersey in their Surrey cottage where Bill ran a nearby watercress farm. He was given a most warm welcome and he sat with them for hours, listening to them tell of their hairsbreadth escapes.

Collier's research over six years was founded on official records, war diaries, military signals, ships' logs etc., as well as extensive personal testimonies. Collier and a nine-person research team covered over 60,000 miles visiting nearly 400 towns and cities in Britain, France and Germany, to hear and document the experiences of more than 1,000 eye-witnesses in the retreat to, and evacuation from, Dunkirk.[22]

Bill and Augusta's story was just one of those, but almost certainly unique.

* * *

Notes:

1. Daniell, *The History of the East Surrey Regiment – Volume IV,* pp.57-9
2. Collier, *The Sands of Dunkirk,* pp.60-1; Evans, *Airmen's Incredible Escapes*, p.11
3. Daniell, op. cit., pp.71-2; Larson, *The Splenndid and the Vile,* p.54
4. Collier, op. cit., p.26
5. Daniell, op. cit., p.72
6. Collier, op. cit., pp.60-1
7. Ibid., pp.48-9
8. Ibid., p.144
9. Ibid., p.72
10. Ibid, p.164
11. Ibid., pp.164-6
12. Ibid., pp.207-8
13. Daniell, op. cit., pp.73-4
14. Ibid., p.74
15. Collier, op. cit., pp.207-9
16. Ibid.
17. Ibid., pp.223-4
18. Ibid., p.225
19. Daniell, op. cit., p.75; Larson, op. cit., p.57
20. Collier, op. cit., pp.240-1
21. Ibid., p.262
22. Ibid., pp.266-7

Chapter 2

Flying Into, and Hoping to Survive, Berlin's 'Wall of Fire'

Author's Note: *Some of the stories in this chapter, and in Chapter 2 on the Nuremberg and Stuttgart raids, rest upon the shoulders of the acclaimed historian Martin Middlebrook (*The Berlin Raids, *and* The Nuremberg Raid*) and those of veteran bomber aircrew who have recounted their eyewitness experiences of those operations. Martin Middlebrook, who died in early 2024, was the doyen of meticulous research and enthralling writing of RAF Bomber Command operations in the Second World War. Middlebrook adjudged the Battle of Berlin as the ultimate challenge of Bomber Command's air war against the Third Reich. His book* The Nuremberg Raid *is judged by many to be the greatest analysis and finest writing on a such a raid.*

* * *

Over the German Bight the Stirling bomber droned onward from a Berlin raid to make a night-time return flight over the North Sea. Despite having been attacked earlier by a German night-fighter, pilot Frank Mulvey felt the aircraft to be flying along quite normally, like a horse heading back to its home stable. On the intercom the crew were quiet; their adrenaline and tensions had dissipated. Now their thoughts turned to anxiety about making it back to their home base. Without any warning, an explosion on the starboard side shattered the crew's calm. The inner engine on the starboard wing cut out. At once, Mulvey and his flight engineer struggled with the controls to feather the dead engine's propellor. When they looked again at the starboard wing, the engine was not there, and the wing was on fire.[1]

* * *

To protect Berlin from RAF Bomber Command air raids the Germans surrounded the 'Big City' with a 'Wall of Fire' in the sky. It did not deter the RAF; rather like a moth to a flame, Bomber Command took up the challenge. The Battle of Berlin was RAF Bomber Command's main offensive to strike a decisive blow against the Third Reich. It was the longest and most sustained bombing offensive against one target in the Second World War. Between August 1943 and March 1944 more than 10,000 aircraft sorties dropped over 30,000 tons of bombs on Berlin. The RAF aimed to end the war by bombing the German capital to destruction.

Following the devastating bombing raid on Hamburg on 25 July 1943, Air Chief Marshal Sir Arthur Harris vowed to inflict the same destruction on Berlin. The raid on Hamburg had resulted in citywide fires killing some 40,000 people and forcing 1.2 million to flee. Harris propounded the view that Bomber Command could bomb Berlin and Hitler's regime into collapse and surrender.[2]

In the battles over Berlin, or in crashes in flights there and back, more than 1,000 aircraft were lost. Officially, 2,690 bomber aircrew died and an unknown number were maimed with wounds and injuries. Nearly 1,000 airmen were shot down and became prisoners of war (PoWs). Yet many aircrew survived near disaster in one or more return flights in damaged aircraft. Fifty-two airmen who were shot down evaded capture and found a way back to Britain.

The following stories of some who survived raids on the 'Big City' in very different ways are examples of those who escaped the indescribable hell of Berlin's air defences.

* * *

In late August 1943, it was less than two weeks since Flying Officer Albert Hollings and his crew of No.207 Squadron RAF had survived their remarkable first operation. On 12 August 1943, Hollings had piloted their damaged Lancaster on a nerve-racking return flight from a night raid on Milan by threading the bomber on three engines through Swiss Alpine valleys.[3]

Now, on 23 August, they waited to hear later that evening the destination for what they hoped would be their third completed operation. Shortly after lunch, prior to a pre-operation briefing at RAF Spilsby in Lincolnshire, Hollings' navigator, Flying Officer Rex Kenyon, was sitting in conversation with the squadron's Intelligence Officer, Joyce Brotherton.[4] Kenyon wondered aloud where they would be sent tonight. Brotherton knew the target destination but did not respond. Kenyon indicated that he did not care too much, apart from if it was Berlin. At the subsequent briefing later that afternoon it was announced that the operation was indeed Berlin or, as it was generally known to aircrew, the 'Big City'.

At a meeting held from 9.00 a.m. to 10.00 a.m. on 23 August at Bomber Command HQ at High Wycombe, Air Chief Marshal Sir Arthur Harris took the decision to attack Berlin that evening. In the opening raid of the Battle of Berlin, a force of 719 bombers would target the south of the city. Planning for the operation commenced, although a final decision on 'Go or no go', would depend upon an assessment of weather conditions over continental Europe and Berlin.

At 12.40 p.m. a Mosquito took off to evaluate the weather over Germany and what would be the likely conditions over Berlin during the night. Shortly before 4.00 p.m. the Mosquito returned. The resulting forecast was for good visibility with only intermittent cloud at low altitudes. Harris gave the go ahead and the plans went out by teleprinter just before 4.30 p.m. to the Bomber Command groups. From there, orders were sent out to squadrons, which left little time for final preparations by air and ground crew. Bombers would begin taking off at 7.30 pm.

Bomber Command was despatching 719 aircraft to attack Berlin, with another sixty-nine in support roles, e.g. route marking, mine laying etc. Most briefings of aircrew did not mention that this operation would be the opening of a lengthy battle to try to bring the Big City to its knees. It was generally recognised that Berlin had the strongest air defences of all German cities. Flak batteries and searchlights stretched in belts across an area up to sixty miles wide. Three huge flak towers held twenty-four 128mm guns, eight in each tower, which could fire up to a height of 45,000 feet. Eight shells from one flak tower fired in a pattern would explode across a zone of 240 metres.[5]

For Hollings and his inexperienced crew, it was only their fourth sortie. As they made their way out to dispersal and Lancaster DV186, J-Johnny, to head off into the night to bomb the 'Big City' there was surely no truer meaning of the term 'baptism of fire'. It is extremely difficult to prepare yourself mentally and physically to go somewhere you have never been before. All aircrew were about to fly into a cauldron of dazzling light, explosions, and flak surging up in incessant waves from Berlin's anti-aircraft guns. The crew of J-Johnny could have no real understanding of what would confront them.

At 8.31 p.m. Hollings took J-Johnny into the air, one of twelve Lancasters from No.207 Squadron to join up with the main bomber stream. The outward route was direct, flying due east after crossing the Dutch coast, then some thirty miles south-east of Berlin, turning north-west to first bomb, then leave Berlin on the same heading.

Aircrew have described the approach run into Berlin as if you were flying towards and into a wall of searchlights, hundreds of them, some in cones and some in clusters. Beyond the wall of searchlights could be seen even brighter lights, but those were red, green and blue – exploding flak. Those who had been to the Big City before knew it would be hell over the target.

With the mistaken complacency of the uninitiated, and an outward flight without incident, Hollings was thinking it a good trip as they began their run in, and were nearly over the target.

> We were suddenly attacked by a Fw190 night-fighter from the starboard bow. I knew nothing about it until it opened fire at about 400 yards. I saw shells exploding in the cockpit, and George Lapham, the bomb aimer, yelled that he was hit, and also Ernie Scott the flight engineer.[6]

Harper and Denton, the two gunners, opened fire, hitting the Fw.190, which they claimed as damaged. But J-Johnny was clearly not unscathed and Hollings was not sure how much punishment the aircraft had taken, nor the state of Lapham's injuries. 'We got George up from his Bomb Aimer compartment, and laid him on the floor behind Rex to keep him warm.'

Lapham had been shot badly in the top of a thigh and was in excruciating pain. Scott, Kenyon and Blake were all suffering from shrapnel wounds to feet, arms and legs but were able to carry on and at the same time try to patch up Lapham. Meanwhile, Hollings was throwing J-Johnny around in corkscrew manoeuvres to avoid another attack. First aid for Lapham was delayed since Hollings' evasion tactics had sent the medical kit tumbling away somewhere. A search for the kit was not helped by a loss of internal lighting in the aircraft.

Although J-Johnny was holed by flak in numerous places, Hollings found that, as far as he could tell, there was no serious malfunction and took the Lancaster into a bombing run. With Lapham unable to fulfil his bomb-aiming role, Hollings planned to jettison the bombs. 'I found that the jettison toggle did not operate, so I sent the Flight Engineer, Scott, down to the bomb-bay to manually push the jettison bars across.'

Despite his injuries, Scott was able to get the bombs jettisoned. Shortly afterwards, they were coned by thirty to forty searchlights, held in a blinding glare for the anti-aircraft guns to pinpoint their range. Instantly, Hollings reacted just as he had been trained.

> I pushed the nose down a long way, and threw J-Johnny into a spiralling dive. The engines really began to scream, and this went on for six to seven minutes before we freed ourselves from those searchlights. As luck would have it we were not hit by any more flak.

About ten minutes later, as they continued to traverse north-west away from central Berlin but still in the Big City's area, Hollings saw a twin-engine Bf.110 night-fighter attacking another Lancaster.

> It was on our starboard quarter, about 800 yards away, and somewhat below us. As he broke away he headed towards us, so I told Cyril, our rear gunner, to give him a burst if he could line him up.

Despite the damage they themselves had sustained, and rather than take evasive action, Hollings instinctively wanted to draw the German fighter away from their fellow bomber crews. Rear gunner Cyril Harper opened fire on the enemy aircraft. Hollings watched it close on them from some 700 yards down to 300 yards and saw Harper aim long steady bursts at the Bf.110.

Smoke began to stream from underneath the German fighter's fuselage. Then flames flickered from the aircraft's underbelly and, a few seconds later, the Bf.110 broke apart. The two sections of the plane fell like stones, before exploding on the ground. With heightened motivation to get them out of the Big City's killing zone, Hollings turned J-Johnny's four Merlin engines onto full power. 'When we finally crossed the English coast, it was with great relief.'

Hollings radioed Spilsby to arrange for an ambulance to be ready on landing for Lapham and Scott to be dashed to hospital. He brought J-Johnny down towards the runway. It was the acid test. What unknown damage to the landing gear might still bring disaster?

> As I was landing the port tyre burst, but I managed to keep her straight and the right way up. It had apparently been hit when we were attacked. We had a hell of a job getting Lapham out, and together with Scott into the ambulance. Only then did I learn that both Kenyon the Navigator, and Blake the Wireless Operator had also been hit, but had not said anything to save worrying me anymore. Good lads all of them. Then to the debriefing by which time I was myself really buggered. But we made it thank God. Our guardian angels watched over us tonight.

Subsequently, Hollings and his crew received a letter of commendation from No.5 Group HQ for shooting down an enemy fighter that was attacking another Lancaster. Their action not only saved the other bomber but almost certainly themselves. As an inexperienced crew on only their third operation, their first to Germany and its most fiercely defended city, Berlin, they had defied the odds.[7]

* * *

On that same night's raid of the commencement of the Battle of Berlin, a Stirling bomber, BK779 of No.90 Squadron RAF, had completed a bombing run over Berlin. The crew were heading for home on their return leg towards the German north coast when they were caught in the bright light of a dreaded cone of searchlights. Canadian pilot Frank Mulvey took immediate evasive action, throwing the Stirling into a heartstopping corkscrew dive. Although a German fighter attacked them with a burst of fire on their starboard side, they escaped the glare and flew on into the dark. Flight Engineer Sergeant J. Burland was unsure whether they had been hit by the fighter, but to him the aircraft seemed to be flying normally.[8]

They flew on untroubled to cross the north coast, with the German Bight below, on a return course for their home base. Without any warning, an explosion on the starboard side shattered the crew's calm. The inner engine on the starboard wing cut out. At once Burland and Mulvey struggled with the controls to feather the dead engine's propellor. When they looked again at the starboard wing, the engine was not there, and the wing was on fire.

Although the aircraft was at 15,000 feet, the problem was how to descend to the sea without the damaged wing falling off. Worse still, to ditch successfully in the sea required the plane's tail to impact the water first, then put the nose down, and to do so with only two engines operating on the port wing and on a pitch-black night.

Against all probability the starboard wing stayed in place, then hit the water first as the bomber ploughed into the waves. Burland and other crew were thrown around like rag dolls. As he climbed out of the aircraft's hatch, the water surged and bubbled up towards Burland's neck.

> I followed the tail gunner out of the roof hatch, and began to slide down the top of the fuselage, but my dinghy pack, attached to my backside, caught under the rim of the hatch. I was stuck and had horrible thoughts of drowning.[9]

When the sea began to envelop him fate intervened. Burland's dinghy pack floated off dragging him away from the aircraft. 'The rear gunner was already in a dinghy. I can't swim but I felt a man alongside me, helping me. It was my pilot Mulvey.'[10]

When the bomber had sunk out of sight almost instantly, Mulvey, despite suffering some concussion from a head knock, had actually extracted himself from the submerged aircraft and swum to the surface. Burland dragged himself into the dinghy and, with the rear gunner, hauled Mulvey aboard. The three of them were soaking, cold and shivering and alone in a dinghy bobbing up and down like a cork. Although groggy, Mulvey estimated that their approximate position when the plane went down was about ninety miles from Denmark, and sixty from the German coast. In their struggles to get out of the water, Burland had seen the dinghy's main ration packs dislodge and float away. As hours fused into days, and nights, they clung together, and Burland wondered how long they could last.

> After five days I think, we only had left two very small 'seat-pack' dinghy tins of food – hardly anything. It rained after five days and we got our first drink. The weather was stormy, and we were always being drenched – the waves breaking on top of the rollers.[11]

One huge wave, perhaps thirty-feet high or more, flipped the dinghy over and the three of them fought to swim to the surface. The water temperature was desperately cold. Luckily each of them had held their grip on the dinghy's rope. Mulvey fought off his lingering concussion and, no doubt helped by his adrenalin, used his strength to refloat the dinghy upright. Clambering back in, the three airmen slumped down, stunned and freezing. Their clothes were sodden once again and caked with salt.

Burland, who was from Yorkshire, became semi-delirious and at times thought he was on a boating lake in Huddersfield. They drifted into an area of flotsam where they saw a floating body, on which stood a seagull. From the harness, Burland identified it as an RAF pilot.

Although they had a cork life-ring on a 100-foot rope to swim out to help any other survivors, none of the three airmen had the strength to do so. As they watched the body float steadily away from them, Burland could clearly see that the man was dead. He regretted that he did not attempt to reach the body and retrieve his dog tags for informing the man's family. The three of them were barely hanging on and would not last much longer.

When their hope of rescue was effectively gone, late on the eighth day a Luftwaffe aircraft flew low over them and, soon after, a German Navy boat picked them up. They were still alive but in a very poor condition, hardly conscious, when they docked at the German port of Cuxhaven. Remarkably, the three airmen were well cared for and recovered. Burland thought they were treated quite well and put that down to being given large quantities of lemon barley water. Against all the odds they had survived and, despite the war, humanity had re-asserted itself.

* * *

One week later, on the night of 31 August 1943, No.35 Squadron RAF, part of No.8 Group, the Pathfinder Force, took part in another raid on Berlin. Flying Officer Herbert A. Penny,[12] accompanied by Squadron Leader W. 'Butch' Surtees, was the pilot of Halifax II bomber HR878, TL- J, 'Johnny'. It was Penny and his crew's eleventh Pathfinder operation after converting from Main Force operations.[13]

For Flying Officer Herbert Penny himself it would be his forty-second operation. He was from Bow in London, over 6-feet tall, with blue eyes, dark hair, and just twenty-one years old. At age 18, he had joined the RAF in 1940. At 8.10 p.m. on 31 August at RAF Gravely near Huntingdon, Penny lifted Halifax J-Johnny into the air.

> The route to and from Berlin took us over the Ijssee Meer – a landlocked bay formerly known as the Zuidersee – and then across the Dutch/German border. It was a route we had flown before.[14]

In another maximum effort operation in the Battle for Berlin, Bomber Command was despatching 613 bombers, which included 331 Lancasters, 176 Halifaxes, and 106 Stirlings. Many crews were tired from the previous night's raid on Mönchengladbach and Rheydt. The outward flight path was to be south-easterly over northern Holland, skirting to the south of Hanover, before approaching Berlin from the city's south. However, the German air defences were tracking the bomber force as it traversed Holland. Helped also by good weather and visibility, Luftwaffe night-fighters found the bomber stream, and attacked them in strength before and during the approach to Berlin.[15]

At around 16,000 feet over Berlin on its bombing run towards the target, J-Johnny was badly hit by flak, crippling the aircraft. Penny attempted to take J-Johnny back on the return flight over Holland and the North Sea but was unable to prevent the Halifax from losing height.

> Somewhere around the Dutch border our aircraft was picked up by searchlights, and flak anti-aircraft batteries, so that inevitably we became an isolated target for a Messerschmitt 110 night-fighter. Its fire hit our starboard wing and fuselage, which were quickly ablaze. We suddenly became uncontrollable, and began spiralling down.

With the aircraft now certain to crash, Penny shouted the order for the crew to bale out immediately.

> In what seemed just seconds available to get out, I managed to clip my parachute pack on to my harness. Struggling against the centrifugal force and buffeting of a large aircraft spinning out of the sky, I sidled crab-like along the floor to the front exit. It had been left gaping open by those crew who had already evacuated.

Penny and Squadron Leader Surtees clawed their way towards the rush of cold air from the open hatch as the stricken bomber corkscrewed into its death dive. In the rush to get out, Surtees inadvertently left his radio intercom cable connected. Peny unplugged it to avoid being tangled up by the long cable, which could easily trip him up.[16]

> 'Butch' and I left the aircraft almost together in a rather undignified scramble, but we were separated in an instant when the gale-like air outside hit us. I can only describe my exit as being like a champagne cork leaving its bottle! Fortunately my parachute opened satisfactorily, after I had reacted to the fact that, in my haste, I had clipped it on my harness with the release handle on the left rather than the required right-hand for right-handed people. The aircraft crashed and began exploding and blazing furiously, while I was still in the air drifting away in the wind from the crash-site.

Penny landed clumsily in the dark on unknown terrain and stumbled into a muddy bank overhanging a dyke. He took some time to collect his thoughts, gave thanks to the Almighty for his survival, and hoped for a similar outcome for his crew.

> I also thought of the reactions of my new wife and parents, when they received official notification from the Air Ministry that I was 'Missing in Action'. Automatically I got out of my parachute and harness, used a knife to cut off the top portions of my flying boots, and with my badges of rank and aircrew insignia, disposed of everything by pushing it all into the mud of the dyke bank.

He was uncertain whether he was on the German side of the border. By rough estimation and using as best as he could the uniform button compass issued for just this dilemma, Penny moved off in a westerly direction,

> It was necessary that I get away from the crash-site as far as possible, but I had to rest from time to time to gather my wits. I moved from cover to cover stumbling into unforeseen obstacles, until it became obvious to me that I was travelling in a wide meandering circle. I began to feel very much lost, alone and desperate!
>
> In that frame of mind I eventually came across what looked to be a small wooden bridge. All was silent, the bridge seemed unguarded, and I decided to try my luck! If I was in Holland and very fortunate, I might find somebody not antagonistic to the British, and sympathetic to my

situation, or at least be picked up by local police rather than a German patrol – not an attractive prospect for Bomber Command aircrew at that time of the war.

After crossing over the bridge, Penny found that he had arrived in what looked to him at the time and in the dark to be a small farming village. Still not sure whether he was in Germany or Holland, and hoping that it was unlikely that there were any German troops in such a small place, Penny thought that he would take a chance, and look for a place to shelter in the village.

> At first, I hid by the bridge and, surveying the lie of the land, I then crept along the darkened streets, ducking from one building to another. In the end, finding nowhere to hide, I decided to knock on the back door of a small house. I did so as quietly as I could so that only any occupant could hear my knocks. Eventually the door was opened by a man. I flapped my arms like a bird and whispered hoarsely, 'R-A-F, R-A-F' spelling out the three letters.

In that instant Penny did not know whether he was confronted by a Nazi supporter or not.

Instinctively, a startled man in the doorway ushered him quickly into his back room. It turned out that he was in the small Dutch town of Ossenzijl, and the houseowner was a Jan de Boer, who seemed welcoming. But Penny could not be sure whether this man was genuine, or a German collaborator feigning his friendship

> Once Jan had apparently satisfied himself that my scruffy appearance and distressed state of mind was authentic, he put me at ease, gave me some food, and did his best to make me comfortable. But I worried what would happen next, but was totally exhausted and in a while I drifted off to sleep.

Penny was fortunate. Jan de Boer and others in the Dutch Resistance sheltered him, and similar supporters of the Allies helped him to escape, in a journey overland through Belgium, France, over the Pyrenees into Spain, and, over three months, to Gibraltar and eventually on a flight back to Britain.[17] By train, bus and on foot, Penny was passed from one resistance group to another in each country, and is described in more detail in my previous book *Airmen's Incredible Escapes.*

* * *

Author's Note: *In a unique initiative in December 1943 a Bomber Command raid on the 'Big City' carried five journalists as observers. The following is a summary extract of part of the experience of one of those five journalists, drawn from the captivating book* Dispatch from Berlin 1943, *by Anthony Cooper and Thorsten Perl.*

The winter phase of the bombing offensive in the Battle of Berlin was recognised as commencing on 18 November 1943. To strengthen support for the bombing campaign by both the British and American people, and their governments, the RAF invited five journalists to fly as observers on the night of 2/3 December 1943 in a Berlin raid, each in a separate aircraft. The five journalists were Americans Ed Murrow from CBS and Lowell Bennett of International News Services, two Australians, Alf King of the *Sydney Morning Herald* and Norm Stockton of the *Sydney Sun*, and Norwegian Nordahl Grieg, an author, journalist and poet.

Only Murrow and King returned from the operation safely in their designated aircraft. The Lancaster bombers of Stockton and Grieg were shot down, and both journalists were killed. Lowell Bennett's fate was to be literally stranger than fiction.

On the night of 2 December, Lowell Bennett stood, because there was no seat for him, in the cockpit of Lancaster B-Bolty of No.50 Squadron. In his appointed position behind pilot Ian Bolton, as they approached the first ring of Berlin's air defences, he stared at the 'Wall of Fire'. Bolton was just 20, already a flight commander, and already fatalistic about survival being just a case of luck.

The glaring kaleidoscope of coloured lights was mesmerising. Innumerable sweeping searchlights, scarlet explosions from anti-aircraft batteries flashed both below and, above B-Bolty, night-fighter flares and the hanging red and green flares dropped by Bomber Command's Pathfinders, were creating an artificial daylight in the night sky. On his first experience of a bomber raid, Bennett was transfixed, almost hypnotised. His senses were too overcome to recognise the mortal danger posed by Berlin's defences.

Bennett gazed down on the blackness of Berlin's buildings, where there was an increasing number of explosions and the crimson red patches of fires started by incendiary bombs. Then his eyes were torn away by the sight of two bombers blasted apart, their dismembered parts spiralling earthwards like the burning fragments of spent fireworks. Suddenly, he became aware of his own mortal danger. B-Bolty was caught like a moth in a car's headlights, trapped by a cone of searchlights.

When the mid-upper gunner snapped out his warning on the intercom that a fighter was coming in to attack from starboard, Bolton threw the Lancaster into violent corkscrew manoeuvres, climbing, diving, turning left and right. It was to no avail. The tail gunner shouted that two more fighters were closing to attack from astern. Bennett could only brace himself, hang on desperately in the careering aircraft, and watch in horror as the fighter's 'long burst of cannon shells slashed into our right wing'.

In an instant, both engines burst into fire, wing panels tore away and a wall of flames cascaded back in the starboard wing's slipstream. Reality hit Bennett like a sledgehammer, consuming him with an urge to panic. They were at 20,000 feet, 'on fire and going down over Berlin, 600 miles inside Germany'.

Over the intercom Bolton told everyone to bale out as he struggled to keep B-Bolty level. The Lancaster flailed against his controls like a wild beast. Bennett had already grabbed his parachute and buckled it on. He could see that B-Bolty, and probably all of them, were doomed. Both starboard engines had fallen away and the wing was disintegrating as fire ripped it apart.

The bomb-aimer opened the forward hatch in the floor, shouted 'Good luck, skipper', and jumped into the night. Bennett shuddered in the blast of arctic air gushing through the plane. He was behind the flight engineer, who went next even while still trying to clip on his chute. He felt the navigator and wireless operator behind jostling him forward. He had to go.

Bennett pulled himself forward, losing both of his too big flying boots, to crouch over the hatch. It was, of course, his first time to parachute out of an aircraft but he had only one thought. He had to get out of this plane. Over the intercom, he heard Bolton shouting that he could not hold up the aircraft much longer. In the split second or two before he fell through the hatch, Bennett looked down on a nightmare, a cauldron of exploding flak, fires, flares, probing searchlights and falling aircraft streaming flames. Over central Berlin he was jumping into an undreamed of hell.

The two crew behind Bennett also managed to jump before Bolton lost control and Lancaster B-Bolty began the dive to the ground and eternity. In a vicious disorientating spin, Bolton tried to pull himself from his seat towards the open hatch. It flashed through his mind that it could not be done. He hit his head and some part of the aircraft was obstructing him. It did not matter – the bomber exploded, sending Bolton and its disintegrating elements into freefall.

Bennet had fallen through the cockpit-floor hatch with his hand on his parachute ripcord and instantly pulled it. The parachute billowed out, jerking and twisting him like a rag doll, so much so he thought his back would be broken. At nearly 20,000 feet, freezing thin air made him gasp. Maybe he would die of oxygen deprivation. In a vast sky of flak and flame he felt he was just a speck of dust to be swallowed up.

A strap of a small shoulder bag had caught across his face and throat, making breathing even harder. The pain from the chafing strap probably helped him stay conscious, despite the encroaching hypothermia. The sight of falling bombers burning with trailing flames as they hurtled to the ground reinforced his feeling of impending doom. Remorse rose in Bennett as to why he had left his young wife and 2-year-old son.

His thoughts were broken when, below his feet, he caught sight of the sheen of moonlight on water. His efforts to tug at the parachute's cords to veer away proved useless. Although he had been around fifteen minutes in descent, time seemed to accelerate and he plunged through thick reeds and into water up to his chest. Instinctively, he remembered to twist the release on the parachute to let it float away and then pull the handle on his lifejacket.

Bennet did not know at the time that he had landed near Potsdam in Lake Schwielow some thirty-five kilometres south-west of Berlin. The bomber stream had gone off course, resulting in many navigators mistaking Potsdam for Berlin. The area around Potsdam was an integral part of Berlin's outer ring of air defences. Half-submerged in Lake Schwielow, Bennett faced a new and immediate threat to his life – he was waist-deep in mud, and then water lapping at his neck. Weighed down by his RAF greatcoat and other clothing, how could he get out of this and where was the shore?

Bennett saw that his watch still worked; it was 10.30pm and for two hours he had floundered, haphazardly struggling from one clump of three-metre-high reeds to another. Only his lifejacket kept him afloat in the deeper water between the reeds. His sodden overcoat and clothing kept dragging him down so that he could see that he had covered only about twenty feet, from where his discarded parachute straggled across some reeds. With the cessation of bombing and flak in the blackness there was no sight of land in any direction, and he had run out of energy.

His legs were frozen from immersion in the mud and water, and he could feel nothing in his fingers. His mind told him that without help the cold would kill him very soon. Despairingly, he clung to a clump of reeds, pulled himself up as high as he could and managed to shout, 'Komm hier, Help!' Very quickly, after a few shouts, his voice gave out and he no longer cared. His grasp on the reeds gradually began to weaken.

On a December night when the temperature was around zero or even below, and the water only a degree or two higher, Bennett was devoid of hope and close to collapse. Hypothermia would soon totally envelope him. Then he thought he heard some distant voices – or was he hallucinating? Somehow, he found some residual spirit and energy to shout once again, 'Komm hier, bitte!' Bennett thought he heard voices shouting back to him, he was not sure.

After some time a boat emerged from the gloom, with two men, one of whom was using a pole to punt the small rowing boat through the reeds and shallow water. Bennett had no strength to grip and hold on to the outstretched pole and the two men punted the boat closer to him. Each of them then grabbed one of Bennett's arms and pulled him into their boat.

Bennett said that he was American. The two men accepted that, one saying, 'Ja, Amerikaner,' before he collapsed into muddy water swishing around in the bottom of the boat. They pulled him up and sat him down and it was obvious to them how Bennett was weak and frozen. So, while one man punted the boat towards the shore, the other rubbed Bennett's legs to restore circulation. Eventually, they reached open water and, at about the same time, the sky cleared to bright moonlight. Bennett's spirits rose, blood flowed in his legs and he felt that he would survive after all.

They began to approach a half-visible shoreline and Bennett felt his legs again, and his strength re-asserting itself. One of the boatmen jumped on to the land and began to pull the boat up from the water. At this moment, Bennett remembered he still had a revolver in his holster under his coat. As one man helped him step ashore, he instinctively let go of the helping hand, grabbed his revolver, and pointed it at the two men. Again, without any hesitation, he shouted at them to get back in the boat, 'In dem boot!' The two boatmen looked on stunned.

Bennett took a couple of steps to free his feet from the mud and water. It was his undoing. He slipped, falling flat and dropping his gun. In an instant, one of the boatmen jumped on his back, knocking the wind out of him. When he was allowed to stand up, he could see one of the men pointing his gun at him.

Bennett was duly taken into captivity as a prisoner of war (PoW). German authorities recognised his potential as a journalist to be exploited for propaganda purposes and decided to take Bennett on a bizarre tour of bombed-out cities. He was shocked and disillusioned at the destruction and suffering of civilians that he saw.

His captors then staged an opportunity for Bennett to escape. While on the run he wrote an article 'Inside Nazi Germany', which was published on 24 January 1944 in the USA. Following this, certain German agencies disapproved of the whole ruse and Bennett was soon re-captured. He spent the remainder of the war in Stalag Luft 1 PoW camp on the Baltic coast where he was re-united with his pilot Ian Bolton. He, too, had remarkably survived after being blasted out of the exploding Lancaster, his parachute opening without his knowledge, but he was the only other member of the crew to survive.[18]

NB. For a full account of the fates of Bennett and the other four journalists on the night of 2 December 1943, read their compelling stories in *Dispatch from Berlin, 1943*.

* * *

In the last days of January 1944, the Battle of Berlin was approaching a tipping point. After more than four months of bombing raids with the objective of bringing Berlin to its knees, there was still no sign of collapse, nor any intimation that the Third Reich regime might contemplate negotiation of surrender terms. The priorities for Bomber Command were changing in preparation for the Normandy landings planned for June 1944.

On the night of 28/29 January in a raid on Berlin, Australian Pilot Officer D. Shipley was a tail gunner on a Halifax bomber of No.10 Squadron RAF.[19] On this raid the planned route to Berlin was a long roundabout flight of more than three hours, first over the North Sea, then across Denmark and the Baltic Sea, before turning south-east to Berlin.

It was a freezing winter night with heavy cloud and icy conditions. Departure of the main bomber force of 677 aircraft – 432 Lancasters, 241 Halifaxes and four Mosquitos – was delayed twice because of the bad weather until take-off began at midnight. Many crews were already exhausted from flying on a raid to Berlin the previous night. On the outward leg over the North Sea the atrocious weather contributed to nearly 10 per cent of the bombers being forced to turn back.

However, the advance force of Pathfinder Mosquitos arrived over the Berlin target on schedule and provided concentrated accurate marking. On the bombing-run approach Pilot Officer Shipley's Halifax was attacked by an enemy fighter and he saw one of the aircraft's engines catch fire immediately. Almost in the same instant Shipley felt the bomber bank violently, like a wounded buffalo veering away from a hunter's rifle.

> Our skipper, Flight Lieutenant Kilsby dived and corkscrewed to evade the fighter, he was a beauty, and that put out the flames. He then flew another circuit on three engines to bring us back on to the bombing run again.

Then, all of a sudden, came the chatter of a fighter's cannon. The cannon fire came from underneath and ignited the overload tanks carried in a portion of the bomb bays. The gunfire almost certainly came from a fighter with the upward-firing gun, known by the Luftwaffe as *Schräge Musik* (jazz music). Kilsby at once gave the command to bale out. Shipley knew he had split seconds to save himself. He threw himself backwards to get out. To his horror, he was caught by his right leg which was trapped in the wall of the turret. 'This was a terrifying experience to me, because the flames and slipstream were overpowering. Even though I clawed at the sides of the turret, I was unable to free my leg.'

Shipley was facing death. Engulfed in flames, the Halifax began to spiral into a death dive.

> I can assure you it is a frightening thing. The last things I can remember are the frantic attempts to free myself ... and my despairing appeal to God ... my life passed before me, people and events of years gone by were graphically depicted. It was so real. My darling mother, father, fiancée and family, all flashing before me. I knew my number was up.

The fuel tanks of the Halifax exploded, and Shipley lost consciousness as he became just another fragment of the falling aircraft parts. He came to, his eyesight clearing enough to see bending over him an ominous helmeted figure, silhouetted against a background of flames. His immediate thought was that he had arrived in hell.

Saved by the inadvertent opening of his parachute, Shipley had landed next to an airfield and was duly taken prisoner. The Halifax's burning shell lay not far away, in which Kilsby and the wireless operator, Dagget, were found, their bodies huddled together.[20]

* * *

For aircrew the raids into the hell of the air defences of Berlin were the most daunting, the most feared. In the five months of the Battle of Berlin 1,128 aircraft of Bomber Command were lost over enemy territory. This amounted to more than the maximum number of front-line strength on any day at that time.

For Bomber Command the raid on Berlin on 23/24 September 1943 was, at that time, the worst night of the war to date. In the heaviest loss by Bomber Command on a single night of the war up to this date, sixty-two bombers were lost, 8.7 per cent of the 719 despatched. A loss rate of anything above 5 per cent was seen as unacceptable and unsustainable. In respect of aircrew, 298 were killed and 117 taken prisoner.

In contrast, the Luftwaffe lost only nine fighters, four aircrew killed and two injured. On the ground in Berlin the bombing killed 854 people and destroyed 2,611 properties. However, analysis of the bombing found it to be very scattered. The section of Berlin which had been intended in the planning as the target was largely undamaged. [21]

Notes

1. Middlebrook, *The Berlin Raids*, pp.335-7
2. Cooper and Perl, *Dispatch from Berlin, 1943*, p.4
3. Veteran's account, Flying Officer Albert Hollings; Evans, *Airmen's Incredible Escapes*, pp.86-91.
4. Brotherton, *Press on Regardless*, pp.127-9; Evans, op. cit., pp.86-91.

5. Middlebrook, op. cit., pp.29-76.
6. NA Kew, AIR27-1234-15/16, No.207 Squadron RAF, August 1943; Veteran's account, Flying Officer Albert Hollings
7. Veteran's account, Flying Officer Albert Hollings; Evans, op. cit., pp.86-91
8. Middlebrook, op. cit., pp.335-7
9. Ibid., p.336
10. Ibid.
11. Ibid.
12. Veteran's account, F/O Penny; Evans, op. cit., pp.92-101.
13. Middlebrook, op. cit., p.1
14. Veteran's account, F/O Penny; Evans, op. cit., pp.92-101.
15. Middlebrook, op. cit., pp.78-84
16. Veteran's account, F/O Penny; Evans, op. cit., pp.92-101.
17. Ibid.
18. Cooper and Perl, op. cit., pp.6-8, 124-31, 145-55, 162-6, 314.
19. Middlebrook, op. cit., 245-6
20. Ibid.
21. Middlebrook, op. cit., p.288

Chapter 3

Escape from the Disastrous Nuremberg Raid, Only to be Blasted into the Night Sky over Stuttgart

In the early hours of 25 July 1944, Halifax bomber P-Peter of No.466 Squadron RAF endures heavy flak as it makes its bombing run to the target in Stuttgart. Several flak bursts are close, and bomb-aimer Keith Campbell hears shell fragments rattle against the bomb-bay. He releases the bombs and begins to turn to move back from the aircraft's nose when there is a heavy but dull explosion from behind him. Over the intercom someone shouts 'Bloody hell!' Within a split-second a delayed shockwave from the explosion blasts him straight through the nose of the Halifax. The next thing he hears is the wind in his ears as he floats in mid-air, hanging from something. Campbell's semi-conscious mind wrestles to clear itself. Is he in heaven or hell?

* * *

On 30 March 1944, soon after 9.00 p.m., the Lancaster and Halifax bombers based in Yorkshire began to take off on a raid to bomb industrial targets in the city of Nuremberg. They were the first of the hundreds in the Bomber Command stream to leave since they had the longest distance to fly to the concentration point over the North Sea where 779 bombers would assemble. From RAF Leconfield, near Beverley in East Yorkshire, the Halifaxes of No.466 Squadron were part of No.4 Group in these early departures.[1]

While most squadrons took a south-easterly course to the stream's assembly point, the bombers of No.4 Group from Yorkshire were routed at first due south so as not to disrupt the departures of Lincolnshire-based squadrons. Flight Sergeant Keith Campbell, at just 20 years old, was the bomb aimer of a Halifax of No.466 Squadron which lifted into the air at RAF Leconfield.

> We took off into a light wind from the north-west, and began to climb on full power to around 2,000 feet, then on lower revs continued to climb in a circle up to about 10,000 feet. This enabled all of our aircraft to reach this

> height in about half an hour, before we set course to the south, and then a turn to the east for the assembly point over the North Sea.[2]

Campbell's Halifax, HK274, took off at 10.38 p.m. and joined the other fifteen aircraft of No.466 above RAF Leconfield. Once they were formed up at 10,000 feet, they set course for the North Sea assembly point. However, when the navigator in Campbell's crew became ill and unable to carry out his indispensable role, the aircraft captain, Flight Sergeant N.J. Walsh, had no option but to abort their flight at 11.47. After their bombs were jettisoned over the North Sea, Walsh took Halifax HK274 back to Leconfield. Keith Campbell and his fellow crew would later learn that, inadvertently, they had avoided what would become Bomber Command's most disastrous operation of the war.

For a variety of reasons, a number of individual aircraft dropped out of the bomber stream and began returning to their base airfields soon after they had taken off. A typical cause was engine failure or a malfunction of oxygen supplies, intercom or a Gee set, injury or illness of aircrew. Of the total force of 779 aircraft despatched on the Nuremberg raid fifty-two turned back, 6.9 per cent of the total, which was about average at that time. The more reliable Lancasters were below average at 4.7 per cent while the Halifaxes were as high as 14.2 per cent.[3]

The other aircraft of No.466 Squadron flew on towards the assembly point for the whole bomber stream, which was about fifty miles off the English east coast over the North Sea. The bomber stream was planned to be sixty miles in length, with the bombing over Nuremberg to take, in theory, seventeen minutes.[4]

Once the stream left the assembly point and was over Belgium near Liège, it turned due east between Brussels and Charleroi and flew on the easterly long leg some 250 miles, passing over the Rhine, then between Bonn and Coblenz, and deep into Germany.[5]

On this long easterly leg of the outward flight between Liège in Belgium and a navigation point south of Eisenach in Germany, where aircraft would turn south towards Nuremberg, the bomber stream suffered heavy attacks by Luftwaffe night-fighters. In the hour following midnight, fifty-nine bombers were shot down, causing enormous casualties among the aircrew. When an aircraft was hit by a fighter's cannon shells, its bombs and fuel tanks were nearly certain to explode and catch fire. If an airman was not directly killed or wounded, there were often only seconds to find a parachute, put it on and get to the escape hatch. Of the fifty-nine bombers shot down, there was only one where all the crew survived.[6]

* * *

Of those bombers that survived the attacks by fighters on the outward and long leg, one of the most remarkable experiences was that of a Halifax of No.578 Squadron of No.4 Group based at Burn near Selby in East Yorkshire. Pilot Officer Cyril Barton was only 22 years old and, as he held the controls crossing the German border, it was nothing new to him. He had completed seventeen operations, five of which had been to the hell of the 'The Big City', Berlin.

Cyril Barton was deeply and openly religious and, despite his young age, was able to persuade his crew to attend the village church in Burn. Yet on this night he was taking them and his Halifax bomber to deliver death and destruction from on high to the inhabitants of Nuremberg. It was a dilemma recognised and felt in the minds of many bomber crews. Barton flew on deeper into Germany, his navigator giving instructions for the planned turn to the south, towards Nuremberg.

Then, with no warning, they were hit. It probably came from a fighter which had approached from underneath and fired its *schräge musik* gun into a wing of the Halifax. The damage was instantaneous and devastating. One engine cut out, two fuel tanks were holed and leaking, the radio and intercom were damaged and out of action, and all gun turrets immobilised. Remarkably, there was no immediate fire.

Barton had an understanding with the three gunners in his crew that, if there was an intercom failure, and the bomber was under attack or in serious trouble, the aircraft's emergency signal system of button-controlled lights would be used. In the ensuing confusion the bomb-aimer, navigator and wireless operator thought there was a signal to bale out, which they promptly did. At the same time, Barton threw the Halifax into corkscrewing evasion twists and turns and got away from the fighter which had attacked them.

What Barton did next defied belief. He ignored that he had lost his three crew indispensable for guiding his bomber to the target, and for dropping its bombs. Inexplicably, he decided to follow to the letter the motto and spirit of Bomber Command, 'Press on Regardless'. Despite the Halifax being seriously maimed, perhaps fatally, he would attempt to fly on, find Nuremberg, and bomb the target.

With the assistance of his flight engineer, Sergeant Trousdale, Barton flew on, intent on reaching Nuremberg. Over what they thought was Nuremberg, Barton released the bombs. However, Barton and Trousdale did suspect that they might have wandered off course and bombed the city of Schweinfurt. This was quickly dispelled from their minds and Barton turned the Halifax onto a long westerly return flight on only three engines, no navigator and no wireless operator. Even if they found an accurate course, they doubted that their remaining fuel would last.

To conserve fuel, anything that was detachable was jettisoned. Using only the compass, sightings of the North Star and his own judgement, Barton kept the Halifax heading westward. Finally, he saw the English coast ahead – and disaster threatened. They were approaching the air defences and numerous anti-aircraft balloons of Sunderland in north-east England and the very real risk of being shot down by friendly fire.

Barton turned the Halifax back out to sea and, although being aware that they were now running on empty, flew south before turning in over the coastline again. He took the bomber down to 1,000 feet looking for somewhere flat to land. Over the small mining town of Ryhope the fuel gave out. The three remaining crew, the flight engineer and two gunners, crouched down next to where the main wing-spar joined the fuselage, waiting for the crash.

Despite the Halifax being in an unpowered dive, Barton managed to lift the nose to avoid rows of miners' cottages. The bomber then dropped, hit a hillside and ploughed across a railway line, before disintegrating as it came to a halt in the coal mine's yard and buildings. One miner on his way to work was killed while the three crew back in the fuselage survived. Barton was found dead in his cockpit.

In Barton's letter left for his mother in case he did not return, he had written: 'Except for leaving you I am quite prepared to die.' Barton was posthumously awarded the Victoria Cross, for completing his mission 'in the face of almost impossible odds'.

Of all the aircraft returning from Nuremberg, fourteen crashed or made forced landings in England.[7]

* * *

Another amazing return flight and survival was made by a Lancaster bomber and recounted by its bomb aimer. On the outward flight's long leg near the Germans' *Otto* beacon, used by the Luftwaffe's fighters, the Lancaster of bomb aimer Sergeant Patfield of No.61 Squadron was attacked by three night-fighters. A huge explosion with shrapnel scorching through the aircraft sent the Lancaster plummeting into an uncontrolled dive. An engine had been hit, there was fire in the cockpit and nose, the astrodome and pilot's windscreen were destroyed.

Four of the crew were wounded, three seriously, one of whom, the navigator, was critical for the survival of the aircraft and crew. Patfield helped give first aid to the four men injured, then struggled to the bloody mess of the navigator's chart table. Although having only basic navigation skills, he managed to give the pilot some kind of course back to home base. Then, because his oxygen mask was damaged, Patfield collapsed unconscious on the floor.

Wireless operator Sergeant C. Chapman, although wounded, was able to maintain radio communications. Luckily, Pilot Officer D.C. Freeman was unscathed but had to endure an arctic-cold wind through his non-existent windscreen, and managed to fly the Lancaster on Patfield's rough course back to England. He found his way to RAF Foulsham where he made a crash landing successfully and safely so that all his crew survived. Freeman, who was on only his third operation, was awarded the DFC, and Chapman received a rare award of the Conspicuous Gallantry Medal.[8]

* * *

From RAF Mildenhall in Suffolk Flying Officer Bryan Good and the crew of Lancaster ED631 B-Beer of No.622 Squadron took off at 11.50 p.m. on 30 March on only their fourth operation. They were setting off unknowingly on an operation that would surpass the horrors of all previous Bomber Command raids on Germany and would come to be referred to as the 'Nuremberg Catastrophe'.[9]

For the raid on Nuremberg on the night of 30/31 March 1944, Bomber Command despatched 781 aircraft. Once over German territory, the bomber stream's planned route took them between the Ruhr and Coblenz areas, which were heavily defended by flak and searchlight batteries. The Ruhr and Coblenz air defences flanked a twenty-mile-wide airspace known as the 'Cologne Gap'.

Knowing that Bomber Command sometimes used this route, the Germans had placed the fighter beacon *Ida* only a few miles from the gap; with a flashing light and a radio signal, it provided a crucial navigation aid for their night-fighters. On this night about fifty fighters on their way to rendezvous at *Ida* came across the bombers by chance. Already at or in the vicinity of *Ida* were some additional 100 night-fighters, most of which were twin-engined and experienced in radar-guided combat within a bomber stream.

With a half-moon's rays illuminating the night's clear skies, the Luftwaffe's night-fighters began their attacks. Having spent little time searching for the bomber stream, some fighters had fuel for up to two hours' flying. In an inexplicable occurrence, the unusually clear weather also made it even easier for the German pilots to find their bomber prey. Vapour or condensation trails, known as contrails, were stretching out behind each bomber. Those contrails were normally only found above 25,000 feet and, although the bomber stream was at around 19,000 to 20,000 feet, the ribbons of vapour marked out every bomber as a potential victim.[10]

Bomber crews were shaken to be attacked by so many German night-fighters before they had even reached the Nuremberg target area. Some of the more experienced pilots did leave the bomber stream to seek an altitude and airspace of their own and avoid leaving a tell-tale contrail. Bombers were being blasted out of the sky in countless numbers and sent plunging to fiery destruction on a scale and intensity never before experienced. Flying Officer Good was stunned by the swarms of attacking fighters and the carnage they were inflicting. His thoughts like so many others turned to a silent plea for divine help. 'It was a night of terror for all participating crews, and one which I will never forget.'[11]

In only an hour and a half, between the German border and Nuremberg, as the near 800 bombers streamed towards the city, eighty aircraft were lost to night-fighters and anti-aircraft defences. Overall, on the Nuremberg raid Bomber Command lost ninety-five aircraft out of 781 despatched, a rate of 13.1 per cent. The total number of airmen killed, wounded or taken prisoner was 723, of whom 545 were dead. It was a disaster far in excess of the supposedly sustainable casualty rate of 5 per cent.[12]

Like so many other new crews in their early experiences of operations over Germany, Good was shocked by the brutal air war and its horrendous casualties.

> Someone's prayers must have been with us to bring our crew safely back from such a hazardous mission. After Nuremberg I was resigned to what I sincerely believed to be the inevitable. How could I possibly expect that we might be spared to survive thirty trips such as on our first four? It was impossible. I was determined therefore, that I would do my duty to the utmost while I could.[13]

The Nuremberg raid truly had been a catastrophe.

* * *

Prior to the Allied invasion of North West Europe on 6 June 1944 and subsequently, Bomber Command was given new priorities for bombing operations. At RAF Driffield, close to the east coast of Yorkshire, in the early evening of Monday 24 July, Flight Sergeant Keith Campbell, one of those fortunate survivors of the disastrous Nuremberg raid, sat and listened. Group Captain Forsyte DFC told the assembled bomber crews of No.466 Squadron, what the target for the night would be. Campbell, like most crews, was expecting another short trip, perhaps in support of Allied forces on the ground.

> When we heard the petrol and bomb load no one could guess what the target was, as we had all tanks and wing overloads, and were carrying HE (High Explosive). Group Captain Forsyte soon settled the many guesses, and announced our target was Stuttgart.[14]

Because Stuttgart was a major industrial centre with automative factories, military bases and an important rail interchange, the city was bombed repeatedly throughout the war. Between 16 and 29 July 1944 bombing raids struck Stuttgart on five nights. By mid-July 1944, to counter the constant attacks, Stuttgart had established very strong defences, including eleven heavy (88mm) and thirty-eight light (20-44mm) anti-aircraft gun batteries, as well as a nearby Luftwaffe night-fighter base. The city's location in a narrow valley also made it difficult to pinpoint.

Campbell was a member of the crew of Halifax LV833, P-Peter, in No.466 Squadron RAAF. The other crew members of P-Peter were pilot and captain, Flying Officer R.J. 'Jim' Walsh DFC, navigator Flight Sergeant Keith Smith, wireless operator Flight Sergeant Pat Conroy, flight engineer Sergeant Bob Palmer, rear gunner Flight Sergeant Mat Whitely and mid-upper gunner Sergeant Howard Lloyd. This night they also had a passenger, a 'second dickey', Pilot Officer W.D. Croft.

Croft was a new member of No.466 Squadron and was flying with P-Peter for operational experience, before going on a raid with his own crew. While a 'Second Dickey' was usually viewed as an unlucky encumbrance, perhaps a more important passenger in the crew's opinion was 'Peter Junior', a toy rabbit mascot, who flew every mission. It was a common practice for many crews to take a mascot which they looked upon as a lucky talisman. Flight Sergeant Campbell liked to keep 'Peter Junior' close by, tucked into his bomb-aimer's position.

Keith Campbell was born in Tamworth, northern New South Wales, in Australia on 18 September 1923, joined the RAAF Reserve at eighteen and, a year later in May 1942, was called up. In November 1942, he left for training as a bomb aimer in Canada, followed by further training in Britain, before joining No.466 Squadron at RAF Leconfield, Yorkshire. From Bomber Command bases at Leconfield and Driffield, before that night's operation, Campbell and his crew in P-Peter had completed thirty-three operations. Earlier in 1944, the number of operations to complete a tour was increased to forty. He was well aware that, inevitably, the odds on them completing a thirty-fourth and even reaching forty were lengthening each time they flew.

> Things went along normally – we went out to the kite, P-Peter, as usual – with 'Peter Junior' our pet rabbit mascot in the nose. We checked everything and went outside for our final smoke. The padre came around and wished us a good trip. Soon it was time to set off, so we took our place in the line to move up to the runway. Then the ground crew, only a few of them as it was about 22.00 hours, gave us the 'thumbs up' and we were in the air. In

> a few seconds we were circling around, waiting until all twelve aircraft had taken off, and gained height before setting course for Stuttgart.

The twelve Halifax bombers flew south over England at about 15,000 feet and then, at the planned turning point, climbed to 20,000 feet on a course over France. With no moon, the night was dark and, as forecast, as they flew on over occupied Europe the cloud below them began to break up.

> Occasionally one of the boys reported sighting one of the 700 bombers close to us. All of the equipment was working perfectly, and P-Peter was behaving well. Once over Germany the flak defences were very active, there were several bursts very close – we could hear shell fragments rattle against the bomb-bay. As usual I was leaning on my chute, in the nose looking down in the bomb-aimer's position. When moving around to see the targets more clearly, the left clip of my harness clipped accidently onto the hook in my parachute. Don't know why I always used my 'chute' to lean on, perhaps it was a feeling of security that its nearness seemed to give.

In some ways when in the target area, the bomb aimer lying in the aircraft's nose, was a second pilot giving the pilot instructions such as 'right a bit, left a bit' on the bombing run, as the pilot was unable to look down on the Pathfinder flares and markers.

Heavy flak was encountered over the target, in loose barrage form, stepped up from 16,000 to 22,000 feet.[4] Despite the flak, Campbell's guidance took them smoothly over the markers.

> The Pathfinder Force had been spot on, and we bombed on the markers OK, hoping as usual that our bombs would land in the middle of some flak battery. We turned after bombing and getting our photo, then Bob Palmer our engineer, said he was going back to check 'bombs gone' as by this time we were past the main defences. I only saw one fighter that night, an ME210, but he didn't bother us.

Bombing drill completed, Campbell turned around to get back to the H2S navigation aid.

> I was just about to unclip the 'chute when there was what seemed to be a heavy dull explosion behind me, and someone saying 'bloody hell … .' The next thing I knew I was in mid-air, floating down swinging on the end of a single strap of my harness!

An explosion, which Campbell at the time thought to be a stray flak shell scoring a direct hit on the Halifax, blasted him straight out of the nose of the aircraft.

> The explosion had blown the kite to hell. Only for the fact that my chute was on, I would have continued down to earth much faster than is good for one's health. I have no recollection of opening the 'chute, and I must have been temporarily knocked out, and the wind opened it. My helmet with its intercom plug and oxygen tube must have pulled out – damn lucky as they usually get hopelessly tangled. They can easily strangle you or break your neck.
>
> It took a long while to come down, and it was a fantastic experience. I could see the last of the raid, all the flak and searchlights at the target, the fires in the city, Pathfinder flares burning out, and strings of bombs bursting. It looked like a fairy land somehow, everything seemed so unreal. Saw several fighters fly past, going up to intercept the rest of the chaps, and an occasional burst of tracer, like a miniature meteorite, streaking across the sky.
>
> There was complete silence except for the creaking of the harness, and it was hard to realise what had actually happened. Luckily the wind was blowing away from Stuttgart, and I seemed to be slowly floating down, suspended in space by a single strap with a layer of thin clouds lazily coming up to meet me.
>
> At first I mistook the clouds for the ground, and made several 'perfect book landings' only to find I went right through what I thought was the ground. Finally when the real earth was about thirty feet away, it seemed to rush up at an alarming speed. Before I had time to do a 'book' landing, I was sprawled out in a wheat field, which was nice and soft luckily. I gradually realised that I was alive, and this was not a fantastic dream.

Campbell quickly remembered the drill on coming down in enemy territory. He removed his harness and bundled it up with his parachute. After taking out the torch from his 'Mae West' life-jacket, he placed the life-jacket and the bundled parachute into a depression in the ground before covering everything as best he could with stalks of wheat. He just had to hope it was not discovered too soon.

> My next thought was a cigarette, so I had one, and found my compass. I set off in a south-west direction to put as much distance between that spot and myself as possible. It was approximately 02.15 hours on the 25 July when I landed, so I had a few hours to walk before dawn. I left the wheat paddock and wandered across more fields until I found a road.

In one direction the road headed south-west and Campbell began to walk that way. The chance of encountering local people, vehicles or troops was a risk but he decided it was worth it. Eventually, he came to a small village. Should he stay on the road, or backtrack and make a detour of unknown length? In the dark he could become totally lost.

> I decided to walk through the village. At the village pump I was very glad of a drink and a wash, as I was rather thirsty and equally bloody from a few small cuts and grazes, received when I made my rather hurried exit from the kite. After washing, I felt I was a bit more presentable again. I continued on, and then saw two 'Jerries' approaching. Didn't quite know what to do, so promptly jumped into a ditch.

Praying that the two Germans had not seen anything, Campbell waited until they had passed. Then he resumed his walking until dawn began to break, when he found a wood with fairly thick undergrowth. He lay down under the cover of some bushes and made himself as comfortable as possible. Exhausted, he went straight to sleep

> I woke up at about 10.30 am, and felt a lot better. Then everything came back in a rush – instead of waking up in my bed, I was in the middle of Germany. And not very happy about things. I thought of the rest of our kites, and the crews who would have arrived back at the squadron. As usual someone would ask, 'Anyone missing?' The Intelligence Officer would say, 'Yes, P-Peter isn't back.' Some chap says 'Bloody bad show, another good crew gone.' And so my squadron career ends after thirty-three trips. And then I thought about the rest of the crew – it was only too obvious what had happened to them. Fortunately it was all over in a very few seconds.

Campbell lit up another cigarette and took stock. His typical escape kit included:

- Maps and compass
- Money
- Rations, which also contained three bars of chocolate, gum, sweets, Horlicks tablets, and other tablets of various medications
- Water bag
- First Aid Kit and a handkerchief
- Cigarettes (around 40) with matches and lighter
- A saw and a knife
- The torch from his 'Mae West'

In the event of capture he had his RAF identity card. He was also rather well off for clothes – being dressed for the cold at 15,000 to 20,000 feet flying altitude, with thick flying sweater, battledress, another sweater, flying underwear, flying and ordinary socks, flying boots and scarf.

> After that I took stock of my 'injuries', which I was very pleased to find consisted of only a few scratches and bumps. Then I cut off the tops of my flying boots, leaving an ordinary looking pair of shoes, removed my rank and brevet from my battledress, and settled down to study my maps. I had to decide on a plan of escape.

Being aware of the approximate position of the aircraft after completion of last night's bombing run, until the explosion, and by studying his maps and compass, Campbell was able to estimate his location. He thought it to be about thirty miles south of Stuttgart, but could not pinpoint the wood in which he lay hidden. Campbell's calculations of where had landed were probably very accurate. He did not know it at the time, but Halifax LV833 P-Peter crashed twenty-seven kilometres from Stuttgart at Plattenhardt.

He spent the rest of the day in a quandary, wondering what to do, and waiting for nightfall. Darkness would be his only friend.

> I finally decided to make for the Swiss border as it was the closest neutral country. However, I realised that it was practically impossible, as I had no knowledge of German, very little food, and the German police would be looking for the crews of planes shot down. I didn't set out again until about 22.00 hours as it was mid-summer, and consequently just getting dark. I found another road going approximately south, so I followed it for about half a mile when two men, probably farmers, turned a corner and walked towards me. It was no use turning around and going back, as they had already seen me.

Campbell kept on going. He did not know whether he should do a 'Heil Hitler' or not, as they got nearer. His escape attempt could soon be over. In the end he casually passed them without a word and they did not seem to think anything was wrong or out of order.

> About two hours later I heard the sirens go, and spent the next half hour watching the boys prang Stuttgart again. It was very interesting to see a big raid from the ground. First the multi-coloured flares, then the searchlights picking out the kites, the flak barrage and noise of the HE exploding, the

> fires and smoke caused by the incendiaries, and the tracers streaking across the sky – and the tragedy of a plane going down in flames.

Campbell was distracted from watching the pyrotechnics of the raid when he saw some lights and figures emerge from a farmhouse perhaps a hundred yards away. They, too, were watching the raid, so he waited until they went back inside before continuing. He had become very thirsty and had no water, so kept on hoping he would run across a stream or pass through another village with a water pump. 'A few more hours of walking passed and I found a small stream, so had a drink and a wash. I filled my water bag and ate a square of chocolate, with a few Horlicks tablets.'

He carried on until dawn, passing through several small villages where everyone was asleep, until just before dawn he found another wood. Breakfast was another piece of chocolate, Horlicks tablets and water, then Campbell went to sleep, hoping for the day to pass. Hunger and tiredness were now his constant companions.

> I woke about 10.00 hours and had another 'meal' – the same again. While I smoked a cigarette, from my maps I at last managed to locate the road, along which I had been walking, and where I now was. I tried to get to sleep again, but couldn't. I sat for about an hour and got thoroughly sick of doing nothing, so decided to explore the wood. I collected my belongings and pushed on.

After coming out of the wood Campbell found another stream, had a wash and replenished his water bag before following its course in good cover and into another wood. A half hour later, he emerged to see a fairly large town lay ahead of him. What should he do now, it blocked his path? Was there some way round it?

> I decided not to risk going through the town, so I retraced my steps for about half a mile, and then went off at right angles to try and go around the town. On this new course I came to some fields at the edge of a wood – I immediately wondered what might be growing there. It proved disappointing however – cabbages. Still it was something to eat, so I picked one and ate it. I was surprised how good it did taste, so I put one inside my battledress jacket for future eating.

He now found that the fields meant that he had approximately a half mile of open country to cross. Although the fields were heavily cultivated, wheat and cabbages mainly, he could not see any farm workers. He took the risk and walked on, grabbing ears of corn to eat as he went.

> I was very hot as I still had my battledress and all my flying clothing on, and it was a glorious summer day. So I threw away my flying boot tops, which I had kept as a comfortable pillow. When I came to a main road, I continued to walk along it. As there was a wood adjacent to the road, I thought that if I saw anyone I could easily divert off into it. After walking for about two miles I saw another town and a wide river ahead, so I walked along the bank of the river for a while. I was feeling tired again so sat down, had another look at my maps, and removed some of my heavy clothing.

In the warm sun he lay down against the bank of the river, and exhaustion soon sent Campbell off to sleep. After a short time, the shouts of some children, who were swimming in the river about 100 yards away, woke him. He picked up his gear and climbed up the bank as they swam in his direction. One of them, maybe after seeing his white sweater, which he had shed and thrown on the ground, began pointing and shouting. Soon all of them were shouting at him.

They might just have been saying 'Hello', but he left in such a hurry that he left his white sweater behind. It might betray him as an RAF flyer, but he was better off without it, he thought. He walked as quickly as he could across more fields, and followed some farm tracks. There were farmers in the fields, and some women cutting wheat, and tying it into sheaves. Campbell kept walking and no one said anything to him.

> I was still quite close to the river, and passed another group of swimmers. They waved and shouted, so I waved and shouted some kind of noise back at them. This seemed to be OK, and no one took any further notice of me. I kept on.

Campbell walked for another two days and nights, keeping to woods for cover wherever he could, or little-used roads. He saw very few people and doubted if they noticed him. One old chap said something to him, so he grunted in reply which seemed acceptable. On the next night he picked up cabbages and potatoes from another field, and in another wood lay down and fell asleep at about 3.00 a.m.

> I woke up at 09.00 hours feeling extra hungry. Breakfast that morning was raw potatoes and cabbage, with a square of chocolate. I ate the last three sweets, and felt a little better. So I set off and came to a road which I

followed for about three miles. The traffic became fairly heavy, passing military trucks, cars, bikes – some waved to me, so I waved back.

Campbell was in trouble. This could not last. At any moment he could be confronted and, unable to speak German, would be asked for his papers. He was on a road with quite busy traffic and decided to get away and make for the next wood. It was too late.

A civilian lorry passed me, and the driver signalled to me that he would give me a lift. I shook my head at him as he passed by, but he stopped anyway. As he was only about ten yards away, I felt that I couldn't do anything but keep on.

To turn away and retrace his steps would only arouse suspicion. Could he keep walking and just mutter something unintelligible again?

When I was level with the driver he said something to me that I didn't understand. But I replied in French, trying to make it seem that I was a French worker. Unfortunately, another chap with the driver said something in French – he knew the language better than me. The two of them had a little conference, and then asked me more questions, and finally taking out their identity cards and pointing at them, then at me. I only had my RAF card.

If I behaved I was likely to get on better, as the civilians weren't too well disposed towards the RAF. I gave him my RAF card, which he couldn't read anyway, but he kept it. Then he said in very halting English, 'You RAF – Englander Ja? Flieger?' I answered 'Ja', and he pointed at his lorry. So I resumed my journey by motor transport.

In the lorry with the driver and his passenger was a little girl. Campbell thought her to be about 5 years old.

I thought it would be a good thing if I gave her some of my remaining chocolate. This put my stocks up considerably, and when I shared what was left with the driver and his mate, they were very surprised, and managed to say 'thanks' in English. After driving on for about half an hour we arrived at Tubingen, where the driver stopped on the outskirts of the town.

The other chap went into a beer garden, and came out with three bottles of beer, one of which he held out to me and said 'beer?' So I didn't lose by investing half a block of chocolate. It was excellent beer, ice cold and

> tasted A1. After finishing the beer, they took me to a house, which had a large swastika on it, so I thought, 'Here's where the Gestapo get me.' They escorted me to the door, exchanged 'Heil Hitlers', and asked for someone there.

They were redirected to the railway yards where, once again, the three of them alighted and the driver pulled out a packet of Chesterfield cigarettes, offering one to Campbell. Ten minutes or so went by before a police officer in a green uniform appeared. He was holding a revolver.

> I was handed over to him, with a long explanation. It must have been a good report on me, as he put away that wicked looking revolver. But I noticed that he left the flap of his holster undone. He indicated that I was to go with him, and after a while we managed to have a very difficult conversation in bits of French, English and German – helped out with signs.
>
> He was quite a good type, but made it clear that I was 'his prisoner', and patted his gun! I was quite happy about being a prisoner, as by then I was very hungry, tired, dirty, and couldn't have carried on much further by myself. I had covered about forty to fifty miles, but would still have had a long way to go, and very little hope of getting to Switzerland. The show was over.

Following the usual interrogation process Campbell was sent to a PoW camp at Bankau in Poland. In January 1945, in the face of the Russian Army's advance, the camp was evacuated, and in the depths of a very severe winter Campbell and the other PoWs were marched to another camp at Luckenwalde some fifty miles south of Berlin. Then, in May 1945, they were liberated by the Russians and Campbell was flown back to Britain by RAF aircraft and, in August, repatriated to Australia.

* * *

Sixty-two tears later, in 2006, Keith Campbell was astonished to learn from the Historical Branch of the UK Ministry of Defence, that his Halifax was not hit by flak. It collided with another bomber of No.466 Squadron. Twelve Halifaxes had been despatched and those two were reported as missing. The rest of Campbell's crew were killed, as were all the crew of the other aircraft.[15]

By the freak chance of being ejected violently from the bomber, his parachute opening by some fluke spontaneously, and hanging from a single strap, Campbell was the only survivor from both crews. Maybe, as Halifax LV833 P-Peter was shot down, the toy rabbit mascot 'Peter Junior' brought Campbell his bizarre good fortune. Yet, once on the ground, it was his spirit, resilience and persistence that enabled him to survive his days on the run and the deprivations of PoW captivity in the freezing winter of 1944-45.

In late 1945, Keith Campbell returned to Australia, left the RAAF and, in 1948, married Berenice. With that same resolve and determination that he displayed in the war, he forged a new life and successful career in hotel and catering management and with Berenice had two children, Fiona and Peter.[16] His son's name would always be a reminder of LV833 P-Peter, his toy rabbit 'Peter Junior', and his miraculous escape.

He had been fortunate to avoid the carnage suffered on the Nuremberg raid and, even more so, his survival after being shot down near Suttgart, so that all his life Campbell considered himself very lucky to be alive. After Berenice died in 2013, Keith remained fit and active, living independently until at age ninety-five he died in July 2019.[17] It was seventy-five years almost to the day since that fateful operation to Stuttgart on 24 July 1944.

Notes

1. Middlebrook, *The Nuremberg Raid*, p.116
2. Veteran's account, Fl/Sgt Keith Campbell; Evans, *Airmen's Incredible Escapes*, pp.165-78
3. Middlebrook, op. cit., p.11/9
4. Ibid., p.117
5. Ibid., p.161
6. Ibid., p.170
7. Ibid., pp.154-5
8. Ibid., pp.121,151-2
9. Veteran's account, F/O Bryan Good; Evans, op. cit., pp.129-39
10. Middlebrook, op. cit., pp.138-40
11. Veteran's account, F/O Bryan Good
12. Middlebrook, op.cit., pp.138-40
13. Veteran's account, F/O Bryan Good
14. Veteran's account, Fl/Sgt Keith Campbell (and all subsequent direct quotes); NA Kew, AIR 27/1928/13, 24 July 1944, No.466 Squadron RAAF.
15. Veteran's account, Fl/Sgt Keith Campbell.
16. *Sydney Morning Herald*, Obituary, 20 July 2019.
17. Ibid.

Part II

North Africa, Mediterranean and Italy

Chapter 4

Escape to Join the Italian Partisans – a Scottish Commando is the Only Option

In the early months of 1942, the Allies' underlying strategy in North Africa was to interdict and strangle the Axis' supply routes from Sicily and southern Italy. As the days went by in May 1942, supply shortages did not prevent the eastward drive of Rommel's Panzerarmee Afrika. In late May, Rommel attacked the Gazala Line in Libya, driving the British Eighth Army back towards the Egyptian border.[1]

The Axis attack commenced on 26 May 1942 and, in the first two days, met stiff resistance from Eighth Army's new American Grant tanks. Because of a lack of any British counter-attack, Italian troops were able to regroup and bring forward new supplies for German armour. On 1 June German panzers surged through a major breach in the Gazala Line. In torrid tank battles in an area which became known as the 'Cauldron', Panzerarmee Afrika gained a crucial victory. Eighth Army lost more than 100 tanks, some 3,000 men taken prisoner and 150 Infantry Brigade effectively destroyed.[2]

* * *

Douglas Davidson from Motherwell in Scotland was a trooper in the Royal Tank Regiment, one of the units bearing the brunt of the Axis offensive. Davidson was born on 4 April 1919 at Motherwell, the third of four sons of well-educated parents, his father being a schoolteacher. He was 6-feet tall with blue eyes, yet had auburn hair, so that, at times, he was nicknamed 'ginger'. At 14 he ran away from home and, by claiming that he was 16, tried to enlist unsuccessfully in the Army. He tried again a year later, once more claiming he was 16, and this time did so successfully, joining the Royal Artillery.

Outwardly, Davidson appeared as someone with a calm and thoughtful personality but beneath the outward expression of those attributes, there was a stubborn streak with a seemingly fearless response to adversity. Despite his formal education being limited, he had an innate ability in mathematics and for planning ahead. In the late 1930s Davidson first served in the Royal Artillery in Egypt. Then, after the outbreak of war in1939, he was posted to 44th Royal Tank Regiment (RTR) in the Libyan campaign.[3]

On 1 June 1942, 44 RTR were overrun in the area defended by 150 Brigade near Knightsbridge in one of the battles for Tobruk, which resulted in Davidson and the majority of 44 RTR being captured. He, with some twenty others who were taken prisoner, met Rommel for whom they had a great respect as a soldier, and who ordered they should be treated well, given food and water, just as German troops were treated.

They were then held by Italian troops in a temporary camp for prisoners of war (PoW) at Derna on the north-east coast of Libya. In barbed-wire compounds men slept on the sand, teeming with lice, fleas and insects with nothing to cover themselves. Some were able to make a tent of sorts from a groundsheet with two metal uprights.[4]

Davidson's subsequent numerous escapes and survival are a story rarely equalled for persistence and an unquenchable spirit not to be incarcerated. The story that follows is drawn from Davidson's personal account, reports from the *Tank Journal* and other publications, and the private collection of his son, Ian Davidson.

One night in the summer heat Davidson and a few other PoWs lay in the open of the Derna camp and hoped for some cooling breeze to help them sleep. Davidson gazed up at the stars, startlingly bright in the desert air. It seemed to him to have gone very quiet and that the other PoWs had gone to sleep. He looked around and could not see any of the Italian troops who were meant to guard them. Perhaps they too had lain down and were asleep? Very slowly, intent on not making any noise, Davidson rolled onto his stomach and began to crawl inch by inch away from the slumbering group. The stars on the horizon were beckoning him.

When he had crawled perhaps twenty yards or so from the sleeping group, he got to his feet and found a way through the camp's temporary perimeter fence. He began to half trot away, veering in the direction of the north star. By dawn, he had reached the north Libyan coast on the Mediterranean. In daylight, Davidson's luck ran out. He was spotted by an Italian military patrol and that same day they returned him to the Derna PoW transit camp. Once again during the night, and undeterred by his failure to get away, he managed to slip away undetected. As before, he was seen walking towards the coast, recaptured, and returned to the Derna camp.

Some men at Derna were confined in cramped rooms and slept on concrete floors. Conditions for PoW officers were often better than for other ranks, but not always. Major Harry Sell and other officers at Derna were crammed into a tiny, narrow and dirty concrete cell which he thought was more like a jail in the London of the 1600s.

Despite escaping and being recaptured twice, Davidson's desire to escape remained unquenched. A few days later, he was plotting another escape attempt with six other PoWs. One of them had got hold of some wire-cutters and they were all desperate to avoid being transferred to a permanent PoW camp in Italy. Once in such a camp in Italy they would be held prisoner for an unknowable number of years, providing they survived. No one knew how long the war would last, or who would win.

Once again at night, Davidson and his fellow escapers cut the temporary wire fence surrounding the camp and all seven of them got away. Davidson decided to separate from the other six who were intent on heading towards the coast. This time he walked eastwards, hoping to reach the Eighth Army lines. When daylight came, he approached an Arab village as he realised that he needed food and water if he was to continue.

Luckily for Davidson, the villagers had no liking for their Italian colonial masters and their German allies. With a smattering of Arabic that he had picked up in his time in Libya, he conveyed his need for food, water and clothes to reach the British lines. With some dates and water, and an Arab *keffiyeh* on his head, he set off again on his easterly trek. Next day his luck ran out. Within sight of British positions, he was stopped by a German patrol and taken prisoner again.

When Davidson was returned to the Derna camp, he was locked up with three of the other escapees, who had been captured separately. The camp guards had lost patience with his repeated escape attempts. They saw him as a troublemaker and ringleader influencing other PoWs to escape and gave him a severe beating.

The scars on his back would stay with him for the rest of his life. Incredibly, Davidson's motivation to escape was still not extinguished. Yet again, a few nights later when the wounds on his back were beginning to heal, he once again found a way to crawl through the camp's perimeter fence of barbed wire. This time he was quickly recaptured in the morning.

Not surprisingly, the patience of the prison camp's Italian commanders had run out. They decided that Davidson should be executed by firing squad. It appeared final. Then, on the day of the designated execution, a senior British officer of the camp's PoWs made a plea for clemency to the camp commandant. His intervention must have been very persuasive for Davidson's execution was cancelled.

In late June, Davidson and other PoWs were transferred from Derna to a larger camp at Benghazi. Despite the blistering heat of the day, the nights were cold and hunger was ever present. There were around 1,000 men in a compound fenced in by barbed wire and with a machine-gun post on top of a 40-foot-high tower, as well as guards patrolling the perimeter. Daily rations were three pints of water per man and a tin of bully beef and two small loaves of bread between three PoWs. The shackles of captivity were tightening and becoming more oppressive, thought Davidson. There was no way he could put up with it.

One of the PoWs, Sergeant John Kelley felt that they had begun their journey to starvation.[6]

> We were searched for anything sharp, and if something was found it was confiscated. A few men luckily managed to keep their jackknives hidden, so we were able to use them to open the bully tins. Profiteering took over, £3 for an extra quart of water, cigarettes which were one piastre each rose to ten piastres. Sanitary arrangements were just a row of open trenches and the smell became unbearable.
>
> Empty day followed empty day, bored, dirty, and unshaven, with the main conversation being on food and how to get more. By early July, morale was low and sickness high. Then on 6 July there was great excitement when the RAF bombed Benghazi Harbour, and did it again on the 9th.
>
> On Sunday 12 July there was a service by a South African padre, but by now many men's health was getting poor. We were dirty, unshaven and lice started to appear. We found the guards would sell forty cigarettes for one Egyptian pound. A cookhouse was built, but we only got one hot meal every third day.

The first hot meal provided by the cookhouse was on 17 July, one pint of rice with a half-tin of bully beef per man, cooked in what looked to Kelley to be a stodge of olive oil.

> Dysentery broke out amongst the weakest of us, but only the worst cases were given medical care. I reckon about sixty died at this time. Our daily routine was, get up when you felt like it, or able to, pass the time somehow until noon when rations were drawn, then go to bed early to escape the day and its heat.

By 25 July the reality of how weak the PoWs had become hit home, when they were required to do some manual work.

> New latrines were needed to be dug, so the labour had to be divided up in a roster, and each man could only dig for two minutes. Many were unable to complete even their two minutes. A couple of guys made an escape attempt hanging on the underside of a rubbish truck. Unfortunately, the

truck went into the next compound, where they were seen and recaptured. The guards brought them back in chains, in which they spent the next forty-eight hours.

The officers' camp conditions at Benghazi were no improvement, thought Major Sell.

Our quarters were grimly overcrowded, lice and fleas abounded, any food was a disgusting mess, an open cess-pit in the yard was breeding millions of flies, which swarmed over everything and everybody. But even this was luxury compared with the compounds of other ranks.

On 27 July Sergeant Kelley and his fellow prisoners saw that groups of PoWs from the next compound were beginning to be moved out and they had heard rumours that it was for transfer to camps in Italy.

On July 31 we were given one tin of bully between two men, so we knew that it would soon be us, and began pooling our food to sustain us on the journey. Next day we were roused and paraded at 03.30 hours and marched to the docks. On the way it was good to see the damage done by RAF bombing. We embarked on the *Rosalino Pilo*, which although modern soon became more of a slave ship, as we were crammed into its holds.

If any of us were slow on the ladders the Libyan crew and dock workers stamped on our fingers and then threw sea water at us through the gratings. A meal of of cold fried bread, bully and water arrived at 11am, before we sailed at noon, but the heat was stifling and we dreaded the night.

The PoWs were told the next stop was Tripoli and then by ship across to Naples.

Rations were lowered to us in the hold in buckets at 4pm – just a tin of bully and biscuits. The dysentery cases became so bad that those cases were allowed on deck. We tried to sleep despite the heat, the engine noise and smell of engine oil – it was a long night, going into the unknown.

As dawn approached the hold was silent save for a few groans and moans. Then I heard an unknown person playing 'solitude' on a mouth organ. My feelings and thoughts were the same, I could sympathise with him. We were allowed up on deck at 8am and managed to stay there all day. One man was hauled up unconscious and taken off when we docked at Tripoli, which we reached at noon.

When Davidson and other PoWs were disembarked in Italy, they were transported to prison camp PG70 at Monturano in the Marche region. Monturano is some fifty kilometres south of Ancona on the central Adriatic coast. Camp PG70 can be best described as part of an industrial complex of some 4-6 acres, with large brick-built warehouses used to accommodate the prisoners next to a railway line.[7]

Conditions at PoW camps in Italy varied but were often little better than in North Africa. Food was meagre and devoid of any necessary daily sustenance. A typical breakfast could be only a cup of pseudo-coffee, made from burnt wheat or barley. Lunch would be 150 grams of bread, 28 grams of cheese and, on occasional days, some scraps of horsemeat. The usual evening meal was a pint of rice or macaroni soup with pieces of a few potatoes, onions and dandelion leaves. Only the delivery of Red Cross food parcels once a week saved the PoWs from mass death from starvation.[8]

Davidson was remarkably undeterred by his series of failed escape attempts in North Africa and began to dream of possible new scenarios to escape once more. This was in spite of the penalty for an escaping PoW who was recaptured having become ever more dangerous. Italian authorities introduced a reward of 1,000 lire to any prison guard who prevented a prisoner from escaping in any way necessary, including lethal force. In some instances, where PoWs bribed guards to turn a blind eye to an escape, the guard broke his word, shot the PoW dead and then claimed the 1,000 lire reward.[9]

Meanwhile, in September 1943, after the Allied landings at Reggio and Salerno in southern Italy, and Mussolini having been ousted in July, on 8 September Eisenhower announced an armistice with a new Italian government under Marshal Badoglio. This caused German forces in Italy to take control of all Italian prison camps, and although some PoWs simply walked out of unguarded camps before the Germans arrived, the transportation began of PoWs by train in cattle trucks to Germany.

In late September, Davidson and other prisoners were boarded onto a train of cattle trucks which pulled out of Monturano and began its journey to a PoW camp at an unknown destination in Germany. Men's thoughts turned to dread of worse conditions, interminable imprisonment and likely death in a Nazi concentration camp. Davidson found the thought totally unacceptable and decided that he must find a way to escape en route.

Bolted into a cattle truck as the train rolled northwards, Davidson examined the inside of the truck's door to see if it could be forced open. He noticed that at the end of one of the door's wooden struts there was a gap wide enough for his hand to penetrate. He began to wrench and lever the strut. With a couple of other PoWs, he also worked on the adjoining door struts, pulling, pushing, twisting and loosening them until they had created a gap large enough for a man to squeeze through.

When the train halted somewhere, it would be an opportunity to struggle out of the cattle truck and make a run for it. But where and when would the train stop? Surely it could not travel non-stop all the way to Germany? Davidson and one or two other would-be escapers were becoming increasingly impatient and willing the train to come to a halt.

As the train approached Bologna it began to slow. Davidson decided there was no point in waiting for it to stop at Bologna station or in a marshalling yard where the gaping hole in the truck door might be discovered. This was a chance that might not re-occur. He thought the train's speed had slowed to perhaps less than 20 mph and there looked to be a grassy verge next to the track. He pulled himself through the gap in the door and, almost in the same movement, kicked himself away from the truck.

He hit the ground hard and, gasping for breath, rolled with his momentum, then flattened himself on the ground and waited for the train to disappear down the line. 'I saw two others make the jump after me, and saw one man hit a telegraph post and likely killed, but another looked to land safely.'[10]

There were no shouts or alarms sounding, so perhaps he had been lucky and his jump from the train had not been seen. Davidson picked himself up and ran into some nearby woods. Running as fast as he could, with no idea whether he was being pursued, he only knew that he had to get away quickly from the railway line. Using a smattering of Italian picked up in the PoW camp, he was able to obtain help from the local population.

He was even luckier when he made contact with some Italian partisans who were fighting against the German occupation. Cold, hungry and dehydrated, he had no choice. He must join their ranks and fight with them if he was to survive. With a workable knowledge of the Italian language, he soon convinced them that he would be a valuable addition to their ranks. They were a motley group of different nationalities and political persuasions.

At the partisans' hideout in the mountains, Davidson's knowledge of the Italian language and his experience as a soldier led to him being given the leadership of about fifty partisans who became known as the 'Davidson commando'. Over nearly a year, Davidson led the commando in sabotage and harrying guerilla attacks on German forces. On three occasions he was wounded in firefights and, in one encounter, broke a leg.

In late October 1943, north of the Trigno river on the Adriatic Coast, the Battle Patrol of the 1st Battalion East Surreys made contact behind German lines with some partisans. One of them was a Scots woman and her husband, a doctor, who had left the surrendered Italian army. He may well have subsequently treated Davidson for his injuries.[11] In late 1944, Davidson and his fellow partisans were able to make contact with the advancing Allied forces in central Italy, and he was able to leave the partisans, and rejoin the British Army.[12]

Davidson had escaped from a PoW camp on four occasions which certainly made him amongst a very small number of PoWs who had done so on multiple occasions – and survived. His 'never say die' spirit in persisting with escaping from PoW camps and then joining the Italian partisans to fight the Germans, led to Davidson being awarded the Distinguished Conduct Medal.

After the war Douglas Davidson threw himself into post-war life with undiminished energy and a desire to explore new opportunities wherever they might be. He was commissioned as a lieutenant in 1946 but resigned in 1947 to take up a position as a colonial police officer in Malaya, with his wife Cecelia, 'Cis', until 1958. After that time, and eighteen months of life in New Zealand, they returned to the UK with their three children, Sandra, Michael and Ian, and Douglas Davidson took positions in management with companies such as Lucas and then Mace until retirement. Even that was hardly retirement, as he then worked as a ghillie on the River Wye in Wales. He died in 1993 and Cecelia in 2000.

Notes

1. Evans, *The Decisive Campaigns of the Desert Air Force, 1942–45*, p.26
2. Collier, *War in the Desert*, p.90
3. Ian Davidson – Private Collection; Green, *Tank Journal – Escapers All*, February 1995
4. Clarke, *Prisoners of War*, p.30
5. *Second World War Experiences Centre*, Major H. Sell (https://war-experience.org)
6. *The Wartime Memories Project*, Sergeant John Kelley, (https://wartimememoriesproject.com/ww2/view)
7. Ian Davidson – Private Collection; Green, op. cit.
8. Clarke, op. cit., p.30
9. Ibid., p.84
10. Ian Davidson – Private Collection; Green, op. cit.
11. Evans, *With the East Surreys in Tunisia, Sicily and Italy 1942–45*, p.94
12. Ian Davidson – Private Collection; Green, op. cit.

Chapter 5

Hi-jacking a Sea-plane, and escaping Italian style

One solitary Italian military guard sat in the aircraft cabin with the four prisoners of war (PoWs), four RAF airmen. They were being flown by seaplane from a Greek coastal air base to Taranto in southern Italy, from where they would be transported to a PoW camp. Silently, they looked on in amazement as their guard slumped forward in his seat, convulsed and groaning with airsickness. The four airmen stared at each other with an unspoken question in their eyes – 'Is this a chance to hi-jack this plane?'

* * *

Embedded in the centuries' old wall of the Grandmaster's Palace in St George's Square in Valletta, the capital of Malta, there is a royal announcement engraved on a stone plaque, that reads:

The Governor
Malta

To honour her brave people I award the George Cross to the Island Fortress of Malta to bear witness to a heroism and devotion that will long be famous in history.

George R.I.
Buckingham Palace
April 15th 1942

At the time of the award by King George VI, Malta had been enduring ever increasing air raids by the Axis powers Germany and Italy, and there seemed no end to the constant interdiction en route to Malta of both airborne and shipping supplies. Malta's survival as a critical base in the Mediterranean for Britain and her Allies hung by a thread. There was a strong view that, if Malta fell to the Axis, British forces in Egypt and Libya would be doomed.

After Rommel with his Panzerarmee Afrika captured Tobruk in June 1942, the Axis army continued the pursuit of British Eighth Army into Egypt. As part of the plan to defeat Eighth Army and occupy Egypt, Axis paratroops were readied to assault the island of Malta.

Essential supplies for Malta could only be brought in by ship, but these were being strangled by Axis attack. Food, fuel, medicines, military equipment, and reinforcements of troops were sent on merchant ships in convoys which the Royal Navy, its Fleet Air Arm and the RAF attempted to protect. Those convoys were suffering severe losses and Malta was being increasingly blockaded and starved towards surrender.

By the end of June Malta's population and military forces were almost out of food, and lacking fuel and other crucial supplies. At the same time Axis convoys between Italy and Libya to re-supply Rommel were also incurring heavy losses from attacks by British aircraft, naval ships and submarines operated from Malta. It was critical for Rommel that Malta was captured, and his supply routes made safer.[1]

* * *

Interdiction of Axis supplies bound for North Africa took many forms but essentially by Royal Navy surface ships and submarines and aircraft of the Fleet Air Arm and the RAF. One of the types of aircraft operated by the RAF was the torpedo-bomber. In an operation by one of those torpedo-bomber squadrons seeking to cut off Rommel's supplies there occurred one of the most bizarre, possibly unique, escape and survival experiences. In July and August 1942 Wing Commander Patrick Gibbs was commander of No.217 Squadron RAF, based in Malta, flying Beaufort torpedo-bombers.[2]

Gibbs arrived at the squadron in the last week of April 1942. After being posted in late 1941 from a squadron of Beauforts in Coastal Command to Cairo, he had spent nearly a year in a desk job. He had kept pressing to no avail to join an operational squadron until 14 April 1942. On that day, No.39 Squadron of Beaufort torpedo-bombers lost many of their best crews and aircraft and Gibbs was tasked with rebuilding the squadron, and the survivors' shattered confidence.

In early August he led an operation of six Beauforts to attack an Italian cargo ship on its voyage from Zante towards Sapienza, at some 300 miles range on the Greek isthmus of Corinth. The merchant ship was escorted by two Italian destroyers and two E-boats. Gibbs' intention was to intercept the convoy and attack it head on. As they neared the island of Prote, close to the Greek coast, he received a message from a reconnaissance aircraft that the Italian ships were farther south. It meant that it must now be a more dangerous attack from astern. From this engagement would arise an amazing escape and survival situation.

Gibbs led his flight past the rear destroyer and began to turn for an approach run towards the Italian freighter's port side, readying to launch torpedoes. The azure blue sky and blue sea belied the violence and destruction that was about to occur. As Gibbs and his section of Beauforts skimmed just above the waves, blistering anti-aircraft fire burst out from the destroyers and the merchant ship turned rapidly to try to sail head-on towards the attack, to reduce the chance of a torpedo strike.

Instinctively, Gibbs took his flight into another turn, then straightened again to aim for the vessel side on. Six torpedoes, dropped into the sea from the Beauforts, surged towards the target. Because of the change of position seconds before release of the torpedoes, Gibbs doubted if any of the six would strike home. As he led the six Beauforts in a tight turn and climb away, he saw an explosion on the port side of the ship. A huge spout of water shot into the air. One torpedo had hit the freighter, bringing it to an abrupt standstill.

The sight of this success was quickly dismissed from his thoughts when he saw that the Beaufort to his right, that of his close friend pilot Ted Strever, had suffered an anti-aircraft hit in its port engine. White smoke poured out from the back of the engine like a vapour trail. Gibbs found his radio was out of action, so did not know if Strever had tried to communicate. Within a minute or so, Strever turned away, losing height, and headed towards the nearest Greek coastline.

In another flight involved in the attack on the cargo ship a pilot of a Beaufighter saw Strever's Beaufort ditch into the sea and had enough fuel to circle the stricken aircraft. He reported that he watched as the crew clambered into an inflated dinghy before the Beaufort sank below the waves. Gibbs did not hear of this until he returned to Malta and assumed that since they had gone down so close to the enemy coast they would be rescued and taken prisoner. Even so he went to bed that evening with the memory of his friend Ted Strever being forced to break away from the formation and head towards the coast. If Strever and his three crew made it, they would be captured and made prisoners of war (PoWs).[3]

* * *

While Gibbs came to terms with losing another Beaufort torpedo-bomber and more good friends, actions were being taken in the UK to strengthen significantly the capability of torpedo-bombers in Africa and Malta. Yet, in mid-1942, the challenge of flying new aircraft to RAF squadrons in Malta and Egypt was fraught with risk and subject to heavy losses from interception by Axis fighters, as well as attrition from mishap en route. Enemy fighters shore-based in Sicily, southern Italy and islands such as Pantellaria were taking a heavy toll on any Allied aircraft that ventured across the Mediterranean skies.

But rather than being sent via the only alternative itinerary, trans-Africa from Takoradi on the African west coast over to Sudan, then north to Cairo, increasing urgency meant that some aircraft were flown through the Mediterranean to Cairo. One such flight was to deliver the latest Wellington Mark VIII torpedo-bomber to Cairo and bolster the interdiction campaign which was seeking to tighten the blockade supplies to Rommel's Axis Army.

In the UK in July 1942 Flight Lieutenant Bill McRae had recently completed his final training as a pilot of a Wellington bomber and he and his crew were awaiting posting to an operational squadron. Without any prior notification, and with him and his crew lacking any operational experience, McRae was given an unexpected and critically important mission.

> We were handed a brand new Wellington Mark VIII, and ordered to fly to Cairo via Gibraltar and Malta. This Wellington was rather a special one – festooned with radar aerials, associated instruments and equipment, and modified to carry torpedoes. It was to be used to locate and attack enemy vessels at night. At the time the equipment was highly secret and we were briefed on how to destroy the Wellington aircraft should we be forced down in enemy territory.
>
> I must say the thought occurred to me that my RAF superiors were taking a bit of a risk in entrusting this aircraft to me. A ferry flight they called it! The later part of the flight would be at night into Malta to hopefully avoid enemy fighters, and I confess I was none too confident of my ability to fly in the dark. My night flying training in England had been limited.[4]

Bill McRae was twenty-nine years old, originally from Sydney, Australia and, at the outbreak of war, was working for the Bank of New South Wales in London. He joined the Royal Artillery and, in November 1940, was temporarily attached to the RAF with whom he learned to fly light aircraft for directing artillery. A year later, McRae transferred permanently to the RAF and, in April 1942 commenced training as a pilot of Wellington bombers.

In the Second World War flying training at every stage was fraught with accidents, injuries and deaths. During aircrew training in the RAF the overall casualty rate was a shocking 13 per cent. There were also many lucky escapes, some quite freakish. Then, if an air crew made it through, they faced that initial and daunting test, a first operation into enemy skies.

Now at 08.00 hours on 29 July 1942, McRae lifted the RAF 's latest radar-equipped Wellington into the air at Portreath in Cornwall. For McRae and his crew, on their first operational flight with a new specially-equipped aircraft, it truly was a flight into the unknown.

> On the flight out to Gibraltar there were no problems, until I asked my navigator to come up front to see the Rock. Suddenly the airspeed fell away and we began to lose altitude. I opened the throttles fully to try and maintain height.

McRae somehow kept calm. Visions swirled in his head of having to ditch in the sea. It could be the end of him and his crew on their first operation. Strong crosswinds around the Rock and across the Bay of Algeciras made landings extremely dangerous. After a couple of minutes on full power struggling to maintain height, McRae realised that the aircraft's flaps were fully down. His navigator had accidentally put his hand on the flap lever when he was leaning over to get a better view!

At 16.00 hours McRae put down and, after England, Gibraltar was another world: sun, clear blue sky, hot weather, plenty of food and drink. However, McRae and his crew got little sleep that night in a hut next to the runway, roused constantly by continuous aircraft landings and take-offs.

> At 16.00 hours the next day we took off on the 1,000 mile overnight flight to Malta. At the briefing we were told to keep radio silence, and call up Malta about half an hour before reaching the island. They would respond to us with a course to steer. We were warned that Malta lay only about eighty miles south of Sicily, and its Axis air bases.

An error in navigation could bring them close to Sicily's southern coast, and the marauding night-fighters of the Luftwaffe.

* * *

Meanwhile in Malta, on the day after the attack on the Italian merchant ship, the aircrew of No.217 Squadron were given the day off for recreation and Wing Commander Gibbs went swimming with another crew member at one of Malta's coves known as the Blue Grotto. When he returned and walked into the squadron's Intelligence Office, he was dumbfounded. For a second or two he thought he was looking at four ghosts.

> Then the ghosts came to life, and I found myself listening to a story such as I never thought could exist outside fiction.[5]

There follows an edited summary of Ted Strever's account of how the four airmen survived and escaped back to Malta:[6]

> After we suffered a hit in the port engine, we had only one option – to try and make for the Greek coast. However, we lost height too quickly, ditched in the sea, and the four of us managed to clamber into an inflatable dinghy before the aircraft sank. I estimated that we were about five miles from the coast. A Beaufighter had seen us and circled around for a while, so we had hope that we might be rescued if there was a Royal Navy ship in the area.

For a few hours they floated in their dinghy, getting no closer to the shoreline. Eventually they were spotted and rescued by an Italian Navy flying boat, which took them back to their naval base. Following questions from Italian intelligence officers, the four aircrew were treated to sumptuous food and wine in the officers' mess. During the evening's hospitality Strever was amazed at a message read out from an Italian admiral.

> The admiral congratulated our squadron on its successful attack on their merchant ship! But in the morning we were taken aboard a flying boat once more, and we took off for Taranto in Italy for further interrogation. From there we were informed we would be moved to a prisoner of war camp. The thought of this made us quickly forget the previous night's joviality.

The aircraft had two pilots and a flight engineer but only one soldier to guard the four airmen in the aft cabin. The stark reality of being prisoners of war hit them. They were being flown by seaplane from a Greek coastal air base to Taranto in southern Italy and were then to be transported to a PoW camp. Silently they looked on in amazement as their guard slumped forward in his seat, convulsed and groaning with air sickness. The four airmen stared at each other with an unspoken question in their eyes – Is this a chance to hi-jack this plane?'

> The four of us looked at each other knowingly. Then I hit the guard hard, down he went, grabbed his gun, and got another surprise. Hard to believe but it was not loaded! I knew we had to act at once. I went forward to the cockpit, my crew behind me. Despite the gun not being loaded, I pushed its barrel into the back of the pilot's neck. When I demanded the pilot change

> course, he shouted something in Italian that was clearly not an agreement. The second pilot got physical so we had to quickly overpower him also.
>
> I took over as pilot, although the controls were difficult to operate, and my navigator tried to assess our position, and set a course for Malta. After a while the Italian pilot must have realised my efforts were becoming risky, and that we all may end up in the drink. By his hand signals, an odd word or two, and a more agreeable manner, he showed that he wanted to help. So I let him take over.
>
> By this time we found that we were now in the Italian Gulf of Taranto, so we persuaded the pilot by various means to change course to the south. It meant we had some two hundred miles to fly south towards Malta, close to the Italian coast, the foot and toe of Italy, on our starboard side. It dawned on us that despite our Italian air force markings on our seaplane, if an enemy aircraft approached us, we had no idea if we would be required to give some kind of recognition signal. Obviously, we could not rely on our Italian pilots to tell us.
>
> I felt sure we would be intercepted, and our nerves began to jangle. First a formation of Luftwaffe Junkers 88s passed by without any interest, and we breathed again. Then some ME 109s streaked past us, also disinterested, and our nerves calmed.

Their relief was premature and Strever's heart rate accelerated 'when an Italian aircraft for a few minutes joined in a friendly formation with our flying boat!'

Amazingly, this close encounter came to nothing. Strever and his crew were stunned both to see their own Italian pilots do nothing untoward to alert the enemy aircraft, and then to see it turn away and fly off on some other mission. Yet as they neared Malta another stark realisation came to Strever. They were in an Italian flying boat, an easy target, a sitting duck for RAF fighters to shoot down. His new fear soon materialised,

> The most scary moment by far arose when we were within sight of Malta. A flight of Spitfires, maybe a dozen at a guess, sighted us and naturally dived like hawks on their prey. Luckily I had instructed our Italian pilot to fly low in case this kind of interception happened. We were fortunate the sea was calm, and I ordered the pilot to immediately to make a water landing. Once we were down we waved white handkerchiefs, anything white, to signal our surrender. However the Spitfires dived towards us, and we expected to be strafed and sunk. With Malta minutes away we appeared to be doomed.

As Strever and crew cowered, trying to take shelter, the Spitfires roared low over the flying boat but, amazingly, did not fire. The white handkerchiefs had saved them. A little later, a Royal Navy launch reached them and towed the Italian flying boat intact into Malta's harbour. Not only had Strever and his crew escaped from capture, they had brought home a prize enemy aircraft and three prisoners.

That night Gibbs laid on a party in the mess for Strever and his crew. The story of this most bizarre escapade and miraculous evasion from captivity spread through Malta like wildfire. No one there knew that there would be some surprise latecomers to the celebrations.

* * *

While Strever told of their miraculous escape, McRae's flight from Gibraltar was seeming to be uneventful, until they believed that they were nearing Malta. Although given a course by radio from control in Malta, almost immediately they were enveloped in low cloud and unable to see the ocean or the horizon.

> We were at 3,000 feet and although there was a half moon, heavy cloud was blotting out any lights of Valletta town and its airfield. After circling around for ten minutes, we thought we spotted it through the cloud. Keeping in mind we might be way off course, and over Sicily, and also aware there were hills reaching up to 700 feet in Malta, we carefully descended. Suddenly there was break in the cloud, and we caught sight of the aerodrome flare path. We touched down at 01.00 hours on 31 July, and I was relieved my night landing was reasonable.
>
> When we reported to the aerodrome control officer, the first thing he said was, 'You seemed to be wandering around a long time. We were beginning to get a bit worried.' I felt like replying, 'So was I'. He told us to taxi the aircraft away into a blast shelter, and be back at daybreak. We then went into the mess for a cup of tea and ran into an enormous and raucous party.[7]

Over numerous drinks, McRae and his crew heard the extraordinary story of the hi-jacking of an Italian seaplane by Strever and his crew. Everyone at these festivities, of course, could not know what a significant impact this new Wellington torpedo-bomber, flown by McRae and his crew to Malta, and others to follow, would have on the North African campaign.

* * *

The third Battle of El Alamein began on 24 October 1942, launched by the British Eighth Army. With the offensive underway it was critical that interdiction of Axis supplies was intensified.

There follows a summary of Flight Lieutenant Wiggins' account, and the Operations Record Book of No.38 Squadron RAF, of the sorties on 24-26 October 1942:[8]

On 24 October at 1800 Wing Commander Pratt of 38 Squadron led four Wellingtons in an operation to locate and attack an enemy convoy, which was known to be heading for Tobruk. They were first ordered to rendezvous with a specially-equipped Wellington of 221 Squadron. Severe electrical storms forced the abandonment of the operation without finding the convoy.

At 23.30 Flight Lieutenant Wiggins and Sergeant Taylor of 38 Squadron, in two stand-by Wellingtons, took off in a second attempt but, because of extensive cloud, were unable to locate the convoy.

On the 26th at noon five Beaufort and four Bisley bombers of No.47 Squadron RAF, attacked the escorted convoy of cargo ships making for Tobruk. Their attack on the convoy included a direct hit on the oil tanker *Proserpina* (4,809 tons), which caught fire. The *Proserpina* had been carrying 2,500 tons of petrol.

So critical was the supply situation for the Axis ground forces that both sides were committing every resource possible in the struggle over Axis supply channels. Six of the attacking aircraft were lost to either enemy fighters or anti-aircraft fire from the ships. A second operation by Beauforts failed to locate the remaining ships, which were still on schedule to reach Tobruk, before night-flying Wellington torpedo bombers would be available to interdict. Since the supplies were so crucial for the Axis army, it was decided to risk an operation by 38 Squadron for the first time at dusk.

Summary of Sortie Details No.38 Squadron RAF, 26 October 1942:

At 1540 Flight Lieutenant Wiggins led three Wellington bombers in formation, with Pilot Officer Bertran and Sergeant Viles in Nos 2 and 3 positions respectively. The weather and visibility were good, with minimal cloud. The three aircraft proceeded at 100 feet until they were about 60 miles out to sea. They then turned westward, and proceeded parallel to the coast until they were approximately 60 miles north east of Tobruk. Navigation was perfect and they were able to make an immediate approach in formation.

In the first dusk attack ever attempted by 38 Squadron, the three planes headed straight for a large merchant vessel, the *Tergestea*, thought to be carrying both army supplies and fuel and lying perhaps two miles outside Tobruk harbour. There were many destroyers escorting the *Tergestea* but they were taken completely by surprise. It was not until the aircraft were beginning their run within two miles of the *Tergestea* that frantic signalling took place from the destroyers to the merchant vessel.

All three aircraft dropped their torpedoes at a distance of around 500 to 600 yards from the target. The three torpedoes were seen to be running straight towards *Tergestea*, which appeared to be stationary, perhaps at anchor in the water. One or more torpedoes hit the ship, causing an enormous explosion. The aircraft crews then observed a huge column of black smoke, surging up from *Tergestea* to an estimated 3,000 feet.

After dropping his torpedo, Flight Lieutenant Wiggins chose to take his aircraft climbing straight over the top of *Tergestea*, attracting the greatest concentration of anti-aircraft fire from the escort destroyers, so as to draw fire away from the other two bombers. Despite his aircraft suffering multiple hits, Wiggins was able to maintain his escape flight beyond the range of the destroyers' guns.

Wiggins' bombing run came in with a dark sky behind the three Wellington bombers, whereas their target, *Tergestea*, stood out against the sun setting in the west. Of six torpedoes launched, three ran well, striking the motor vessel *Tergestea* (5,890 tons).

Sergeant Bertran was able to turn away to starboard and received lighter anti-aircraft fire. After releasing its torpedo, Sergeant Viles' aircraft was seen to stagger, probably from receiving fire from the destroyers. The last that was seen of Viles was his aircraft breaking away to port. Both Wiggins and Bertran safely completed their return flights to base.

The cargo of *Tergestea* comprised 1,000 tons of petrol and 1,000 tons of ammunition. A further operation that night reported that there was no sign of *Tergestea* which must have sunk. Nothing remained of the convoy except for the tanker *Proserpina*, now settling low in the water and still burning after the earlier Beaufort attack.[20]

Such was the strategic importance of denying these fuel supplies to Rommel's Axis forces that General Montgomery expressed his personal gratitude for the outstanding efforts of 38 Squadron and 201 Group RAF in assisting Eighth Army's offensive:

> Recent attacks carried out against enemy ships so vital to his effort were a wonderful achievement. I would be grateful if you would convey to those responsible our gratitude for operations carried out which must be epic against ships at sea.[9]

On the other hand, Rommel felt that the fuel supply shortage, by constraining his actions, was making his position increasingly untenable.

> The tanker *Proserpina*, which we hoped would bring some relief in the petrol, had been bombed and sunk outside Tobruk. There was only enough petrol to keep supply traffic going between Tripoli and the front for another two or three days, and that without counting the needs of the motorised forces, which had to be met out of the same stocks.[10]

If equipped with sufficient petrol supplies, Rommel would have been able to move substantial forces from the south to mount a major counter-attack in the north. As it was, he only risked moving 21st Panzer to the north, knowing they could not return. He also reported directly to Hitler's HQ that, unless supplies improved significantly, the battle would be lost. That evening he wrote to his wife telling her that the situation was critical.[11]

On 27 and 28 October Rommel wrote to his wife again, in a near defeatist mood, and doubting that he would survive. When he heard of the loss of *Tergestea*, coming only twenty-four hours after the destruction of *Proserpina*, Rommel must have been despondent. His last hope of any extra fuel supplies, in time to make a difference to his army's plight, was gone. On 4 November, with his forces under threat of encirclement, Rommel ordered a retreat.[12]

Flight Lieutenant Wiggins thought that the loss of *Tergestea* was probably the last straw for Rommel and had condemned his Panzerarmee to retreat. Wiggins, of course, had a personal interest. He knew that Australian troops were fighting and dying on the Alamein battleground.[26] What Wiggins did not know was that there was also another Australian connection. Three months earlier it was fellow Australian, Flight Lieutenant Bill McRae, who had flown the first radar-equipped Wellington Mk VIII torpedo-bomber out to Egypt,.

Notes

1. National War Museum (NWM), Malta
2. Gibbs, *Torpedo Leader*, pp.145-52
3. Veteran's account, S/Ldr McRae
4. Evans, *The Decisive Campaigns of the Desert Air Force 1942–1945*, pp.20-4
5. Gibbs, op. cit., p.149
6. Gibbs, op. cit., pp.149-51
7. Veteran's account, S/Ldr McRae
8. Veteran's account, F/Lt Wiggins, and Evans, op. cit., pp.45-51
9. Evans, op.cit., pp.45-51
10. Ibid.
11. Ibid.
12. Ibid.

Chapter 6

Surviving a Day at a Time – the Fragile, Knife-edge Life of a Bomber Pilot

Despite the port engine of the Wellington bomber spluttering and sporadically cutting out, pilot Bill McRae had taken it into the approach, a night bombing run on the Tunis docks. As he climbed the aircraft away, so much slower than he wanted, the port engine shut down completely. Seconds became an eternity – the Wellington was becoming a sitting duck for the Axis anti-aircraft gunners. And even if they could get clear of the enemy defences, he knew that on only one engine they would keep losing height all the way on the return flight to Malta – and they might not make it. For two and a half hours, they would be descending all the time towards a dreaded ditching in the sea.[1]

* * *

The following is a summary of interviews with Squadron Leader Bill McRae DFC AFC and extracts drawn from his memoir writing, diary and logbook during his deployment to No.104 Squadron RAF in Malta in December 1942 and January 1943.[2]

For a bomber pilot and his crew every day staying alive was an escape and another day of survival. In the North African campaign and related operations from Malta, crashes and subsequent deaths arising from poor aircraft serviceability and the resulting accidents and mechanical failures were common, in addition to being shot down by enemy fighters and anti-aircraft fire. There were horrendous losses of aircraft and airmen in the North African, Mediterranean and Italian campaigns. In 1943 alone, Allied air forces lost over 700 aircraft in operations to cut off enemy supplies and to gain air superiority to support the Tunisian and Italian campaigns.

Compared to today's sophisticated aviation technology with such as GPS and electronic communications, the challenge of navigation over huge expanses of featureless desert and sea could mean flights veering off a planned route, running out of fuel or being forced down in the desert or ditching in the sea.

After reaching Malta and refuelling, Pilot Officer Bill McRae and his crew flew on to Egypt and, in early August 1942, joined No.148 Squadron RAF. Operating conditions were very different from those prevailing for Bomber Command crews flying from Britain on operations over Europe. McRae thought that the only advantage in the North African and Mediterranean theatre was that the average flight tended to be somewhat shorter, while there were many disadvantages and hardships in the harsh desert conditions.

> The squadrons of a mobile bomber force were based on tents, trucks, and improvised runways scraped from the desert surface. Airfield equipment if any was primitive, maintenance of aircraft engines and airframes very difficult, living conditions always uncomfortable, 'gippy tummy' and chronic skin troubles common, relaxation time in a city rare indeed, sand blowing and getting into everything, hot humid days, and freezing nights. Flies were everywhere, and a fly swat was an absolutely essential item of personal equipment.
>
> The tents, each one shared by two men, were scattered over the desert about fifty yards apart, as a precaution against air raids. The Officers' Mess was simply a larger tent with trestle tables, benches and a few wicker chairs. The staple food was 'bully' corned beef, as it came out of the tin, or cooked in many disguises, stewed, fried, grilled, boiled etc. Sleeping was on a camp bed or in a sleeping bag, having first checked that there were no scorpions in residence. We sweated by day and froze at night.

At El Alamein in late October and early November 1942, the British Eighth Army turned the tide, won a famous battle and forced Rommel's forces to retreat. The Axis plans to assault and take Malta were cancelled. In early December 1942 No.148 Squadron and its Wellington bombers were based at Landing Ground (LG) 157 a few miles south of Tobruk. Rommel's forces were farther west of Benghazi, retreating from El Alamein towards Tunisia. Pilot Officer Bill McRae and his crew were enjoying a break in air support operations, and awaiting their next orders.

> At 14.00 hours on 7 December an order came through, '12 planes with crews having operational experience of 15 trips will take off for Half-way House immediately.' The name Half-way House was derived from the fact that Malta was about 1,000 miles distant from both Gibraltar and Alexandria. Having done about 30 operations our crew was one of those 15 chosen.

Although McRae recalled the riotous party he had encountered there, celebrating the amazing escape by airmen hijacking an Italian air force seaplane, he did not look forward to this redeployment move.

> I also had in my mind the unhappy experience of a friend I had trained with. Our two planes took off from Gibraltar for Malta on the afternoon of 29 July. Our plan had been to fly in loose formation until dark. He turned back after about half an hour, and I later learned the hatch above the pilot had blown open, and could not be closed.
>
> He arrived in Malta the next day after we had left, and was detained by the AOC in Malta, who had the authority to commandeer aircraft. Subsequently after returning from a bombing operation, he crashed on landing, and while trying to extricate his rear gunner from his burning turret he was badly burned. Then unable to rescue him, he used his revolver to put him out of his misery.
>
> For our redeployment flight to Malta we were briefed at 16.00 hours and took off at 17.30 – the Met weather report was somewhat vague. The distance to Malta was about 650 miles – the first 100 to the Med coast then 550 over the sea. Besides our crew of six, we had seven ground crew as passengers, who had no parachutes or Mae West life vests. As a gesture we took ours off and stowed them in the back of the aircraft.
>
> At the briefing we were told that we should see a beacon flashing 'P' near the coast to the north of Benghazi. We did sight a beacon but it was flashing a 'V'. My navigator Ian Gould wanted to be sure of our direction before crossing the sea, so we flew back south then north and along the coast, before he was able to figure out where we were, and give me a course to fly.

Malta is a small island, only seventeen miles long and nine miles wide, and for McRae and his crew it was some 500 miles distant. Their only previous flight to Malta was a flight from Britain four months earlier, and this was on an unknown route, and at night variations in wind direction could cause an aircraft to drift off course. To monitor this a flame could be dropped every 100 miles or when needed, and then wind direction assessed visually.

> When we were about an estimated fifty miles from Malta we switched on the IFF automatic radio signal, which should be picked up by radar in Malta. Our wireless Operator Ernie Howden requested Luqa aerodrome in Malta for a course to fly. We were unable to get any reply from Luqa, and as our estimated time of arrival drew near, I spotted a lot of lights ahead. They were so bright I thought I must be hallucinating, or we had

strayed well off course and were back over Alexandria in Egypt. As we got closer I just decided we could not be that far astray, it had to be Malta.

There were a lot of aircraft circling around, so I turned on all our lights. As we had no radio contact we had to circle the flare path and tap out in morse the letter of our aircraft, and wait for a green light from the Aldis lamp of the control pilot at the beginning of the runway. It took us about half an hour to get a green.

While circling I noticed that there was no glide path indicator at the beginning of the runway, which should have beams of light, red, amber, and green, that show the angle of approach to be taken by a pilot. When we finally got a green, and were approaching to land, I noticed a fire at the side of the runway. My landing without the glide path indicator was not good, too low on final approach, and I had to use a lot of power to correct,

We were directed over to one side of the aerodrome and then waited a long time for a truck to take us to a mess building. We learnt that the fire I had seen at the side of the runway was one of our aircraft. Apparently, the pilot came in well to the side of the runway, and hit a sand bag shelter. He and three or four others were injured and in hospital, the other crew and passengers killed.

We had a long wait until a truck turned up towing a very long loader, used for transporting crashed aircraft, and about thirty of us climbed aboard. We were driven through the suburbs to Balluta Bay about four miles north of Malta's Grand Harbour. Our billets were a block of flats, and what a contrast to our last couple of months in tents in the desert – large, rooms, tiled floor, beds, indoor toilets, plenty of water, and water views. We got to bed about four in the morning, and then an air raid siren sounded at 4,30am, but nothing came of it.

For McRae and his aircrew, compared with living in tents, and constantly moving to a new landing ground in the desert, the contrast was even more stark when they were awakened next morning by women cleaners.

Breakfast was provided in another house a couple of hundred yards away. Food was reasonable, weather fine and cool, no flies, streets clean and hilly. We wandered around and came upon some soft green grass in a park and rolled in it. We found a picture show late in the afternoon, where the six of us made up about 50 per cent of the audience. After the show we visited three little water side cafes, but alas no liquor was available.

The next day 9 December we reported in, and found we were now attached to No.104 Squadron. Their Wellingtons had the latest Rolls

Royce Merlin engines, whereas we would continue flying our existing aircraft with the older Pegasus engines. We were told to report the next day for briefing at 14.00 hours, for an operation that evening.

We assembled on 10 December for the briefing, which I thought was not very informative. Our target was the wharf and warehouse area of Bizerte near the Gulf of Tunis. Supplies for the retreating Axis armies were being shipped in there. The weather didn't sound the best, so if we couldn't locate Bizerte in Tunisia, the alternative target was the Italian occupied island of Pantellaria, which was heavily fortified with air defences and fighters. If that was not possible we were instructed to return with our bombs.

Since all countries to the north of Malta were enemy occupied, the weather forecasters in Malta were handicapped by not having access to weather reports in the region on which to base their forecasts. This uncertainty was exacerbated by seasonal instability at this time of the year, such as sudden wind changes, rain and electrical storms.

We were ordered to taxi our aircraft onto the aerodrome from the horse shoe shaped sand bag shelters, which were scattered around about 400 yards from the runways, so that trucks could reach them for loading the bombs. The taxi-ing was not easy as it had rained heavily, and I feared we might get bogged down before reaching the runway.

After warming up the engines we took off with the others on time and very quickly ran into cloud and extreme turbulence. Then we blundered into a storm cloud with hail hammering the aircraft, and electricity flashing around the engines. Our air speed was jumping up and down by fifty knots or more, and similarly the aircraft's height was varying suddenly without warning by 500 feet or so. With the temperature around zero there was a danger of icing on the wings.

I dodged around clouds we could see, and bumped through others, and we fortunately soon got out of the worst of the storm. It was still impossible to fly the correct course and air speed, which did not help Ian's navigation. We were at 8,500 feet, still in cloud and had reached our ETA, when we should be over Bizerte.

McRae was reluctant to descend below the cloud without any knowledge of how far it went down, and to do so could make them an easy target for search lights and anti-aircraft fire.

> We decided to give up on Bizerte, and try for Pantellaria. There was no break in the cloud, and we could not get a glimpse of the island. With the crew's agreement we decided we should best head for home.
>
> When I checked the petrol in the port tank I got a shock – the gauge was on the red zero! I hoped it was just faulty, and we turned on the fuel balance cock hoping that would keep both engines going.

They flew on, the whole crew tense and anxious about running out of fuel. Eventually, around an estimated time to be nearing Malta, McRae thought he saw a glimmer of light ahead. Because of the persistent cloud the Luqa air base at Malta had turned on some searchlights for the returning aircraft. Luckily, McRae spotted the blur of light through the murk.

> We descended and I prepared to enter the circuit, levelling at 1,000 feet. I then noticed we were still going down, now at 900 feet. I pulled the nose up and pushed the speed back up to 110 knots, but we were still unable to climb. The port engine began cutting out, and the engine rev counter was jumping around. I felt pressure on the rudder, which meant the port engine was losing power.

He knew there was only one thing to do, in spite of their briefing instruction.

> I turned the aircraft around, and headed back towards the coast. When I saw the white of waves hitting the shore below, I quickly opened the bomb doors, and pulled the bomb jettison toggle. As we flew back towards the aerodrome, the engine picked up somewhat. I asked Ernie, the wireless operator, to fire a red Very flare.

The Very pistol was kept in the wireless operator's 'office' position, and Ernie fired it through an opening above his head. A red Very flare indicated an emergency and that an immediate landing was being requested.

> We got an immediate green from the flarepath control pilot. Very worried about the engines cutting out again, I didn't put the flaps down until we were well into the approach. We landed but it was not smooth. Next day we heard from the ground crew that the problem was probably due to water getting into the petrol, plus the wrong mixture settings!

McRae's next operation was on 12 December and, once again, the weather was poor, putting the raid in doubt. Depending on the latest forecasts a decision had to be made between proposed targets at Bizerte or Palermo in Sicily.

Bill Hersey – Infantry soldier in the 1st Battalion East Surrey Regiment in the evacuation from Dunkirk. (The History of the East Surrey Regiment, *Volume IV*)

Augusta Hersey – Wife of Bill Hersey in the evacuation from Dunkirk. (The History of the East Surrey Regiment, *Volume IV*)

HMS *Ivanhoe* – Royal Navy destroyer bombed and disabled while evacuating Bill and Augusta Hersey and other troops from Dunkirk. (*Public domain/IWM FL 22376*)

Flying Officer Albert Hollings (kneeling, right) with crew at RAF Spilsby 1943. (*Private collection, Geoff Hollings*)

Flight Sergeant Keith Campbell in 2016. (*Private collection, Keith Campbell*)

Halifax LV-833 P-Peter of Flight Sergeant Keith Campbell No.466 Squadron RAF, 1944. (*Private collection, Keith Campbell*) NB. Also published in *Airmen's Incredible Escapes*.

Douglas Davidson (second from left) with Italian partisans. (*Ian Davidson*)

Pilot Officer Bill McRae underneath the nose of a Wellington bomber seated on bombs to be loaded. (*Private collection, Bill McRae/Sue Templeman*)

Peter Craig, Royal Navy and Royal Australian Navy, aged 99 at ANZAC Memorial Day in 2021. (*Private collection, Bryn Evans*)

Pilot Officer Bill McRae leans out of the cockpit of a Wellington bomber. (*Private collection, Bill McRae Sue Templeman*)

he *Scharnhorst*, battleship of the Kriegsmarine, which was later sunk in the Battle of North Cape. *Bundesarchiv DVM 10 Bild 23-63-07*)

lying Officer Robert 'Slim' Sommerville (far right) with Robert Gregory (middle) and Graham Richardson eft). (*Private collection, Lesley Sommerville*)

Major W.G. 'Bill' Gingell (right), British Battalion Reunion Dinner, 26 November 1946. (*Surrey Hist*
Centre ESR/3/8/3)

David Clemens, aged 23, East Surrey Regiment in 1938. (*Private collection, Harry Skilton/Bryn Evans*)

tan Durston (middle) loading 15-inch guns of Johore Battery in Singapore. (*Private collection, Debra* *rittingham*)

uy Sebastian in Japanese PoW camp wearing
ave labour clothing for mineworking.
Private collection, Ivan Sebastian)

General Douglas MacArthur, Commander US Army Forces in the Far East (USAFFE). (*MacArthur Museum, Brisbane, Australia*)

Allan Gardner after the war. (*Private collection, Rhyll Hansen*)

George and Mary Keeling in the 1970s.

Stan and Pat Durston with daughter Barbara freed from Changi leaving Singapore in September 1945. (*Private collection, Debra Brittingham*)

Guy Sebastian post-war in civilian life in Malaya.

> Finally, the decision was made, Palermo capital of Sicily. At the briefing the CO of No.104 Squadron Wing Commander Saville addressed us. He was very insistent that we must make sure that we dropped all our bombs on the target, the Palermo Harbour, any ships and its docks. A check would be made later by a photo reconnaissance aircraft to see if we had done so, or strayed from the docks area. One of crew joked afterwards that Saville had recently been awarded a DFC, and he is now after a DSO!

Wing Commander Saville did get a DSO later in the war but, tragically, it was posthumous. He suffered the all too typical fate of bomber aircrew when flying a Stirling bomber in a raid over Germany. He was shot down and did not survive. Two of the crew parachuted down near a Luftwaffe air base, while two others came down near a town, and were hanged from a lamp post by the local people.

McRae and the other Wellington bombers took off heading north from Luqa and soon ran into turbulent cloud. Their course was taking them parallel to the east coast of Sicily, then a turn west through the Straits of Messina with the Italian coast on their starboard side and along the north coast of Sicily towards Palermo. McRae was happy that the variable cloud cover was persistent, which was helpful to avoid interception by enemy fighters.

> As we neared Palermo the cloud cleared, so we were able to identify some islands, and work out the wind direction for the bombing run. We circled around off the coast until our designated 'blitz time', when we began our approach run to the target, the docks area in Palermo Harbour.

As expected, the radar of the Italian air defences detected McRae's aircraft and the flak was reaching up towards them, although at first it seemed light.

> The light flak was unusual as anti-aircraft batteries had a habit of firing at anything within range – and we soon would be! We were at 10,000 feet and I told Ian that we would turn left over the coast, then right towards the docks losing height down to 8,000 feet, and increasing our speed to 160 knots. With the nose down on the bombing run, I had a good view of the harbour, where there was a ship moored at the wharves. Ian let the bombs go in one stick. I immediately opened the throttles, and did a climbing turn – hoping to evade the increasing flak.
>
> When we were back at 8,000 feet, I eased back on the throttles, and pushed the nose level. Suddenly both engines cut out! It flashed through my mind – had we been hit? Incredibly after a few seconds, that seemed like an eternity, both engines picked up again. As usual when getting

> clear away from a target without being shot down, my mouth had gone completely dry.
>
> As we flew on the return course along the north east coast of Sicily, Ian our bomb aimer decided to look into the bomb bay with a torch, to make sure all the bombs had dropped. He informed me that there were a couple of 'hang ups'. Remembering the CO's insistence on dropping all our bombs on target, I thought it best to jettison these two bombs over the sea, rather than land at Luqa with them.

As they left Sicily behind and were on course for Malta, McRae ran into very unpleasant weather – rain, cloud, turbulence and poor visibility. With thoughts of the erratic engines in mind, he hoped it would soon become clearer so that they could look for the lights of Malta.

> Then Sid our front gunner reported seeing lights, which he thought were a runway flare path. It confused us as it was far too soon, and we thought we were off course, until Ernie made radio contact with Luqa in Malta – we were still on course. We decided that maybe Sid caught a glimpse of stars on the horizon through a break in the clouds. Eventually it was a relief to see the glow of Malta's searchlights.
>
> We joined the circuit for landing, only to find that the hydraulics had failed, meaning we could not lower the undercarriage and had no wing flaps. It meant the crew having to pump the wheels down by hand, and land without any flaps!
>
> Had to use a lot of brake, and pulled up at last with no more runway left. After five hours and forty minutes it was a relief to get home. Then we got a surprise. We found out that a wireless recall signal had gone out to all planes on the operation, but due to the deteriorating weather we and one other aircraft had not received it. We should not have carried out the lone bombing raid! Hence the light flak at Palermo for a single aircraft attack! We had been incredibly lucky, a lone bomber over Palermo should have been a sitting duck for the Italian anti-aircraft batteries.

The contrary possibility was also true, for if the enemy anti-aircraft defences had been fully manned they may have been able to concentrate all their fire onto McRae's Wellington.

> On 14 December our aircraft had an elevator change, and other adjustments, so for an operation that evening we were not able to air test until around five pm. On running up the engines oil was leaking, and there was a mag

drop. I talked to the ground crew who were of the opinion that the aircraft was not serviceable.

The wing commander was becoming impatient as the operation take-off time got nearer and sent a message to McRae telling him to air test the machine, or he himself would come out and do so if not.

The flight sergeant in charge of the ground crew agreed with me that it was unserviceable. I wrote this down with the problems, and had the flight sergeant sign it. I then took this to the Wingco in the mess – in the event he was quite understanding. We were out of that night's operation. However, it rankled – especially when it was found next day that there was metal in the oil filter. This meant that the cylinder was breaking down, and the engine could have failed on take off or soon after. They had to replace the engine, and so I was vindicated.

The spirits of McRae and his crew rose when they moved to better accommodation, the New Imperial Hotel in Malta town, an old colonial building with large china urns in its imposing entrance and reception area. They found the food reasonable, although most meals contained goat in some form. On preparing for their next operation, they narrowly avoided another disaster from an unexpected incident.

On 15 December the operation was to La Goulette and its docks on the Gulf of Tunis. Take off was scheduled for 17.15 hours but repairs to the hydraulics meant our air test was delayed until 17.00. Just as we were about to turn onto the runway for the test, a returning Beaufighter fired a couple of red distress signals, and then made a weaving approach to land. Its undercarriage was not down, and it looked as if he was going to hit us, so I told the crew to evacuate.

I scrambled out the last one after the rest of the crew, and in the panic got the inter-com cord tangled around my neck. I almost choked. Luckily the Beaufighter made a belly landing, slewing off the runway in a cloud of dust away from our aircraft. We finally did the air test, and got away at 18.15, joining 40 Squadron who were on the same target.

It was a clear night with a near full moon, and the area around La Goulette very visible. The flak was light, and we dropped a flare before making three bombing runs. Ian said he thought we hit a ship moored at the wharves, and it appeared to be burning. As the pilot I cannot see the bombs hitting, as I am concentrating on flying straight and level on the nominated course.

> On the way home we flew in clear air through some magnificent cloud formations – 'feathered canyons in the sky' in the words of the song. We had no trouble in finding our way back, a round trip of four hours, but once again we had to lower the undercarriage with the hand pump, and land without flaps.
>
> We were transported from our aircraft as usual by a truck to a dispersal shelter well away from the aerodrome runways, to wait for another truck to take us to the debriefing room. We waited and waited, in all about an hour and a half before it came. When we at last got to the debriefing room the Intelligence Officer had left, while on his blackboard list of aircraft returned from the operation, ours was written off as 'Missing'! When we got to the Mess we told everyone it was our 'Lazarus' act, before relating the true cause of our delayed departure, and late return.

On 20 December it was another raid on Tunis, and the weather forecast was only fair.

> We found the cloud cover to be quite high, so I decided to stay below it at around 5,000 feet. As we passed over Lampedusa Island I began to gradually climb up towards 10,000 feet, as this was the height at which we usually bombed. It was difficult to coax our tired old aircraft much above that. But if you remained at 5,000 feet over a defended target you were within range of the light flak.
>
> At 6,000 feet the port engine was running rough, and I was keeping an eye on the gauges. The oil pressure gauge started to fall, and asked Henry Langton, our second pilot on this flight, to pump some oil from a tank in the aircraft.

In Wellington bombers, after three hours' flying, it was the job of the second pilot to go back to the centre of the aircraft and hand-pump more oil to each engine. This oil pumping procedure was repeated hourly thereafter. 'I was hoping the trouble might be a faulty gauge, but then the engine rev counter began to wander.'

Despite the struggling port engine, McRae took the Wellington into the bombing run over Tunis docks. If the engine cut out, he knew they would be in big trouble trying to climb away – a slow moving target at a low altitude for the anti-aircraft batteries.

> I opened the bomb doors, pulled the jettison toggle and dumped the bombs. There were a couple of flares with the bombs, and they lit up the docks and sea below.

McRae was able to climb the Wellington, albeit slowly, and they were fortunate not to be hit by flak. They were even luckier that the port engine held up until they were clear of Tunis, before it cut out completely.

> It was not possible to feather the dead engine, in which case the drill was to put it into coarse pitch, and with the throttle fully closed let it windmill. To compensate I ran the good engine at climbing revs and boost – not that we would be able to climb. Then I remembered there were nasty stories of propellors running on boosted and oil-starved engines falling off and hitting the side of the aircraft. Such a possibility suddenly seemed very real, because the propellor was quite close to the pilot's position. I felt as though I could just about reach out and touch it.
>
> On one engine it was not possible to maintain our height, so it was going to be a gradual downhill trip home – if indeed we could make it. Ernie radioed Malta and told them of our desperate plight. The thought of having to ditch in the sea was a sobering thought. On we went, everyone tense – not much being said. When we were about ten miles, according to our navigator, from Malta, I switched on our lights, and hoped we were on course.
>
> Very quickly in the distance I saw a green landing permission light begin to blink at us from the Luqa runway. Yet again the wheels needed some help from the hand pump, but I made one of my better landings.

Relief on making it back was palpable all round, and McRae was flattered when the crew came up with 'Good show Mac'.

> We were unable to taxi off the runway as the port propellor had stopped completely, oil was splashing over the wheel, and the engine was smoking.
>
> As you switch off the engines, it is very nice to hear the airscrews give their death rattle, and then be aware of the contrasting silence that follows. It is one of the two best times of a trip. The other is when you clear the target after putting the bombs in the right place.

Bad weather grounded all operations for the next few days, until 20 December when McRae and his crew were scheduled once more for a raid on Tunis.

> Because a couple of weather fronts were predicted around Tunis, the target was changed to Palermo in Sicily. We stood by for a couple of hours, until electrical storms were forecast on the route to Palermo, and the operation

> was scrubbed. It was noticeable how everyone's spirits lifted, and showed me again how our underlying tensions were lifted.

In December 1942 the Allies' air operations against the Axis armies retreating to Tunisia, which aimed to cut off their supplies and reinforcements being shipped and flown in from Germany and Italy paid no regard to any possible crew leave for Christmas and New Year functions. McRae did not expect anything else.

> We celebrated Christmas Day on an operation, and missed out on the evening dinner. Because the weather was not promising, we had a choice of targets – we could take our seasonal goodwill greeting to Tunis, or as an alternative Sousse. On the way to Tunis we ran into cloud over the coast, very bumpy with rain and hail at 6,000 feet. With the temperature around zero there was a danger of icing, so I turned back 180 degrees hastily into the clear. I then tried to climb over the cloud and struggled up to 11,500 feet.
>
> After cruising around for a while I still came into cloud and we had no visibility. I came back out again, and decided we should try for Sousse. As we approached I descended to 5,000 feet, and again ran into more cloud and rain, with zero visibility. Finally, we agreed to call it a night and bring our 'Christmas gifts' bombs back home. We landed in rain, which made taxi-ing in the blackout to the dispersal pens very trying.

On 27 December, after McRae and his crew had taxied a Wellington bomber out to a runway, ready for take of at 17.15 hours, there was still work needed on its trimming box, and they were told to switch to another aircraft.

> When I started the motors the starboard engine began to bang like a motorcycle engine. An engineering officer diagnosed a blown plug, which could be quickly replaced, for us to join forty other squadron aircraft. Fortunately for us the officer in charge of night flying was against the risk, and decided our trip should be scrubbed.
>
> Next day on 28 December we were briefed again for Tunis. On take off the revs on one engine were a bit low, and a worry. Nevertheless, we got off, and at first kept under some dark cloud, and then climbed to 7,000 feet where the sky was clear. Suddenly the starboard motor cut out, emitted sparks, and then picked up. After about five minutes it cut out again.

McRae and his crew thought that trying to limp home on one engine yet again, if it held up, was to tempt fate too much.

I dumped the bombs and turned for home. Hoping we were on course, we descended through a storm, rain, hail, severe turbulence, and static electricity around the propellors. We got below it, found Luqa, and landed on the one engine, relieved to be on the ground again.

The coastal port of Sfax, in the south-east of the Gulf of Gabes, was the target on 30 December and McRae was delighted to be in a Wellington aircraft that he was familiar with from previous operations in Egypt.

Take off was at 17.00 hours still in daylight, and we flew low over the sea in the Gulf of Gabes, before turning east towards Sfax. It was dark as we neared Sfax, and we were able to pinpoint our position in relation to some islands to the east of Sfax town. We had climbed to 6,500 feet, and Ian had identified the wind direction for the bombing run. The weather was clear and we could see our target, the buildings in the port.

As we began our run exactly on scheduled 'blitz' time, another aircraft dropped a string of flares. Surprisingly no flak was coming up at us – I did a couple of bombing runs, and in a quiet sky Ian thought he was back home on a bomb aimer's training exercise. Then as we were turning over the sea for a final run we spotted a ship offshore. We circled around to line it up but the flares had gone out, and we couldn't locate it.

We had our own flares stowed in the aircraft, and Ernie was able to launch a few but they all turned out to be duds. So that ship was lucky. We returned to the port at Sfax and dropped our remaining bombs. On the way home the aircraft ran like a bird. Maybe she knew it was her last return flight, for on the next night she crashed, killing Flight Sergeant Iremonger and his crew. I remember him so well, for it could so easily have been me and my crew.

It triggered a distressing memory for McRae, from a few months earlier on a previous operation at a base in Egypt.

I was lined up for take off waiting for an aircraft ahead of us to lift off, and our clearance to go. Suddenly in the distance seemingly beyond the end of the runway, there was a burst of flames and explosions, which lit up the night sky. We waited and about five minutes later our Wing Commander drove up to us. He said that the Wellington in front of us 'went in' about 300 yards past the end of the runway. Despite the orange hue in the sky ahead of us, he said it was safe for us to take off. As we climbed above the fire of the burning aircraft, I felt us lift in an updraft of hot air.

> When the fire and ambulance ground crews got to the wrecked aircraft, they found that the nose section had detached from the fuselage and been blasted at least thirty yards ahead of the burning wreck. The pilot was Flight Sergeant Iremonger sitting in his seat and uninjured. To recover, Iremonger was sent on leave for a couple of weeks in Cairo, where unfortunately he broke his ankle rollerskating. His luck ran out fatally that night in Malta.

There was another consequence of frequent aircraft mechanical failure, which McRae and all aircrew were well aware of.

> Poor aircraft serviceability was not good for one's nerves or one's morale. There was a nasty thought at the back of your mind that your superiors might think that you were not 'pressing on' sufficiently. The greatest disgrace in the air force was to be branded as 'lacking in moral fibre' (LMF). We were fortunate that our fellow pilots and superiors were sympathetic, and realised our run of bad luck with aircraft problems was caused by tired old aircraft.

* * *

Malta itself had survived 1942, a year of hell. In 1943 Malta became the Allies' HQ for the invasions of Sicily and mainland Italy later in the year.

In December 1943 the President of the USA, Franklin D, Roosevelt, put on record his recognition of Malta's heroic resistance:

> In the name of the people of the USA I salute the island of Malta, its people and defenders, who in the cause of freedom and justice and decency throughout the world, have rendered valorous service far above and beyond the call of duty.
>
> Under repeated fire from the skies, Malta stood alone but unafraid in the center of the sea, one tiny bright flame in the darkness – a beacon of hope for the clearer days which have come.
>
> Malta's bright story of heroism, fortitude and courage will be read by posterity with wonder and with gratitude through all the ages.
>
> What was done in this island maintains the highest traditions of gallant men and women, who from the beginning of time have lived and died to preserve civilization for all mankind.
>
> December 7th, 1943
> *Franklin D. Roosevelt*

That message of rich appreciation is also commemorated in a stone plaque on the wall of Grand Master's Palace. Once again, as it had so many times over the centuries, Malta had survived. And so had McRae.

* * *

Bill McRae completed forty-three operations and the story of just a few of those flown from Malta, gives us a vivid illustration of the never-ending daily challenge and ordeal – 'dicing with death', as he once described the daily life of a bomber pilot and his crew. He thought that survival as a bomber pilot was luck and, early on, realised that aircrew were expendable. McRae spoke of operations as a 'very worrying time', and how, on walking out to the aircraft before an operation, the crew did not talk much, and some would have a smoke, others a nervous wee on one of the plane's tyres. In two years of operations from Malta, No.104 Squadron alone lost 108 aircraft destroyed or missing and 206 crew killed or missing.

In mid-1943 McRae was transferred to the UK to be a training instructor and was eventually promoted to squadron leader. He married Joan Stockton later that year and, at the end of the war, resumed employment with the Bank of NSW in London. They returned to Sydney in 1947 with their daughter Susan where, after retiring from the bank, he worked with Coca Cola. In his hundredth year in 2012, he attended the opening of the Bomber Command Memorial in London. Bill had a welcoming smile and engaging personality with everyone he met, right up until he passed away in 2019 at age 106. McRae's awards for his service included the DFC, Air Force Cross, Malta George Cross, the French Legion d'Honneur and Croix de Guerre.

Notes

1. Veteran's Account, Sq/Ldr McRae
2. Ibid.

Part III

At Sea

Chapter 7

Hunting U-boats – Facing Life or Death in the Battle of the Atlantic

U-226, seeking a clearer view of its prey, came to the surface. Through its periscope the U-boat captain glimpsed a fat prize, an aircraft carrier. As the carrier, HMS *Tracker*, sailed onward oblivious to the danger, *U-226* emerged from a patch of fog, intent on closing to a position for firing its torpedoes. More than two miles away, on the sloop HMS *Kite*, a radar echo of *U-226* was registered. Then a reconnaissance aircraft from *Tracker* and a lookout on *Kite* saw *U-226* on the horizon and soon after *Kite* fired a starshell to alert the other ships in the flotilla. The hunter had become the hunted.[1]

* * *

In the Second World War Peter Craig became an able seaman and gunner on HMS *Woodcock,* in the Royal Navy's long war in the Battle of the Atlantic against Germany's U-boats. He was born on 4 November 1922, in Uddingston, Lanarkshire, near Glasgow in Scotland.[2]

Craig first tried to enlist in the Royal Navy at age eighteen, then again at nineteen, but was rejected on both occasions because he was employed in construction, a reserved occupation. He was influenced by his elder brother, who was in the Royal Navy, and his father, who had served in the Cameronians.

Finally, at age twenty, Craig was successful and, after training, was posted to HMS *Woodcock,* an anti-submarine sloop deployed in the Royal Navy's 2nd Support Group, known as the 'Johnnie Walker Group', hunting U-boats in the Atlantic Ocean. Craig thought it was just the right thing to do. 'It was just the fashion when the war started. All the young fellows thought they'd be brave.'[3]

HMS *Woodcock* was commissioned in May 1943, built as a specialised escort ship, a sloop in the Black Swan class, 300 feet in length, with a range endurance of 7,500 miles and a maximum speed of 20 knots. *Woodcock* was armed with ten 20mm Oerlikon and six four-inch guns, a minimum of 180 depth charges and a crew of 240 seamen or more.[4]

In early October 1943 Peter Craig's HMS *Woodcock* undertook working-up training with three other sloops of 2nd Support Group, HMSs *Wild Goose,*

Magpie and *Kite* at the port of Tobermory on Scotland's Isle of Skye. Later in October the 'Johnnie Walker Group', under the command of Captain Fredric 'Johnnie' Walker in HMS *Starling*, came together off the north coast of Ireland where they were joined by the aircraft carrier HMS *Tracker*.[5]

Despite the moonless night, *Tracker*'s profile was easily visible as she approached to meet the flotilla. As the group set sail for the North Atlantic, the five sloops – *Starling*, *Wild Goose*, *Magpie*, *Kite* and *Woodcock* – took up a line-abreast formation, two either side of Walker's *Starling*. *Tracker* followed them up to two miles astern and each ship maintained its own continuous zig-zag course, wary of any U-boats which might lie in wait.

For a number of days, the group encountered horrendous weather that meant the only objective was self-preservation, keep afloat in the storms and avoid collisions. Fifty-foot waves in rolling swells of maybe 500 yards crashed across the ships' decks. Engines struggled to maintain a forward speed of only around three knots, and to keep ships' bows heading into the mountainous waves. In HMS *Woodcock* Peter Craig, like other men on watch and on deck, was constantly sodden and frozen. In storms that reached Force 10, hardened sailors were continuously seasick.

Although it was known that they were in the vicinity of U-boats, the weather was in control. Meanwhile the U-boats were inhibited from surfacing to find targets as they would roll excessively in the heavy seas. By the first week of November Walker's group was still battling the elements east of Newfoundland. Then, during the night of 6/7 November, the wind at last dropped. For fleeting moments a few stars could be seen through breaks in the cloud. There was still a high swell, but not as savage, so that Craig and other seamen not on watch could finally grab some sleep.[6]

The improved weather allowed Walker to restart search operations for U-boats and reconnaissance aircraft were able to take off from *Tracker*. It paid dividends when an aircraft spotted a U-boat on the surface. When *Kite* fired starshell it sent *U-226* diving for the safety of the depths. This was not before the U-boat captain had fired a torpedo at *Tracker* which, fortunately, had already turned away from the threat. Walker began the hunt for the fleeing *U-226* with *Kite* and *Woodcock* in support of *Starling*.

While the sloops *Wild Goose* and *Magpie* escorted *Tracker* away from the pursuit, *Kite* made a depth-charge attack in the area where the U-boat had submerged. There was no discernible result. Determined not to lose contact with the U-boat, Walker instigated his own innovative attack approach with patient stalking or creeping tactics. *Kite* and *Woodcock* were ordered to keep well away and switch off their ASDIC equipment. Meanwhile, Walker in *Starling* fell back about 1,000 yards astern of the U-boat but maintained ASDIC contact.

The maximum speed of a U-boat when submerged was about 4 knots. For whatever reason, *U-226* was moving even slower. It may have been damaged by *Kite*'s attack or was merely trying to slink quietly away and evade the range of *Starling*'s distant ASDIC contact.[7]

The captain of *U-226* may not even have known or been unsure that he was being followed by *Starling*. Walker was aware that, below seven knots, his sloop's propellor was not audible above normal water noise.[8]

Some four hours went by as *Starling* stalked its prey and Walker waited for the dawn. At first light, Walker signalled for *Woodcock* to approach within hailing distance and gave *Woodcock*'s Captain Ginnifer the approximate position of *U-226* for an attack. *Woodcock* began a stealthy approach at no more than five knots with its ASDIC switched off. Walker in *Starling* continued as before, tracking the U-boat with its ASDIC contact but keeping well distant astern. The captain of *U-226* was lulled into thinking that there was no change in the cat-and-mouse game and that *Starling* was the only threat well in arrears. He was totally unaware of *Woodcock* silently closing at an angle towards him.

Slowly and quietly, *Woodcock* glided into the designated area and, over a grid of around 400 by 100 yards, dropped a pattern of depth charges. *Woodcock* was carrying out Walker's innovative creeping attack, hopefully to make the kill. The depth charges had been set at their maximum operational depth of 700 feet, to reach the U-boat, and they began to explode.

Shortly after 07.00 hours *Woodcock*'s ASDIC signals indicated that the U-boat might be breaking up. Soon after 07.30 there were two explosions, one erupting above the waves, and, fifteen minutes later, came the evidence it was over. Debris from *U-226* began to float to the surface.[9]

Peter Craig watched as the wretched remains of *U-226* popped up to the surface. 'At first, from the large amount of wreckage we thought it to be a milch cow, or a large supply boat. We later learned that it was the standard type VII U-boat.'[10]

With the U-boat destroyed, the group took up their line-abreast formation ahead of *Tracker* and resumed their sweep. Alan Burn, who was the Gunnery Officer on Walker's *Starling*, had begun to relax.

> Captain's rounds had just been completed. The wind was down to force two, and even the swell had flattened out, …when at 13.03 Archie Pitt's team picked up an HF/DF bearing of another U-boat transmitting on the surface about twenty miles away.[11]

For two and a half hours, the group searched with no contact. Then *Wild Goose*, which was about a mile away on *Starling*'s port beam, reported an ASDIC contact at 1,800 yards. Walker sent *Wild Goose* into another creeping attack. Due to some kind of malfunction, a planned fire of twenty-six depth charges discharged only ten. Nevertheless, before Walker could send a message of admonition to *Wild Goose,* the air reverberated from loud underwater explosions.

Oil and wreckage soon came to the surface. The U-boat, subsequently identified as *U-842*, had been destroyed. Walker's personally devised tactic of a creeping attack had proved successful on its fourth consecutive application. It was also the second time the 'Johnnie Walker Group' had sunk two U-boats in twenty-four hours. And it was in the one available break in horrendous weather.

The group set course for Argentia, the US Naval base in Newfoundland and, from the effects of the severe storms, all the sloops were in bad need of repair. Peter Craig was well aware that *Woodcock* was one of the worst damaged.[12]

While the group sailed on in formation once again, there was no help from the elements. In Walker's words, 'quite the fullest gale I have yet met,'[13] the sloops made little headway. As the seas crashed into the ships' sides, Alan Burn described their designated course as no more than hopeful.

> Much of the time the sloops could not see each other. Their small outlines were obscured by the driving spray, appearing occasionally on the crest of a wave, and then disappearing behind the crest as they sank down into a trough. In these conditions, radar was of limited assistance. The only method of keeping in touch without chattering on the radio or flashing lights, was to endeavour to keep *Tracker* in sight, since she was the most visible and least maneuverable of the ships. She appeared from time to time through the spray, heaving and twisting in her agony. For the second time on the patrol the majesty and ferocity of the Atlantic had become our chief adversary.[14]

On his first operational voyage and engagement with German U-boats, Peter Craig on HMS *Woodcock* realised that the North Atlantic and its ferocious weather were as dangerous as the enemy below the waves.

> I had just turned twenty-one and thought it was the end of me. The seas pounded us so hard they forced our forward guns into their full elevation. They were jammed and unusable. To make it worse our ammunition lockers, although made of steel and welded to the deck, were torn loose by wave after wave, and washed overboard. We were at the mercy of the sea and the enemy.[15]

Besides the weather damage, all the group's ships were running out of food and ammunition. Furthermore, all the sloops had suffered structural damage from depth-charge explosions, while they were moving so slowly in the creeping attacks. When the five sloops sailed into the US Navy base at Argentia in Newfoundland, they were unrecognisable from the flotilla that had set out a few weeks ago from Scotland. Captain Walker wrote of some of the incessant rain and its continual storms:

> Perpetual paddling in water, snatches only of sleep in wet blankets, no radiators for drying and warming, a succession of long faces reporting, one dynamo flooded out, gyro, director and radar out of action, three depth charges chasing each other around the quarterdeck; but what are such things compared with satisfaction of having given the Boche another mouthful of dust to bite.[16]

Peter Craig described being scared during operations against the enemy at sea but with no time to think about it.

> You never knew what was going to happen, when you were chasing U-boats. Especially when they used to operate in packs, maybe six, seven or eight, all together so they could get amongst convoys and cause havoc. When you go to sea, you're on edge all the time.[17]

While the sloops *Starling, Wild Goose, Magpie* and *Kite* were able to use the stay in harbour for repairs and re-supply, *Woodcock* joined a convoy back to the UK for more substantial repairs and the replacement of damaged guns and other equipment.

* * *

In January 1944 the 2nd Support Group, now comprising *Starling, Wild Goose, Magpie, Wren, Kite* and *Woodpecker*, joined the escort carriers *Nairana* and *Activity* to hunt down two groups of U-boats which were waiting across the line of advance of a merchant convoy. On 21 January a U-boat was detected and attacked at once by *Wild Goose*, which was quickly joined by *Starling* and *Magpie* in heading directly towards the ASDIC contact.

The three sloops and the carrier *Nairana* were tempting targets for the U-boat captain to loose off a GNAT (German Navy Acoustic Torpedo), an acoustic-homing torpedo. *Magpie* fired its new Hedgehog battery, which launched twenty-four mortars into the air, dropping them into the sea at the location of the submerged U-boat. If a GNAT was fired at the sloops and the carrier, it missed its mark. In a later report, Walker said that *Nairana* was probably saved by *Wild Goose*'s quick decision and speedy attack.

No debris emerged to indicate any damage to the U-boat from the Hedgehog rounds. The only conclusion was that its captain had dived deep to evade his attackers. In response, Walker committed the group to a stealthy long hunt and a variation of a creeping attack. While *Wild Goose* tracked the range of the fleeing U-boat, *Starling* employed its ASDIC Q attachment, which calculated the estimated depth of the U-boat.

Depth charges were thrown out from the stern of each sloop at five-second intervals, each one set to explode at 700 feet deep. Eventually, after one such underwater blast, there came an unexpected yet almost immediate second explosion. Alan Burn watched, stunned, as a huge mountain of water climbed into the air like a monster from the deep, a mere ten yards from *Starling*'s starboard quarter. 'The great mass of water climbed higher than the ship's masthead and seemed to hang for seconds over the quarterdeck.'[18]

The ship jerked as if it had hit a rock, which loosed two primed depth charges, one of which fell five feet onto the steel deck. Miraculously, it did not explode. Burn could only hang on and watch.

> Tons of solid green water began to descend on top of the depth-charge crews. As the water cascaded over the side, they emerged, soaked, shaken, some badly bruised, but still pushing out the remainder of the pattern.

As water drained from the quarterdeck, *Starling* seemed to shake herself, before continuing to release depth charges in the planned pattern of the creeping attack. A few minutes later, a series of heavy underwater explosions were heard. Debris of all kinds, including personal effects, oil and bodies of the U-boat crew began popping up to the surface. Those were the last pathetic remains of the U-boat, later identified as *U-592*.

* * *

As days went by the challenge for the sloops' crews on watch was to stay alert. On the night of 8 February *Wild Goose* was some eight miles from the convoy on her port bow. It was fine weather with a smooth swell, but visibility was deceptive as moonlight fused with patches of mist. The eyes of the port look-out, Able-Seaman Wall, saw it first, and reported a black object ahead on the bow. A signalman on watch confirmed it as a U-boat, about a mile away, on a converging course and diving. Captain Wemyss reduced *Wild Goose* to seven knots, wary of being a target for a GNAT that might be fired by the U-boat.

ASDIC operators were tracking the submerged U-boat on a course which was coming head on towards *Wild Goose*, as if it was oblivious of the sloop. Lieutenant Commander D.E.G. Wemyss and his crew tensed. A GNAT homing on *Wild Goose* was but one fear. Now the range between them and the U-boat was shrinking so fast, such that the U-boat might collide with *Wild Goose*, or pass underneath bow to stern.

There came a shout from a lookout. He had sighted the periscope of the U-boat, which had surfaced to look around. It was a mere twenty yards away passing *Wild Goose* in the opposite direction. An Oerlikon gun opened up on the area of sea around where the periscope was seen as the U-boat crash-dived.

Wild Goose was quickly joined by *Woodpecker*, and the two sloops began a co-ordinated depth-charge attack to saturate the likely position of the U-boat. It was not long before hydrophones picked up the tell-tale sounds of the U-boat blowing its tanks. Then came five unmistakeable underwater explosions, followed by the inevitable surfacing of wreckage and bodies from the destroyed U-boat. It was over. By 02.00 hours on 9 February the two sloops were on their way to rejoin the convoy which had changed course to avoid the U-boats' threat.[19]

* * *

Early on the misty morning of 9 February, *Kite* headed towards a contact of a U-boat, estimated to be nine miles distant and on the surface. For twenty-five minutes or so, *Kite* nosed its way warily but quickly through the banks of mist. Visibility remained patchy and the atmosphere tense. Suddenly, the long grey shape of a U-boat was discerned only about half a mile away. It looked as though it was near to full speed, sailing towards the convoy. The U-boat captain must have been so intent on his attack on the convoy that he was unaware of *Kite*'s approach. Hearing of this from *Kite*, Walker on *Starling* sent *Magpie* racing to help make a kill.

In another direction *Starling* had set off to support *Wild Goose*, which had detected another U-boat by radar. It was 3,000 yards away on the surface and attempting an attack on the convoy's port side. When the distance had been closed to 2,400 yards, *Wild Goose* opened fire which sent the U-boat into an emergency dive. Before submerging, the U-boat fired a GNAT at *Wild Goose*. Luckily it exploded some distance away.[20]

Keeping the U-boat in its ASDIC contact, *Wild Goose* followed it slowly and stealthily, waiting for *Starling*'s support. Two hours later *Starling* caught up and, using Walker's creeping attack tactic, the two sloops began to stalk the U-boat.

Wild Goose used flares to indicate the U-boat's underwater position which allowed *Starling* to go in at an angle and fire a pattern of depth charges. The deadly cat-and-mouse game went on for another hour, before a depth-charge attack caused the U-boat to change course and fire a GNAT. It exploded harmlessly some way off *Starling*'s stern. It proved to be the U-boat's death throes. Soon after an enormous underwater explosion sent the usual debris bubbling up to the surface.

Some miles away in a break in the misty conditions *Kite* and *Magpie* had finally spotted a U-boat on the surface. Lieutenant Commander Segrave on *Kite* increased the sloop's speed and went straight into attack, dropping a single depth charge with shallow settings, and opening gunfire at the ominous grey shape.

In a matter of seconds after this one depth charge disappeared below the waves, the sea erupted as if from an underwater volcanic explosion. A mountain of water tore into the air, far higher than the top of *Kite*'s masts, and obliterating any sight of the ship. It seemed time stood still as foam and spray dispersed, drifting like a fog back down to the sea. *Magpie*'s crew felt sure that *Kite* must have been hit by a GNAT and had capsized or at least was mortally damaged. Surely *Kite* was lost?

As the visibility cleared, *Kite* appeared like an apparition. Although there was some minor buckling of the hull's plates, and the crew members on the quarterdeck were stunned and shaken, *Kite* was undamaged. The U-boat had indeed fired a GNAT at *Kite* before crash-diving but it had been counter-mined in effect by the single depth charge, setting off a combined explosion of the two weapons. *Kite*'s Lieutenant Commander Segrave brushed off the narrow escape and sent *Kite* racing into an immediate pursuit, following the ASDIC contact of the U-boat.

In sea and weather conditions which were making it very difficult to maintain ASDIC contact, *Kite* made three attacks firing ten depth charges each time. When *Magpie* arrived to assist, the two sloops combined over more than five hours, putting in a creeper and a follow-up attack with depth charges, a Hedgehog salvo and two more attacks of ten depth charges each time.

At midday Walker brought *Starling* into the hunt and, since *Kite* had only seventeen depth charges remaining, ordered Segrave to leave the pursuit and join up with *Wild* Goose in patrol. Because the U-boat was moving very slowly and very deep, *Starling* found it difficult in the poor sea and weather conditions to pinpoint its position and direct a creeping attack accurately. Walker decided to try a new tactic, using *Magpie*'s new Hedgehog weapon.

Magpie was directed by Walker to sail at slow speed until it was around 1,000 yards from the U-boat's approximate position and given a range to fire the Hedgehog. The Hedgehog twenty-four were launched. No one thought that such a hit-or-miss approach could be lucky enough to hit the hull of a U-boat. Mouths were agape after only a matter of a few seconds when two underwater explosions were heard. *Magpie* followed up with a typical creeper attack and then also *Starling* with targeted depth charges. Wreckage, oil-soaked items and debris of all kinds from the destroyed U-boat soon began popping up on the surface.

This pursuit showed the extraordinary persistence of Captain Walker. It had lasted some eight hours, using up 252 depth charges and two Hedgehog salvos. In just fifteen hours across 8 and 9 February the Johnnie Walker Group had sunk three U-boats, later identified as *U-762, U-794* and *U-238*. There were no survivors from the U-boats' crews. As so often at sea victory was merciless.[21]

* * *

By 20 February the Johnnie Walker Group had sunk six U-boats and suffered no losses or casualties. One of those sunk was *U-204*, which was forced to surface by damage, and then scuttled itself, allowing the crew to be rescued and taken prisoner. Yet both *Starling* and *Kite* had been lucky to survive near misses, thought Alan Burn. 'On this grey February evening, the Atlantic Ocean was cold and menacing. It could not go on like this.'[22]

While the group had accounted for six U-boats, at least twelve GNATs had been fired at them and all crews were mentally and physically drained. Nevertheless, the ships had reformed and were in a routine patrol and watch mode. The crews hoped the group would soon be on course for Liverpool for re-supply and shore leave. This routine surveillance was shattered at 22.00 hours when the radio transmission of a U-boat on the surface was detected.

The group changed course immediately and increased speed to seventeen knots towards the U-boat. All the sloops went to action stations at once. A hunt was on again. *Woodpecker* registered an ASDIC contact but it was too late. A matter of seconds later at 22.16 there came an explosion and, from *Starling*, flames were seen on the port beam. It was *Woodpecker*, from which came a signal that it had suffered a torpedo hit. As *Starling* went to her aid, Burn saw the damage at close quarters, 'the aft fifty feet of the quarterdeck had been blown into the air and folded back … forty feet of the stern had vanished ….'[23]

Miraculously, however *Woodpecker* was able to stay afloat. In due course she was taken under tow by the oceangoing tug *Storm King* which then set sail for Falmouth in Devon for repairs or salvage. The rest of the group, low on fuel, ammunition and food, headed for Liverpool which was reached on 25 February. On 27 February some 120 miles from Falmouth deteriorating weather conditions meant that *Woodpecker* had to be cast off its tow. The remaining crew were taken off and *Woodpecker* was sunk reluctantly by gunfire.

That same day in Liverpool Walker and his wife celebrated their wedding anniversary with a dinner in *Starling*'s wardroom with some of the group's officers and their wives. Walker paid tribute to all his ships' crews but mentioned especially *Woodpecker* and *Wild Goose*. *Woodpecker* had directly contributed to the sinking of five U-boats. Some of those present in *Starling*'s wardroom thought Walker looked exhausted. The group's success in hunting U-boats had come at a cost.[24]

* * *

For the planned Normandy landings to take place in early June 1944, the Royal Navy would have the indispensable role of protecting the Allies' invasion fleet and preventing any U-boats from entering the English Channel. Intelligence had detected that many U-boats were regrouping in the Bay of Biscay to move on the invasion fleet.

The sloops of 2nd Support Group were valued highly for the protection tasks required, not only to hunt U-boats, but also because of their strong anti-aircraft guns which were superior to many of the escort ships of convoys. To take up their new roles for the invasion of Normandy, the Johnnie Walker Group was split into two. *Starling*, *Wild Goose* and *Wren* joined up with three frigates. Four of the other sloops, *Kite*, *Magpie*, *Whimbrel* and *Woodcock*, which had returned to the group after completion of extensive repairs, were attached to other groups for training exercises in early spring 1944.[25]

On 6 June, D Day, the first day of the Allied landings in Normandy, thirty-five U-boats sailed from Brest and other Bay of Biscay ports. They headed for the western approaches to the English Channel and the invasion fleet. Those U-boats not yet fitted with Schnorkels prowled forward to intercept those ships of the invasion fleet which were sailing south from the Irish Sea. Alan Burn, who was on Captain Walker's *Starling*, described the potential danger and challenge that they faced.

> The most immediate threat to the landings came from the eight Schnorkel-equipped U-boats from Brest, only two hundred miles from the Normandy landing beaches. The Second Support Group's days and short midsummer nights became one headlong chase from one sighting position to the next.[26]

Because of the combined operations of aircraft and ships, there were no losses of Allied ships until 15 June when U-boats sank two ships and a landing craft.

On 2 July *Starling* docked back in Liverpool and Walker learned that he had been awarded his fourth DSO. In the four weeks from 6 June to 2 July, twenty-six U-boats had been sunk by Allied aircraft or ships. On the same day the Kriegsmarine ordered all U-boats back to harbour. After a few days' leave, Walker and his wife Eileen lunched with other officers at the Adelphi Hotel in Liverpool. Their relaxation was curtailed when an order was received for the support group to put to sea next day. They did so without their leader Walker who, on that very evening, was taken into hospital. On 9 July the Johnnie Walker Group received a signal that Captain Walker had died at 02.00 hours that day. The men were stunned, for Walker was only forty-eight, and they had been fully expecting him to resume command within a few days.[27]

* * *

Peter Craig was on *Woodcock,* which was in another group with *Kite, Magpie* and *Whimbrel* when, on 27 May 1944, it was accidentally rammed by HMS *Venus.*

> Once again we suffered serious damage, and this time we returned to Hull for repairs. From there we sailed around the north of Scotland, and back down to Liverpool.[28]

The repairs also included fit-out measures for service in the Pacific. When seaworthy again *Woodcock*, with Craig in the crew once more, was ordered to sail for the Pacific to join the war against Japan. 'We joined the British Pacific Fleet in March 1945 at Manus Island in New Guinea, and sailed with them into operations in the Pacific war zone.' Soon after the news in August 1945 that Japan had surrendered, *Woodcock* was ordered to sail at once for Tokyo and its port of Yokohama.

> In Tokyo Bay three high-ranking Americans whom we had on board, were taken off and transferred to the USS *Missouri*, where the surrender and peace agreement was signed. That same afternoon we entered Yokohama and were the first British ship to tie up in Japan.

On return to Britain with *Woodcock* in late 1946, Craig went back to his old job but, before long, responded to a recruitment drive for the Royal Australian Navy (RAN). In six years in the RAN, he served in the Korean War before becoming an instructor. Craig married and made a new life in Australia where his spirit and resilience, so tested at an early age in the sea battles of the Atlantic and Pacific oceans, remained with him all his life. He was still driving in his hundredth year when he died.

Throughout the Battle of the Atlantic, Alan Burn was the Gunnery Officer on Captain Walker's ship *Starling* and continued to fill this position after Walker's death. He used his own accounts of the engagements in the hunt for U-boats and Walker's official reports of the patrols and U-boats sunk to write his enthralling book *The Fighting Captain: The Story of Frederic Walker RN CB DSO*, and also *The Fighting Commodores.* Burn's passionate and gripping story of *The Fighting Captain* illustrates indirectly his own prowess and excellence as *Starling*'s Gunnery Officer.

Captain Walker lay in state at Liverpool Cathedral, before being taken on a gun carriage in a procession to Prince's Pier, then carried and piped aboard HMS *Hesperus*. Beyond the entrance to the Mersey, he was given a ceremonial Royal Navy burial and committed to the deep. His wife Eileen, who had walked behind the gun carriage with their children, cast a single wreath into the sea.

Eileen Walker knew how much her husband loved all the men who served with him. While Walker was in command of 2nd Support Group, not a single ship, not one man had been lost to enemy action. When *Starling* returned from its patrol and docked at Plymouth, Commander Wemyss addressed the ships' companies and told them of Walker's funeral. Eileen Walker made a point of going down to *Starling*'s messdeck. She spoke to the crew despite her raw grief, and described how her husband's greatest happiness was his pride in all the sailors of the Johnnie Walker Group.[29]

Captain Frederic J. Walker RN did more than any other man at sea to win the Battle of the Atlantic, a vicious and unrelenting struggle which Churchill described as the dominating factor throughout the Second World War. He was a formidable figure and one of the greatest fighting captains in the history of the Royal Navy, sinking twenty U-boats. For this he was awarded a CB and appointed DSO with three Bars, only the second man in the history of the Royal Navy to receive this award four times.

Notes

1. Burn, *The Fighting Captain*, pp.112-13
2. Veteran's Account, Peter Craig
3. Ibid.
4. Burn, op.cit., pp.133-4
5. Veteran's Account, Peter Craig; Burn, op.cit., p.109
6. Burn, op. cit., pp.109-13
7. Doherty, *Churchill's Greatest Fear*, pp.231-2
8. Burn, op.cit., p.195
9. Burn, op.cit., p.113
10. Veteran's Account, Peter Craig

11. Burn, op.cit., p.115
12. Doherty, op. cit., pp.231-2; Veteran's Account, Peter Craig
13. Burn, op.cit., pp.115-17
14. Burn, op.cit., p.116
15. Veteran's Account, Peter Craig
16. Burn, op.cit., p.118
17. Veteran's Account, Peter Craig
18. Burn, op.cit., p.127
19. Ibid., pp.128-9
20. Ibid.
21. Ibid., pp.130-2
22. Doherty, op. cit., pp.231-2; Burn, op.cit., p.136
23. Burn, op.cit., p.137
24. Ibid., pp.136-43
25. Ibid., pp.160-1
26. Ibid., p.165
27. Doherty, op. cit., p.253; Burn, op.cit., pp.171-5
28. Veteran's Account, Peter Craig
29. Doherty, op. cit., p.253; Burn, op.cit., pp.171-5

Chapter 8

Death and Survival in Arctic Waters

The Battle of North Cape

The most northern part of Norway and Europe, Nordkapp, or North Cape, deep in the Arctic Circle is a breathtaking promontory which overlooks the meeting of the North Atlantic and Arctic oceans and the Barents Sea. It is a magnet for tourists and cruise ships and a perfect vantage point to observe the Northern Lights. Even in July at the height of the summer season of the Midnight Sun, when the sun does not dip below the horizon, it is a desolate, windswept and freezing stretch of barren land with cliffs dropping over 300 metres to the ocean below. Luckily, as a tourist you can limit your exposure to the freezing elements and take shelter in a large modern building which houses a restaurant, souvenir shop and viewing gallery.

In this tourist complex there is also an extensive Memorial, a display which gives a detailed explanation and account of the Battle of North Cape. On Boxing Day, 26 December, 1943 a major naval battle was fought off North Cape between the UK's Royal Navy and Germany's Kriegsmarine, in the complete darkness of the Arctic winter. It was a brutal battle fought to the death which has been largely forgotten, yet which had a significant strategic influence on the remaining course of the Second World War.[1]

* * *

By late 1943 the Allies' Arctic convoys, which were taking military and other supplies through the Barents Sea to Murmansk in Russia, were proving crucial for the Soviet Union to counter and turn back the German invasion of their country. While merchant ship losses from the convoys to U-boats was a constant risk, there was a more lethal threat. Lurking in the Norwegian fjords were the Kriegsmarine's modern and powerful battleships, *Tirpitz* and *Scharnhorst*. Despite the risk of battle with the Royal Navy, in December 1943 the German High Command was demanding that the 'state of the art' battleship, *Scharnhorst*, be deployed to attack the Allied convoys.[2]

Russia needed the weapons, equipment and ammunition from the convoys to sustain their forward momentum against the Germans. While the Luftwaffe had transferred many of its aircraft from northern Norway to the Eastern Front against Russia, their remaining reconnaissance planes were active in monitoring Allied naval and merchant ships, so as to relay their location to U-boats and, potentially, *Scharnhorst.*

During 1941-42 the Red Army had suffered tremendous losses. For a winter offensive to be maintained in 1943-44, it required large amounts of new war materials, tanks, aircraft, artillery ammunition etc., but for the Allies to ship those supplies to the Soviet Union was very difficult. The only way to reach the Russian Arctic ports of Murmansk and Archangel was by crossing the North Atlantic and the Barents Sea, and hoping to avoid German aircraft, U-boats and ships. Losses to German attacks, as well as the effects of bad weather, were taking a toll.

In July 1942 convoy PQ17 carried one of the most valuable total cargoes, including 300 aircraft, 600 tanks and 4,000 other vehicles. Of the thirty-five ships that sailed from Iceland, only eleven reached Archangel. If the Arctic convoys were significantly disrupted by the Germans, Russian capabilities on the Eastern Front would falter and allow Germany to transfer some forces to north-west Europe, which would imperil the Allies' planned landings in Normandy in June 1944.[3]

In December 1943 the warships of the Kriegsmarine, such as *Tirpitz* and *Scharnhorst* at harbour in the Altafjord close to North Cape, were a constant threat to the convoys. *Tirpitz*, which was seen as the pride of the Kriegsmarine, was moored behind the protection of torpedo nets in the Käfjord, an arm of the Altafjord. However, *Tirpitz* had been under major repairs for several months after an attack by British midget submarines and was not yet seaworthy.

Scharnhorst lay at harbour, similarly protected in the Langfjord, another arm of the Altenfjord. A powerful battleship, *Scharnhorst* was armed with nine 11-inch guns in three triple turrets, twelve 6-inch guns in eight turrets and fourteen 4.1-inch guns, as well as anti-aircraft guns, torpedoes and two Arado sea-planes. Its maximum speed of 32 knots enabled it to outpace, although not outgun the Royal Navy's battleship HMS *Duke of York,* which had a top speed of 28 knots, but was armed with ten 14-inch guns. The Kriegsmarine recognised that it could not match the overall scale and expertise of the Royal Navy, and so had a strategy of maintaining U-boats, and a few powerful warships, to inflict losses and disruption on the Allies' supply convoys.

Unknown to the Kriegsmarine, Norwegian spies were monitoring their ships in the Altafjord and sending reports by radio to Allied intelligence. In the town of Alta, two employees of the local council, Karl Rasmussen the paymaster, and Torstein Räby, a roads office employee, were agents spying for Britain. There were two more agents in the branch fjords, Harry Petterson in Käfjord and Jen P.

Digre in Langfjord. On Christmas Day 1943, at 7.00 p.m., Digre called Pettersen who then called Rasmussen with the coded message 'Grandmother has left on her Christmas holiday'. Räby immediately telegraphed British intelligence.

Scharnhorst and its five destroyers had sailed for the open sea. This was confirmed by British intelligence through interception of *Scharnhorst*'s own radio communications. Later, while Räby was able to elude German investigators, Rasmussen was arrested and tortured until he committed suicide so as not to reveal his contacts.[4]

* * *

During mid-winter in the Barents Sea, between Bear Island and North Cape, it is continually pitch-dark except for two hours of dusk or pre-dawn twilight around noon. Temperatures were below freezing. In stormy weather and, often, driving snow, visibility was very poor, making radar essential to detect surface vessels.

On Christmas Morning 1943, the Arctic convoy JW55B was expected to pass between Bear Island in the north and the North Cape of Norway on its course to Murmansk. Eight U-boats were deployed on the convoy's route, but rough weather was impeding their operations. The Royal Navy's *Duke of York*, the cruiser *Jamaica* and three destroyers under command of Admiral Fraser departed the harbour at Akureyri Island in Iceland to protect the convoy and attack *Scharnhorst* should the battleship leave Altafjord.

At 7.00 p.m., *Scharnhorst* and five destroyers under the command of Admiral Bey sailed from Altafjord to attack the convoy. However, the orders from the head of the Kriegsmarine, Admiral Karl Dönitz, also stated that Admiral Bey should withdraw if more heavily-armed Royal Navy ships were to intervene. Unknown to Admiral Bey, the Royal Navy cruisers *Norfolk, Belfast* and *Sheffield* of Force 1, after escorting the previous convoy RA55 away from the danger zone as it returned from delivering cargo to Murmansk, turned around to escort convoy JW55B to Murmansk.

On Boxing Day, at 3.39 a.m., *Duke of York* received a message from its HQ that *Scharnhorst* had left Altafjord. Despite winter's total polar dark, with the high winds of a storm and snow, German aircraft and U-boats reported on the course of convoy JW55b and its escorts. However, *Duke of York*'s departure in Force 1 from Iceland to protect the convoy and engage *Scharnhorst* was not detected.[5]

By 7.00 a.m. *Scharnhorst* was closing in on convoy JW55b and its accompanying five destroyers of the Kriegsmarine, the 4th Destroyer Flotilla, were taking up a course parallel to the convoy. Still unknown to Admiral Bey, the cruisers of the Royal Navy's Force 1, *Belfast, Sheffield* and *Norfolk*, continued to track *Scharnhorst* and were coming within range. At 9.15 a.m. on *Belfast* a radar contact registered the range at six and a half nautical miles (13,000 yards) which was followed, at 9.21, by a lookout on *Sheffield* sighting a dark shape on the port beam. It could only be *Scharnhorst*. At once Rear Admiral Burnett in command of Force 1 gave the order for *Belfast* to fire a 4-inch star-shell on the bearing and range of the radar contact.

As soon as the shell burst and lit up *Scharnhorst*, *Norfolk* opened fire with its 6-inch guns. Because Kapitän Hintze reacted immediately to the star-shell by turning his battleship to port onto a new course, *Norfolk*'s first salvo fell 500 yards adrift. However, further adjusted gunfire was thought by *Norfolk*'s crew to be on target, straddling the German battleship.

Hintze's new course meant that Force 1 was between *Scharnhorst* and convoy JW55b. To escape the threat of the British cruisers, which could only manage 16 knots in the gale force seas, *Scharnhorst* increased its speed to 24 knots. By 9.40 *Scharnhorst* was some twelve nautical miles distant from Force 1 and increasing the gap minute by minute. While *Norfolk* was out of effective range and ceased firing, its gunnery observers had been right – its third salvo had hit home.

One 8-inch shell from *Norfolk* fell on *Scharnhorst*'s upper deck and into a mess deck, where it started a fire. A second shell destroyed the Seetakt radar on the forward deck, which left only an aft-mounted radar that had a range limited to only six miles. While Admiral Bey maintained his intent to intercept and attack the convoy, his ship was severely handicapped in trying to detect the enemy ships which had launched the attack, or any other Royal Navy force that was seeking to engage *Scharnhorst*. The brief engagement was in effect the first shots in the Battle of North Cape.[6]

With *Scharnhorst* now sailing away from Force 1 at maximum speed, Admiral Fraser on *Duke of York* waited in suspense. Would *Scharnhorst* continue northwards to find and attack convoy JW55b or seek to return to the Altenfjord?

Around 11 o'clock, Admiral Bey received an incomplete report from German aircraft: Royal Navy ships had been seen approaching from the west of North Cape. Nevertheless, Bey stuck to his plan to attack the convoy. He remained unaware of the whereabouts of the *Duke of York* and its Force 2, and that Force 1 had sailed a course which put the three Royal Navy cruisers between *Scharnhorst* and the convoy. At 12.04 *Belfast* picked up a radar contact at a range of 26,000 yards, of what again had to be *Scharnhorst*.[7]

When the range came down to 11,000 yards at 12.21, *Norfolk* fired a star-shell to again illuminate *Scharnhorst*. *Norfolk* immediately followed this with a full salvo of 6-inch shells. Once more, *Scharnhorst* was taken by surprise. A new battle with the three Force 1 cruisers and their accompanying four destroyers, *Musketeer, Matchless, Opportune* and *Virago*, was under way.

Both *Norfolk* and *Sheffield* saw flashes of shells hitting home on *Scharnhorst* but appearing to do little damage. As the gap between them fell to not much more than 4,000 yards, 11-inch shells from *Scharnhorst* hit *Norfolk*, causing significant damage to its aft X turret and to the secondary control centre amidships.

Scharnhorst increased speed to 28 knots, close to its maximum despite the heavy seas, and sped away, leaving the Force 1 cruisers and destroyers in its wake. By 12.40 *Scharnhorst* was some 13,000 yards distant and putting down a smokescreen.

Around 1.00 p.m. Admiral Bey gave up the search for the convoy and signalled that he was under attack by a stronger force which had superior radar capability. *Scharnhorst* turned onto a course to the south-east and, maintaining 28 knots, headed back for Altenfjord. Bey and Kapitän Hintze remained unaware that the Force 1 British cruisers were following about eight miles astern. This change of course meant that *Scharnhorst* was detached from its five destroyers of 4th Destroyer Flotilla, which were continuing to search for convoy JW55b.

It seems that Bey and Hintze were confident that they could not be intercepted and did not ask themselves the key question: 'Can we reach the safety of the Alta fjord before Force 1 is strengthened by the possible arrival of the *Duke of York*?' Bey had no knowledge of the location or the course of *Duke of York*, yet he must have assumed that it would have been responding to the reports from the Force 1 cruisers concerning their engagements with *Scharnhorst*.

In contrast, on *Duke of York* navigators calculated that, based upon the information received from Force 1, the revised courses of the two ships meant that they and *Scharnhorst* should converge around 5.15 p.m. Despite receiving a communication at 1.30 from the Luftwaffe that *Duke of York* had been sighted in the south-west, *Scharnhorst* sent a signal to its base in Narvik in the Altafjord that they expected to arrive soon after midnight. Bey and Hintze thought that they had escaped both Force 1 and any threat from the distant *Duke of York* and Force 2.[8]

* * *

While *Scharnhorst* sailed on towards Altenfjord in blissful ignorance of its persistent pursuers, at 4.17 p.m. *Duke of York* picked up a radar contact. It confirmed information supplied earlier by *Belfast* and its own convergence estimates. Although the radar contact was detected at maximum range of 46,000 yards (23 nautical miles) to the north-east, it had to be *Scharnhorst*. Admiral Fraser ordered the four destroyers of Force 2 to split their positions, HMS *Savage* and HMS *Saumarez* off *Duke of York*'s port bow, HMS *Scorpion* and HMS *Stord* off the starboard bow. The cruiser HMS *Jamaica* followed in line astern of *Duke of York*. All ships maintained a speed of 25 knots in the heavy seas – uncomfortable on *Duke of York* but much worse for those on the destroyers. The trap was taking shape.

By 4.43 p.m. the gap between the converging *Duke of York* and *Scharnhorst* had closed to 16,000 yards (8 nautical miles). Fraser wanted to get as close as possible while *Scharnhorst* was ignorant of the growing threat of Forces 1 and 2. On *Duke of York* Admiral Fraser planned to open fire on *Scharnhorst* at a range of 13,000 yards and then, soon after, launch the two forces' destroyers in a torpedo attack. The two groups of predators were closing in while it appeared that their prey was only aware of being shadowed at a distance by the three cruisers of Force 1.

At 4.47 the range from *Duke of York* had come down below 13,000 yards and Fraser ordered *Belfast* in Force 1 to fire a star-shell over *Scharnhorst*. Once again, the German battleship was taken by surprise and was lit up in artificial daylight like a silver ghost. It is believed that neither Admiral Bey nor Kapitän Hintze were on the bridge at the time and *Scharnhorst*'s guns were not even pointed towards the potential threat from the shadowing Force 1. Expecting an immediate course change as before by Kapitän Hintze, Fraser on *Duke of York* waited four minutes.

With no course change detected, *Duke of York*'s first salvo from its 14-inch guns fired at 4.51 were on target, straddling *Scharnhorst*. One shell hit the forward Anton gun turret, killing its crew and putting it out of action. Perhaps barely a minute later the cruiser *Jamaica* also opened fire and, with its third salvo, claimed a hit on *Scharnhorst*.

Admiral Bey and Kapitän Hintze on *Scharnhorst* were caught unprepared. Yet they surely were beginning to realise that they were in a trap which was rapidly closing in. *Scharnhorst* began to fire back at *Duke of York* and, four minutes later at 4.55, Hintze turned the battleship to the north. At top speed, *Scharnhorst* began to extend the range from the British battleship, but only nine nautical miles to the north was Force 1, in which *Belfast* led with *Norfolk* close behind and *Sheffield* further back. To the west were the four destroyers of 36th Destroyer Division. To the south were the pursuers *Duke of York* and *Jamaica*, hungry to exploit their maiming of *Scharnhorst*. To go due east and away from Altenfjord, which lay to the south-south-east still some five hours sailing away, was the only slim chance for *Scharnhorst* to escape the trap.

The third salvo from *Duke of York* had hit the aft superstructure of *Scharnhorst*, so that it poured smoke fore and aft. Even so, despite the damage, as *Scharnhorst* began to increase the distance from *Duke of York*, it was still dangerous and, like a wounded buffalo, her crew fought back hard. Even before turning to the north, and just six minutes after being surprised by the bursting incandescent light of the star-shells, *Scharnhorst* opened fire with her main 11-inch guns at *Duke of York*. In the ensuing exchange, two of those 11-inch shells hit *Duke of York*'s foremast, destroying the air-warning radar and damaging the surface search radar, although the latter was soon repaired. However, despite using its superior speed to turn away, the northerly course was taking *Scharnhorst* closer to Force 1, prompting *Belfast* and *Norfolk* to open fire as well.

At 5.05 p.m. a 14-inch shell from *Duke of York* hit *Scharnhorst*'s Bruno turret, putting it out of action. Faced with the pincer attacks from Forces 1 and 2, there was only one option left and, at 5.08, Bey and Hintze turned their ship due east. The distance between *Scharnhorst* and *Duke of York* stretched out to 17,000 yards (8.5 nautical miles). The widening gap caused Admiral Fraser to order the destroyers in to a torpedo attack, although to do this for an effective launch in the heavy seas they needed to get within 2,000 yards of *Scharnhorst*. Ten minutes later, it was evident that all the destroyers and cruisers were losing speed on the new course, which left them in danger of capsizing against seas which were hitting them beam on. It left only *Duke of York* and *Scharnhorst* within range of each other's guns.[9]

As *Scharnhorst* kept lengthening the gap from its pursuers, Admiral Fraser began to realise that the German battleship was escaping. There was nothing to block its path to the Altafjord. At 6.19 Admiral Bey signalled to his base at Narvik that *Duke of York* was having to resort to firing only by radar at a range of 19,000 yards. A few more minutes and *Scharnhorst* would be well out of range. Escape to Altenfjord was seemingly almost within their grasp.

Then one minute later everything changed. In one of *Duke of York*'s last despairing salvos, a 14-inch shell hit *Scharnhorst*, seriously damaging a boiler room. *Scharnhorst*'s crucial remaining advantage, a higher maximum speed, was lost and reduced to only 22 knots. It meant the pursuers could catch up – a denouement was surely imminent.

Not surprisingly in the Arctic night and gale force seas, this profound change in the fortunes of the two sides was not immediately apparent. It was not until twenty minutes later, after 6.40 p.m., that it was noticed on *Duke of York* that *Scharnhorst* had lost speed. On radar the four destroyers were seen to be edging closer, *Savage* and *Saumarez* at 9,000 yards to the north-west, and *Scorpion* and *Stord* 10,000 yards away to the south on *Scharnhorst*'s starboard beam. When they closed to a range of 8,000 yards, *Scharnhorst* sighted their vague shadowy outlines.

In the heavy rolling seas, however, *Scharnhorst*'s gunners had great difficulty even seeing the destroyers. When *Scorpion* and *Stord* were detected at 6.49 at 6,000 yards to the south the *Scharnhorst* opened fire, first with star-shell. The four destroyers held their course, despite being dazzled by star-shell and then by the battleship's gunfire and were rapidly shortening the range. Three minutes later, at 6.52, *Scorpion* and *Stord* unleashed eight torpedoes at a range down to 2,100 yards, less than one nautical mile away from *Scharnhorst.*

As *Savage* and *Saumarez,* in the north on *Scharnhorst*'s port beam, closed to a similar range, an 11-inch shell hit the director tower of *Saumarez* but did not explode. Even so, it pierced the deck and damaged the starboard engine, killing eleven men with a similar number wounded badly, causing a reduction in speed to only 10 knots. Nevertheless, the captain of *Saumarez,* Lieutenant Commander Walmsley, carried on the attack, and at 6.53 fired four torpedoes. *Savage* fired eight so that a spread of twelve torpedoes headed towards *Scharnhorst.*

In a timespan of about a minute, four torpedoes hit *Scharnhorst,* one on the port side forward of the bridge, two to starboard, one on the bow and another back from the funnel and a fourth into the stern. The resulting explosions caused flooding and damage to the propulsion system, reducing *Scharnhorst*'s speed to around only 10 knots. Was the ship now fatally crippled?

For about twenty minutes, while the destroyers were attacking, *Duke of York* and *Jamaica* were sailing directly towards *Scharnhorst.* At a range of 10,400 yards (5 nautical miles) at 7.01 p.m., *Duke of York* and *Jamaica* opened fire. *Duke of York*'s fire-control radar had been repaired fully and, in conjunction with optical range-finding, its guns and those of *Jamaica* at once found their target. For the next twenty-five minutes, *Duke of York* fired a salvo of ten 14-inch shells every minute, of which only four missed their mark. *Scharnhorst* became a mass of flames and smoke yet kept firing back with whatever smaller guns remained operable, and even managing to fire a torpedo at *Duke of York,* although it passed wide.

Even though the 14-inch shells were not penetrating its armour belt, *Scharnhorst* became practically defenceless. Yet it was still moving at about 8-10 knots. At 7.20 p.m. Fraser ordered *Jamaica* and *Belfast* to go in and launch torpedoes to hit her hull below the waterline. They each fired three torpedoes, but Kapitän Hintze turned the battleship so that it threaded between the torpedo paths and so none hit home.

Since the four destroyers of 6th Destroyer Division, previously attached to Force 1, had arrived within striking distance, Fraser ordered them also to undertake a torpedo attack. He was determined not to allow even a wrecked *Scharnhorst* to limp back to Altafjord. *Opportune* and *Virago* to the north and starboard of the stricken battleship launched first at 2,100 yards range, then, within a minute or so, *Musketeer* and *Matchless* fired their spreads from the south on the port side. There was no escape for Bey and Hintze this time. In around three minutes, five torpedoes hit *Scharnhorst,* three to starboard and two to port.

In hindsight, those three torpedoes probably sealed *Scharnhorst*'s fate. Uncertainty still hung in the air, and *Jamaica* came in again. At 7.37 p.m. on

Scharnhorst's port side, it fired a spread of six more torpedoes. By then, *Scharnhorst* was heeling over so that the remaining small-calibre guns could not sight on *Jamaica*. Two torpedoes bore into the lower hull on *Scharnhorst*'s aft port side at around 7.40. It was the finish, and Kapitän Hintze gave the order to abandon ship. When the smoke cleared on *Jamaica* its crew gazed on a blazing hulk lying on its side. *Scharnhorst*'s crew jumped from either side, many dying as they hit parts of the ship underwater.

Scharnhorst sank about five minutes later. The sea was littered with its debris, the dead of her crew and those still alive screaming for rescue. Even those clinging to rafts were freezing to death quickly in the icy water and many did not have the strength to climb the ropes and scrambling nets dropped from destroyers such as *Scorpion*. Of the total complement of crew and staff of Admiral Bey on *Scharnhorst* estimated at 2,029, it is thought around 1,000 managed to throw themselves clear of the sinking ship. Nevertheless, there were only thirty-six survivors.[10]

* * *

The Battle of North Cape was a pivotal strategic naval victory for the Allies, which allowed the Arctic convoys to continue supplying Russia with critical military supplies.[11] Those supplies fed the great Russian offensive Operation BAGRATION which defeated the German Army in Belorussia in the summer of 1944.

To read of the experiences of those on both sides who took part in this battle, described in the Nordkapp Memorial on North Cape, in Angus Konstam's gripping and engrossing *The Battle of North Cape* and in other sources is to marvel at the skill, fortitude and incredible spirit and endurance of the sailors on both sides in the most extreme conditions imaginable.

Even in the high summer month of July, North Cape is freezing and inhospitable. The interminable Arctic December night, gale-force storms and seas, blizzards, below freezing temperatures, the battle's death and destruction are incomprehensible, except to those who went through it – and survived,

* * *

Arctic Rescue

In July 1944, although the *Scharnhorst* threat had been eliminated, it was still critical for the Allies to protect the Arctic convoys from attack by U-boats and the Luftwaffe. In addition, the brooding menace of *Tirpitz* still lay at anchor in the Altafjord. It was not known whether *Tirpitz* was seaworthy again and, if so, would the Kriegsmarine decide to send it into an attack on the convoys. Operations by the Royal Navy and RAF continued to counter any such interdictions. The following story is drawn from the experience of Flying Officer Bob Sommerville in those anti-submarine patrols by the RAF and from *Shot Down and in the Drink*, by Graham Pitchfork.

* * *

At RAF Tain in Ross-shire, Scotland, on 18 July 1944 at a little after 2.00 p.m., Squadron Leader Reg Nelms of No.86 Squadron lifted Liberator F-Freddie, FL907, into the air. Nelms' co-pilot was Flying Officer Robert 'Bob' (or 'Slim') Sommerville in a nine-man crew; the Liberator was fully laden with anti-submarine depth charges.

Other crew members were: flight engineer – Jock Toner; first navigator – Flight Lieutenant Ken Gray; second navigator – Sergeant Graham Richardson; flight engineer –Sergeant Peter Toner; flight engineer/rear gunner – Sergeant Dennis 'Dan' Cossey; wireless operator/air gunner – Sergeant Robert Gregory; wireless operator/air gunner – Flight Sergeant Joseph 'Cliff' Contant; wireless operator/air gunner – Flight Sergeant L. Daley

Their mission was to undertake an anti-submarine patrol, part of a larger operation providing protection for a large Royal Navy force. The patrol area was designated east of Iceland, north-west of the Lofoten Islands on the northern Norwegian coast, and some 700 miles north of the Arctic Circle. For six hours in the patrol area the flight was uneventful and the extended daylight of summer in the northerly latitudes helped to keep the crew alert.

The Arctic Circle cuts through the Nordland region of Norway where, on the fissured coastline, the string of Lofoten Islands stretches from the north-east to the south-west into the Norwegian Sea. On a fine sunny day, the Lofotens and their mountains can look like a paradise of wild beauty. At other times, storms can sweep in from the Atlantic, North Sea and Barents Sea and envelop the archipelago in a hell of driving rain and snow.

The Liberator's four engines droned on unremittingly while, at 1,000 feet above the waves, Nelms followed a pre-determined search pattern. Then the calm routine of surveillance was broken when a U-boat was sighted some eight miles away on the surface. Immediately, Nelms banked the Liberator in a turn towards the U-boat which went into a crash dive.

A buoy marker was dropped on the estimated position of where the U-boat submerged and Nelms began a box-grid search of the surrounding sea's surface. For two hours, the crew stared at the waves 1,000 feet below as the Liberator flew up and down the search pattern. Just as hopes were evaporating, the rear gunner, Flight Sergeant Cliff Contant, spotted the U-boat once more on the surface. Nelms at once climbed the Liberator, preparing to position the aircraft for a bombing run on the U-boat.

To conceal an attack run, Nelms first took the bomber into some cloud cover. On sighting the Liberator emerging from the cloud and dropping down into a fast approach, the U-boat captain turned hard to port. At the same time, with the Liberator at around 3,000 yards range, the U-boat gunners opened up at the aircraft with 30mm cannon fire. Nelms kept steady on the bombing run and released six depth charges, which exploded some way off the U-boat's starboard side.

Nelms pulled the Liberator around in a tight turn and began a second attack. A few seconds after six more depth charges were dropped, the U-boat's anti-aircraft fire hit the bomber in the starboard wing and engine. Almost instantly, the wing and engine were on fire. Nelms told the crew there was no option but to ditch the aircraft. Immediately, Wireless Operator Sergeant Robert Gregory, while looking at the flames from the wing searing past his cabin window, sent out an SOS signal of their plight.

The Liberator was dipping down toward the sea. Because the wing flaps had been damaged, effectively disabled by the U-boat's anti-aircraft fire, Nelms was prevented from slowing the aircraft. At such a low altitude, only seconds before hitting the waves, he could only try to keep the aircraft as level as possible. The bomber smashed into the sea far too fast, causing the fuselage to split in two. The rear part submerged almost immediately while the nose and front section churned through the waves for a second or two before coming to rest, rapidly filling with water.

When the Liberator broke apart, the second navigator, Sergeant Graham Richardson (RNZAF) was sucked down with the tail section. Six of the crew were in the forward section and were fortunate to have valuable seconds to free themselves. Bob Sommerville was unconscious, trapped in the cockpit, and only just in time was dragged free and out of the rapidly sinking Liberator. More luck smiled on them when they were able to grab three one-man 'K' survival dinghies from amongst the floating wreckage.

Despite a lifejacket to stay afloat, a man immersed in the freezing Arctic water would not last long. A swimmer in such cold water would only survive on average around twenty minutes as the cold water removes heat from the body some twenty-five times faster than cold air of a similar temperature.[12]

A larger dinghy with survival kit and rations had sunk with the broken fuselage. Two other crew members, Flight Sergeant Daly and Sergeant Cossey, who had escaped from the rear section, were seen drifting away and soon out of sight. The six surviving crew in their three dinghies were on their own. Their sole companions were the sea, the wind and the freezing cold.

Two men were able to share each of the one-man dinghies, only by way of the smaller man sitting on the legs of the larger man. They tied the three dinghies together with a rope. Reg Nelms shared with Robert Gregory, 'Slim' Sommerville with Jock Toner and Ken Gray with the badly-injured Cliff Contant. They sat huddled together in sodden uniforms, whipped by the wind and sea spray, frozen to their bones.

To share amongst the six men there were only two small ration packs of Horlicks energy tablets and no water. The navigator, Ken Gray, estimated that they had ditched north-west of Iceland, some 700 miles from RAF Tain in Scotland, and around 200 miles inside the Arctic Circle. Although their predicament seemed near hopeless, at that time of year there was no night. Only a few weeks after high summer's longest day, it meant that the near twenty-four hours of daylight would assist an air-sea-rescue search. They had to hope that their SOS signal had been received and acted upon.

In each of the three dinghies, they held on to each other, one man on top of another, barely able to move; if they did so they feared a capsizing of the dinghy which would be fatal. The cold threatened them with hypothermia and sending them into unconsciousness, which would be the end. They clung to the hope of a search being underway. At least because there were six of them, there was more chance of there being someone talking, to keep everyone awake. Nelms and Gregory began a competition to recall every Latin phrase that they could remember.

There was a three-way contest taking place for their lives. What would kill them first, the cold, the clutches of the sea or thirst? The lack of any liquid to drink meant that dehydration and its torturous effects were intensifying. After two days, fate intervened when some drizzling rain began to fall. Six mouths gaped towards the heavens to catch some moisture. Gregory used a handkerchief to soak up the fine rain droplets, then screwed it into a ball to suck.

They knew that they had been drifting in their dinghies away from where the Liberator had ditched, making any search increasingly unlikely to sight them. On two occasions, aircraft were seen in the distance. Flares were fired but they were too far away to be seen, and their dinghies were but minor specks in the vast rolling seas. While the six men clung precariously to life, Gregory's quick reaction in radioing an SOS signal moments before they hit the water, sustained them in some slim hope of being found.

As soon as the SOS signal was received at RAF Tain, a request was made to the Royal Navy for HMS *Duke of York* and three aircraft carriers to commence a search in the area of the co-ordinates stated in the signal, latitude 68.46N, longitude 09.53E, some 100 miles west of the Lofoten Islands. Unfortunately, the Navy's operations in protecting the Arctic convoys, and other priorities, prevented it from assisting which delayed the start of an air-sea-rescue search.

Other Liberator aircraft of the survivors' No.86 Squadron began the long flights to the ditching area. Eventually, a Catalina flying boat from No.210 Squadron, capable of landing on the sea and picking up any survivors, took off from RAF Sullom Voe in the Shetland Islands. After conducting a search to the limit of its endurance, the Catalina radioed that no survivors could be seen. A more extensive search operation was planned for the next day, using a number of aircraft.

Hopes of finding any survivors were dimming when, in the afternoon of the second day, a Liberator from No.86 Squadron reported that it had caught sight of the three dinghies. Despite the vast expanses of the North Atlantic, it was as if some unseen hand had guided one of the squadron's aircraft and crews to miraculously fly over their six despairing comrades.

The pilot, Flight Lieutenant Ross, circled around the dinghies with the six survivors, transmitted a signal to RAF Tain of their position and dropped a packet of food and an emergency radio. However, the packet broke apart on hitting the sea and was lost. It was still long odds against the dinghies being located again and the six survivors being rescued by ship or flying boat.

Into the fourth day at 2.00 a.m. at RAF Sullom Voe a Catalina of No.210 Squadron took off to search again for the Liberator's survivors. The pilot, 25-year-old Sergeant Frank French, was an experienced Catalina pilot, having earlier been awarded the DFC for sinking a U-boat. French flew for some six hours on a course plotted by his Canadian navigator, Flight Lieutenant A. Jackson, to the search area some 540 miles north of the Shetlands.

The long daylight hours of the Arctic summer stretched on interminably. A brief dip by the sun below the horizon around midnight before it rose again for the dawn of another day was the only indication that the six survivors faced another day at the mercy of the cold and sea. Around 8.00 a.m. on 21 July, their fourth day in the dinghies, they still clung on to life. Then they saw a moving dot on the horizon, an aircraft which appeared to be heading towards them. The silhouette was growing larger. It was a Catalina. They fired the last remaining distress flares. It was now or never. They could not last another day. Had the Catalina seen them, or the flares in the bright Arctic sky?

When French and Jackson in the Catalina saw the flares, they knew there were some survivors still alive. French circled the Catalina around the dinghies and, to gauge the strength and direction of the wind and assess the sea's strong swell, dropped a number of smoke-floats. The six men watched in hope and could only pray that there would be a decision to land the Catalina. The wind was about 8 mph, but at right angles to a fair north-westerly swell. When the flying boat came around again, as if to make a landing but then aborted, it appeared the decision was negative. If so, it would surely condemn them.

In fact, French had been making a further assessment in a dummy run, and now looked for a lull in the waves. He dismissed from his mind the pre-flight orders that on no account must he hazard the Caralina or risk its loss. His next approach was judged to perfection, landing smoothly on the water, before taxiing around to be close to the three dinghies. One of the Catalina's crew climbed out on a wing, threw a rope to the six men and pulled all three dinghies up to the side hatch in the Catalina's fuselage.

With the help of lowered ropes, five of the six men were hauled aboard. The injured Cliff Contant had to be lifted fully into the flying boat. While French discharged some excess fuel to compensate for the additional weight of the six men, they were each stripped of their wet clothing, dried off, given a warm kapok sleeping suit to put on and hot beef tea to sip. It would be around a six-hour flight back to the Shetlands before they could receive medical care.

By the time French was satisfied with the necessary amount of fuel remaining, and with the aircraft's overall reduction in weight, the Catalina had sat on the choppy Arctic sea for some forty-five minutes. The challenge was for it to take off safely from an unruly unpredictable sea. A rocking swell, which had increased in intensity, meant that there could be no more delay before departure on the return flight. It was not until after a successful take-off that French finally radioed RAF Sullom Voe that six survivors had been taken onboard and that the Catalina was in the air heading back to base.

He thought the rescue had been very lucky, as the weather conditions at such a northerly latitude inside the Arctic Circle are often much worse, which would have prevented a landing and take-off. While the skill of French and his navigator in flying such a precise course was remarkable, as was French's landing and take-off in a dangerous swell, they were also very lucky to spot the flares and tiny specks of the dinghies.[13]

The survival and rescue of the six airmen is considered the most northerly and fully successful air-sea rescue in the Arctic Circle. In this most unlikely rescue operation against all the odds, the recognition of indomitable spirit and selfless determination came in a number of awards: Squadron Leader Reg Nelms – DFC; Sergeant R. 'Bob' Sommerville – MiD MBE; Sergeant Robert Gregory – MiD; Squadron Leader John 'Frank' French – AFC.

Clearly all involved, Liberator survivors and Catalina aircrew, deserved the highest commendations.

Notes

1. North Cape Memorial, *'The 1943 Sea Battle by North Cape'*, Nordkapp, Norway
2. Konstam, *The Battle of North Cape*, pp.1-11
3. Kennedy, *Menace*, pp.66-93
4. North Cape Memorial, op.cit.
5. Ibid.
6. Konstam, op.cit., pp.78-82
7. North Cape Memorial, op. cit.
8. Konstam, op.cit., pp.96-109; North Cape Memorial op.cit.
9. Konstam, op.cit., pp.113-22; North Cape Memorial op.cit.
10. Konstam, op.cit., pp.130-49; North Cape Memorial op.cit.
11. Konstam, op.cit., p.2
12. Ibid., p.149
13. Veterans' Accounts, Flying Officer R.'Bob' Sommerville, and Squadron Leader John 'Frank' French, Private Collection, Lesly Sommerville, and Pitchfork, *Shot Down and in the Drink*, pp.122-6

Part IV

Far East

Chapter 9

The Malaya Campaign – A Fighting Retreat from the Japanese Invasion and a Mysterious Letter

(This summary of the Malaya Campaign is based upon the perspectives and eyewitness accounts of Captain W. Gingell, David Clemens and David Scott Daniell's *The History of the East Surrey Regiment*, Vol IV.)

Eighty-two years ago a letter was lost. It was a mystery letter, written at sea on 8 April 1942 and began:[1]

> My Dear Tommy,
> You will, I know, be surprised to hear from me, but I could not arrive home without letting you know, I hope to reach England once again in a few days time.

The writer was Captain W.G. 'Bill' Gingell, an officer in the 2nd Battalion of the East Surrey Regiment (Surreys). He gives no further details in regard to 'Tommy' and only signs the letter as 'Bill'. In the letter he briefly recounts the role of the Surreys in the disastrous Malaya campaign and the fall of Singapore.

> At the start of the war we were in North Kedah, about ten miles south of the Thai-Malayan border, and it wasn't many days before the Battalion got into action.

After just a few lines on the torrid battles against the Japanese during December 1941 to February 1942, and how he came to survive, Bill finishes the letter:

> I shall post this as soon after landing as possible .... Kindly remember me to Mrs Thompson and Joyce. I do hope they are fit, Yours ever, Bill.

What follows is the story of those months when the world changed for Bill Gingell and everyone.

* * *

The Breaking Storm

In early November 1941, as the threat of war with Japan in Asia and the Pacific grew alarmingly, Prime Minister Churchill decided to deploy the capital ships HMS *Prince of Wales* and HMS *Repulse* to Singapore as a deterrent. HMS *Prince of Wales*, nearly 44,000 tons and commissioned in January 1941, was then one of the largest ships in the world and Britain's most modern battleship. The two capital ships, together with their destroyers and other support ships, were codenamed Force Z and should have included the new fleet aircraft carrier HMS *Indomitable.* After commissioning in October 1941, *Indomitable* ran aground on a coral reef near Jamaica during its work-up, which resulted in postponement of its deployment with Force Z.[2]

At the time there was still a substantial body of opinion in Royal Navy circles that believed that battleships could be protected from aircraft attack by their anti-aircraft guns. Thus, Force Z sailed for Singapore as planned without HMS *Indomitable* and, consequently, lacking any air support.

Once Force Z was docked in Singapore and when it was learned that, early on 8 December, Japanese forces were landing near Kota Bharu on the Malayan east coast, the C-in-C of Force Z, Admiral Phillips, was not deterred by its lack of air support and protection. Assuming the benefit of a surprise attack, Force Z had the potential to damage seriously the Japanese invasion fleet, destroy its troop transport vessels and curtail the amphibious landings that were underway.

That same day at 17.25 hours Force Z departed Singapore to prevent the Japanese establishing a bridgehead. The Japanese attack on Pearl Harbor in Oahu, Hawaii, on 7 December began at about 07.55 local time, actually only an hour or so later than the invasion of Malaya (ignoring the distortion of the International Date Line). Phillips may not have known or been fully aware of the Japanese attack and its catastrophic destruction of US Navy ships.

Certainly the threat of attack on *Prince of Wales* and *Repulse* by Japanese aircraft, if considered at all, was not seen as sufficient for Phillips to call for any delay in Force Z's departure. He planned for the capital ships to sail north all day on 9 December to reach and attack the Japanese invasion fleet the next morning in the region of Singora on the Malayan east coast.

Early in the morning of the 10th however, a Japanese reconnaissance flight spotted Force Z. The consequences were immediate. A little after 11.00 hours thirty-four Mitsubishi G4M 'Betty' bombers, and fifty-one 'Nell' torpedo-bombers, from the 22nd Air Flotilla of the Imperial Japanese Navy Air Force (IJNAF), based at Saigon, dived into an attack on Force Z. A torpedo hit *Prince of Wales*, cutting its power in half and disabling its steering while a bomb crashed through the deck of *Repulse*.

A second wave of Japanese bombers first dived on *Prince of Wales*, unleashing torpedoes one after another into the wallowing battleship, as if it was a mortally wounded wild beast needing to be put out of its agony. Its remaining anti-aircraft guns again fired in vain. With *Prince of Wales* lying dead in the water, the Nells turned on *Repulse*. Two aircraft were shot down and Captain Tennant of *Repulse* twisted and pulled the more manoeuvrable battlecruiser first one way, then the other, to evade the torpedo paths. It could not last. Simultaneously, enemy aircraft launched torpedoes from both port and starboard approach runs. In quick succession, six or more struck home. *Repulse* was hammered into a 40-degree list and Tennant gave the order to abandon ship. Within a minute, *Repulse* keeled over 70 degrees, and Tennant went down with his ship.

Prince of Wales would stay afloat for nearly another hour, allowing the rescue of survivors but, at 13.20, it too sank into the depths. *Prince of Wales* was the first modern battleship to be sunk by air attack on the open sea and this would have far-reaching implications. Coming just a few days after Pearl Harbor, the loss of *Prince of Wales* and *Repulse* was a near mortal blow to Allied naval strength in the Far East. There were no longer any Allied capital ships in the Indian Ocean or in the Pacific west of Hawaii.

The land forces of Britain and its Commonwealth Allies in Malaya and Singapore now faced the full force of the Japanese offensive without effective naval or air support. Japanese air and naval power had struck across half the globe. There was no way to prevent multiple landings of Japanese forces in Malaya. So how would Captain Bill Gingell in northern Malaya escape with his life from this maelstrom that Japan had launched against Britain and its colonies in the Far East?

* * *

East Surrey Regiment leaves Shanghai and prepares for war in northern Malaya

In 1940 the 2nd Battalion East Surrey Regiment (Surreys) was based in Shanghai where Captain Bill Gingell was serving as the quartermaster. From their arrival in November 1938, they were based at the Bubbling Well Road barracks in the British and American sector of the International Settlement. The Surreys' control area boundary of the British sector ran along the Hangchow railway line, on the other side of which was the Japanese sector. There were five level crossings along the rail line and boundary where armed sentries of both countries stood within a few yards of each other.[3]

Private David Clemens of the Surreys described it as a highly charged international situation. The Japanese were in a most arrogant mood and looking for trouble, making the task of British soldiers standing face to face with Japanese troops extremely difficult. A false step could cause a flare up with worldwide implications. There were more than thirty nationalities living in the International Settlement which was patrolled by British Military Police, US and Italian Marines, while the French had their own concession area. The tense urban security environment meant that the Surreys were unable to undertake any field exercise training.[4]

Because of the growing threat of a Japanese attack on Malaya and Singapore, in September 1940 the Surreys were transferred to Singapore where their stay would be brief. On 20 February 1941 the Surreys sent Captain Bill Gingell in an advance party by rail from Singapore north up the Malay peninsula to Tarjan Pau. This was close to Jitra and twelve miles from Alor Star, the main town in the state of Kedah in the far north of Malaya.

> Once across the causeway from Singapore to Johore … the train journey was some 500 miles to Tarjan Pau, which was only a few miles from the border with Siam (Thailand). We made camp in a rubber plantation, where the full Battalion would take over a number of huts which had been vacated by an Indian Army unit.[5]

The Surreys joined 1st/8th and 2nd/16th Battalions of the Punjab Regiment in 6 Indian Brigade, part of 11th Indian Division. Two other Indian infantry brigades made up 11th Division, 15 Brigade and 28 Brigade which included three Gurkha battalions. In 15 Brigade there was the only other British battalion in 11th Division, the 1st Leicesters.

In overcast stifling heat and with no power in the plantation huts for lighting or cooling fans, it was extremely hot, humid and debilitating. Daytime temperatures were usually over 30C, no lower than 20C overnight, and humidity hovering at 90 per cent all year round. In areas where the jungle had been cleared the land looked like a green sea of rice padi fields. Nevertheless, training commenced, and Captain Bill Gingell sensed there was an urgency in everyone to adapt to the tropical weather and terrain.

> Training in rubber plantations and rice padi fields was of a different kind to what we had experienced in Shanghai and before, but both officers and all ranks very soon got to know the country, and how to get around this terrain.[6]

Over the following months of 1941 the Surreys undertook battle training in conjunction with the Punjabi battalions with an emphasis on jungle warfare and defending against enemy assaults. Construction commenced on defensive positions around Jitra with an eye on the threatening posture and likely deployments of Japanese forces into Thailand. In their training exercises and 'war games', the Surreys took on the role of an attacking Japanese force, a simulation which gave them some ideas on what tactics the Japanese might use in an attack.

Instruction courses were held in the use of all weapons, vehicles and other equipment, even throughout the oppressive midday heat. Yet, within a few weeks, the troops became acclimatised to operating in the high temperatures. Months went by in work and training and at one stage an inter-brigade exercise was attended by the GOC Singapore, Lieutenant General Percival and other staff officers. Like everyone, Gingell was aware of the threat that could come from Japanese forces crossing the border only a few miles away.

> We all took our turn at digging. Parties went off at 7am and returned at 5pm. Working in the sun all day, not only digging but felling trees, is no easy task. However, grumbles were few as the men realised why it was needed. And so we came to December, and we all felt the tenson increasing.[7]

To forestall a Japanese invasion into Thailand, and probable landings on its east coast at the ports of Patani and Singora, the British Army had developed a plan, Operation MATADOR, to invade Thailand first. In order to confront such a Japanese attack, British forces would cross the border from northern Malaya into the south-eastern coastal strip of Thailand and construct defensive positions at Patani and Singora.[8]

On 6 December an RAAF reconnaissance aircraft from Singapore sighted the Japanese naval fleet and troop transport ships about 180 miles north of Kota Bharu, Eleventh Indian Division was placed on the highest readiness for Operation MATADOR and preliminary moves towards the Thai border took place in driving rain.[9] No decision was taken by the Royal Navy to attack the Japanese fleet.

At first light on Sunday 7 December the Surreys were ready and awaited the order to move out of Tarjan Pau. They had no knowledge of the Japanese attack on Pearl Harbor in Hawaii which would come later that same day and, in the early hours of 8 December, an invasion of Malaya. In trucks and other vehicles, and two sections in armoured troop carriers, the Surreys deployed to the main road and waited for the order to proceed across the border to Singora. Gingell knew the redeployment could mean an engagement with Japanese forces attacking from Thailand. 'We briefed all our men on the locations to occupy when we reached the vicinity of Singora, and with the rest of the Brigade we waited for the order to move out.'[10]

Gingell's thoughts wandered. They had risen in the dark and assembled while it was still cool. Would their positioning be in effect a tripwire, making them a sacrificial goat to give early warning of a Japanese invasion into Thailand and also Malaya? Singora was only about fifty miles from Jitra. As the sun rose, so did the heat, and still no word came for the column to move.

> Instead later in the day an order came to withdraw, to go back and take up our defensive positions, which we had prepared around Tarjan Pau. This required us to transport all our supplies, weapons, guns, food, clothing and other equipment back over rough roads and ground several miles from the main road.[11]

An order cancelling Operation MATADOR was not received until the afternoon of 8 December, which was twelve hours after the Japanese landings at Patani and Singora on the narrow south-eastern coastal strip of Thailand. It meant that the laborious withdrawal to defensive positions along the Jitra line was also hampered by the continuing torrential rain. Redeploying from an offensive stance of readiness to a defensive one in the atrocious weather affected morale badly. To then attempt to complete unfinished defences around Jitra, which were water-logged from the monsoon rains, made it worse.[12]

Operation MATADOR had been called off without a shot fired and the RAF evacuated its airfields at Kota Bharu and Kuanton which meant no air support for the ground troops. From that Sunday night of 8/9 December onwards the four Surreys companies, A, B, C and D, worked feverishly to re-establish themselves in a defensive deployment, much of it in and around rice padi fields. Over the next days, to urgently strengthen defences, D Company alone laid over 1,500 land and anti-tank mines.

Japanese Invasion

At 00.25 hours on 8 December the Japanese Army landed their first troops at Badang near Kota Bharu on Malaya's north-east coast and, soon after, on the Thailand coastal strip at Patani and Singora. It was one hour and ten minutes before the surprise attack on Pearl Harbor. Because of the International Date Line, and the different time zone, in Pearl Harbor it was still 7 December. On 8 December the Japanese also invaded Hong Kong at dawn, and bombed Shanghai, Singapore and the US Clark Air Force Base in the Philippines, synchronised to be near simultaneous with their surprise attack on Pearl Harbor. The Japanese landings at Badang were aimed at capturing the RAF airfields around Kota Bharu, and secondary to the main landings at Patani and Singora. The British Army's forces in Malaya were widely dispersed with multiple objectives such as the protection of Johore Bharu across the strait from Singapore, defending three RAF airfields at Kota Bharu and one at Kuanton on the east coast and the now aborted plan to launch Operation MATADOR.[13]

Disaster at Jitra

On 10 December the demoralising news came through to 11th Division that the IJNAF had sunk the Royal Navy's HMS *Prince of Wales* and HMS *Repulse*. As if it had been choreographed, in the early hours of 11 December the Japanese Army attacked Jitra in strength. Making a cacophony of noise, their troops screaming and even using firecrackers, rattles and raucous music, Japanese forces drove down the main road and across country in an outflanking movement from the east and attacked 11th Division's positions around Jitra. They broke through the lines of 15 Brigade so that, on 12 December, the Surreys were detached from 6 Brigade and ordered to pull back to protect various bridges, to allow for a total withdrawal from Jitra of 11th Division. The Surreys would in effect be a rearguard and, on the heels of the Division, would destroy the bridges before making their own withdrawal to the south.[14]

In the Surreys' withdrawal Corporal David Clemens was a driver/mechanic with C Company, which also involved being a motorcycle messenger.

> At night … we just slept on a groundsheet in our uniform and boots, weapons at our side, using our pack as a pillow, but with exhaustion we slept, not bothering about mosquitoes and creepy crawlies.[15]

But in the few seconds before sleep came, Clemens thought back to his time in Singapore, where he had met a Eurasian girl, Norah, who lived with her family in a large house on Orchard Road.

> I was free … from six pm each evening and at least three times per week I would visit Norah. By giving favours to a local taxi company, I received a car with free petrol, which made my journeys to Singapore town much easier. Our main entertainment in the evening was to visit one of the massive entertainment centres, Happy, New or Great Worlds, where you could dance, eat, play the machines, and generally have a good time – unfortunately it didn't last too long.

At Christmas 1940 Norah invited me to attend Midnight Mass at the Roman Catholic Cathedral, where the service lasted about four hours and all in Latin, what an ordeal.

* * *

To facilitate brigade orders for withdrawal, Gingell was selected to travel in advance with a small party drawn from the Surreys south to Kebalas Batas to reconnoitre possible defensive positions for two companies around two bridges. The Surreys B and D Companies travelled by armoured train to Anat Bukit where there was a railway station about three and a half miles south of the two bridges at Kebalas Batas. To get there sooner, Gingell took an advance party of eight men by motor transport.

> On arriving at Kebalas Batas my small party of eight men was shot at by an advance Japanese patrol, who were obviously trying to get behind us to blow up the road, to block our withdrawal. As soon as we came under fire we took cover. We did not know their strength, but we had only one option, to engage and try and drive them off.[16]

Gingell and his small group went to ground, stayed still, watched and waited. The buzz and whirr of insects, bird calls, and the rustle of unseen life in the undergrowth seemed magnified and all around them. Sweat dripped under men's arms and mosquito bites were borne in silence. After a while, the Japanese troops showed themselves, at first in ones and twos, and advanced warily. Gingell, breathed in, held his breath, and held his nerve.

> I thought there were maybe twenty to thirty, and allowed them to come on, holding our fire, so that they too would be unsure of our number and exactly where we were positioned. When they were at about 150 yards distance, and clearly unaware of our exact location, I gave the order to open fire. Our fusillade of rifles and one Bren gun killed or wounded eighteen enemy troops.[17]

Those Japanese who survived withdrew rapidly into the jungle. The train with the Surreys' B and D Companies, equipment and other motor transports subsequently arrived without incident at Anat Bukit where Gingell briefed their commanders. The two companies were ordered to move to protect the bridges while a platoon of Gurkhas was sent out on patrol to ensure that no more Japanese forces were able to approach undetected.

A further train arrived with A Company, while C Company came in by evening on 11 March after a forced march. Yet another setback befell the Surreys when their CO, Lieutenant Colonel Swinton, broke his leg in a motor vehicle accident. He was riding as a pillion passenger on the back of a motorcycle while visiting various deployments and, as a consequence, was evacuated to a hospital in Singapore. Major Dowling took over as the Battalion CO, whom Gingell had previously found to be an excellent deputy commander.

> Major Dowling had no time to adjust as next morning the whole Surreys Battalion was ordered to Alor Star, where we engaged Japanese forces in a great deal of close fighting. Among our casualties was Lieutenant Sear, who died from his wounds, before we withdrew to south of the main river bridge.
>
> We prepared this bridge to be destroyed, and we waited for more of our troops to arrive and cross. After a Japanese patrol on motor cycles suddenly appeared, and tried to cross the bridge, we blew it up immediately. All the enemy riders were killed in the explosion, or shot before they could head back to report to their main force. Unfortunately, it meant nine carriers of our troops were left somewhere on the wrong side of the river.[18]

After the Surreys' engineers blew up the bridges on 13 December, they followed the remnants of 6 Brigade and the rest of the badly mauled 11th Division some forty miles south to Gurun. The Battle of Jitra had been a disaster. The effectiveness of all three brigades of 11th Division had been nearly destroyed, losing hundreds of men similar to 15 Brigade, which was reduced to only a quarter of its troops. Inevitably there were also heavy losses of guns, equipment, ammunition and transport.

Gurun – an attempt to regroup

As the Surreys withdrew from Alor Star down the road south towards Gurun, they and other divisional troops were continually repelling enemy attacks that were trying to harass and delay their retreat. At Gurun the main road south straightened to run past the town's railway station and continued south parallel to the railway line. Either side of the road and railway lines lay jungle. To the west, thickly clad slopes climbed up to the 4,000-foot-high Mount Kedah.

On 15 December, some three miles to the north of Gurun, the Surreys' four companies moved into positions to block both the railway line and the road. Around a mile further north of the Surreys were the remaining infantry of

2nd/16th Punjab and 2nd/9th Gurkha battalions and to the east were remnants of 2nd/1st Gurkhas on the east-west road from Jitra.

The Surreys' D Company was deployed with 1st/8th Punjabis furthest to the west of the main road. In the night, at around 03.00, Major Dowling learned that messengers had been unable to make contact with either D Company or the Punjab Battalion HQ. To investigate the breakdown in communications, and the exact location of D Company, and fearing a Japanese breakthrough, Dowling himself went south to 6 Brigade HQ.

He was unaware that the officer commanding 1st/8th Punjabis, believing that a Japanese force had outflanked his position, had withdrawn his troops, including the Surreys' D Company, further away to the west. This created a large gap in the defensive lines. The Japanese quickly grasped the opportunity and surged through the undefended area. Using light armoured vehicles, they broke through to attack and destroy 6 Brigade HQ. Major Dowling, with more than a dozen senior officers and NCOs including the battalion's Medical Officer and Padre, as well as many other men were killed or wounded. Most of 6 Brigade HQ staff were killed in the surprise onslaught, in effect eliminating the brigade's leadership.

Although the Japanese had nearly surrounded all of 6 Brigade's surviving troops, and destroyed their command structure, the Surreys' B and C Companies, embedded in a rubber plantation to the east of the main road, held firm in their positions. It prevented further infiltration by the enemy which would have threatened to outflank the rest of the division.

With 6 Brigade's troops completely cut off from the rest of the division and the Surreys' Battalion HQ almost surrounded, there was no alternative for the Surrey companies but to retreat further south. Those left in A Company struggled south sixty miles through the jungle to try to reach Taiping. The Japanese were waiting for them en route where the few Surreys to survive the encounter were taken prisoner. Some men of D Company, under command of Captain Cater, managed to flee to the west and, on reaching the west coast, were helped by local villagers to cross to Penang in small fishing boats.[19]

The loss of so many of the Surreys' leaders reflected the intensity and desperation in the battles to hold the Japanese at bay. Yet it meant that the Surreys had been destroyed as a functioning battalion. Gingell was one of those lucky to survive and, with the remaining Surreys and other remnants of the brigade fell back gradually, all the time fighting off enemy attackers.

> From the morning of 16 December we had to fight back steadily, with what men who were capable, and who we could get together. Eventually we were ordered to Bukit Mertajam, and the next day we moved on to

> Taiping, where we were joined by our C Company. I had lost touch with them, and assumed they had been scuppered. From Taiping we went on south again to Ipoh [20]

The two remaining companies, B and C, were joined by some surviving Gurkhas. They were a valuable addition to the Surreys' troop count which had been eroded to just ten officers and 260 other ranks. All the division's battalions had suffered similar losses and were also in disarray. In the face of the continuing advance of the Japanese forces, the full division fell back once more some sixty miles south to Ipoh.

Ipoh to Kampur – Reorganisation to fight on as the British Battalion

During a stay of three days in the vicinity of Ipoh the division's battered units were restructured. The two Indian brigades were amalgamated as one into 6/15, and 1st Leicesters and 2nd Surreys were merged and renamed the 'British Battalion' under the command of Lieutenant Colonel Morrison. Unexpected arrivals of small parties of men from the fragmented retreat from Gurun gradually brought the strength of the British Battalion (the Battalion) in all ranks up to around 700. A mix of officers from both the Leicesters and Surreys were appointed to command positions in the battalion, in which Captain Gingell was made quartermaster.

The order for 6/15 Brigade and the newly-formed British Battalion to pull back again came on 23 December, so as to try and halt the Japanese advance some forty miles to the south at Kampar. Barely a mile north of Kampur, the Surreys' C Company deployed in positions stretching some 800 yards west of the main road where they had an open field of fire across cleared ground of old tin-mining terrain. Meanwhile, east of the road the Leicesters' two companies climbed to the tops of some low hills, Thompson's, Green, and Cemetery ridges. Farther east, a jungle-clad mountain, some nine miles long and six wide, rose up to 4,000 feet. To the south-west the Punjabi battalions straddled across part of Kampur town and the congruence of the road and railway lines.[21]

Gingell and his fellow officers of the British Battalion were ordered to hold Kampar for at least ten days.

> In and around Kampar it is hilly country, and when we got there we were able to prepare some fine defensive positions. The Battalion was now about 740 strong as we dug in.[22]

Across the hills and ridges the Leicesters' and Surreys' companies of the British Battalion cleared the ground in front of their positions manually, dug in and laid telephone cabling for their communications. The frequent sight overhead of reconnaissance flights by Japanese aircraft photographing their defensive positions let everyone know that the enemy would be upon them again very soon.

Although the hills and ridges to the east and west of Kampur's main north-south road and railway line were steep and thick with jungle, the troops' patrols discovered many paths used by local villagers. While the Kampur area provided good defensive positions for a division at full strength, the fragmented and battle-worn units of 6/15 Brigade would be a threadbare force to halt a Japanese onslaught in greater numbers. The only support weapons remaining from battle losses and hasty withdrawals were Vickers machine-guns and Lewis guns.

Christmas day came and went, as intermittent mortar fire by the Japanese inflicted some casualties and kept men's nerves on edge. Yet Captain Gingell maintained his reputation as an excellent quartermaster by providing a Christmas dinner for all ranks in the British Battalion, somehow conjuring up roast turkey from local poultry farmers and free beer. Morale was further boosted by the miraculous arrival of ninety-four additional men, both officers and other ranks. Some were released from medical care and some had found their way back through enemy lines. But when would a Japanese attack come again?

It came at 07.00 hours on 1 January, New Year's Day 1942, initially in a barrage of heavy shelling onto Thompson's ridge. As the shelling finally ceased, Japanese troops stormed out of the jungle to the east of both Thompson's and Green Ridges. Despite suffering considerable losses from the Battalion's fire, the Japanese still came on and on. Gingell thought that their casualties must have been considerable.

The enemy infantry was attempting to cross narrow strips of cleared land where, in certain places, there was no more than thirty yards between the edge of the jungle and the British Battalion positions. By 09.00 the Japanese succeeded in gaining hold of a part of Green Ridge. At once two platoons of D Company from the Leicesters, led by Captain Vickers, counter-attacked, drove the enemy troops back and regained possession of the whole of Green Ridge.

As the day wore on against repeated forays by screaming Japanese troops trying to surge across the bare stretches of no man's land, the Battalion's platoons stood fast repelling attack after attack. By nightfall the Japanese infantry, drawn from the deployment of two divisions, had only gained a foothold on the northern edge of Thompson's Ridge. For the first time since their landings on 7 December the Japanese had deployed fully two divisions and would have been surprised that their attacks had been turned back. While it may have seemed to some men in the British Battalion to be a small victory, and an assault of little gain for the enemy, it was only a beginning.

At dawn on 2 January, following more heavy enemy shelling during the night onto Thompson's Ridge, the Japanese attacked again, forcing one of the Leicesters' platoons to abandon their positions. Once again, it was Captain Vickers with Sergeant Craggs who led a platoon and a section of D Company in a counter-attack. One of his men, Private Graves, who had reconnoitred a track through enemy-occupied ground, led them to where they could launch the attack. In a charge with fixed bayonets Vickers shot a Japanese officer and, in close contact fighting, seized the enemy unit's standard in regaining the whole of Thompson's Ridge.

Despite losing half his men in the fighting, Vickers and his remaining troops held the regained positions for the rest of the day. However, they were under continuous fire and resisted several enemy attacks attempting to drive them out. Captain Vickers was awarded the MC, Sergeant Craggs the DCM and Private Graves the MM. In the Surreys Corporal Clemens thought the battle at Kanpur was the most successful so far, but not without many casualties.

Meanwhile the Japanese had gained ground elsewhere. By nightfall word came that the Japanese were bringing in fresh troops, and that the whole Kampur position could not be held any longer. During the night of 2/3 January the British Battalion pulled back from all their positions around Kampur, to avoid being cut off by Japanese attempts to surround them.[23]

Nevertheless, Gingell was a little surprised by the order to resume the retreat.

> When we were ordered to withdraw from Kampur, it seemed an awful pity as our positions were sound, and we were not short of supplies. The reason for our withdrawal from Kampar was owing to both our east and west flanks coming under attack by superior forces. The Japanese had made more landings on the coast in large numbers, and it became imperative for the Battalion to fall back again. We fought a delaying action at Temah, following which we continued south once more.[24]

Only determined rearguard actions, including hand-to-hand fighting in places, allowed a successful withdrawal. As the Battalion bore the brunt of the Japanese attacks, Lieutenant Colonel Morrison was constantly found in the front lines, co-ordinating orders and tactics, and inspiring his men. Nevertheless, the amalgamated companies of the Leicesters and Surreys lost more than 100 men.

The general retreat to the south of the British Battalion and the rest of the three brigades became a confusing and long snaking column of intermingled troops, guns and vehicles of all kinds. As well as the inevitable 'traffic jam' of stoppages, continual harassing attacks by Japanese patrols were fought off. These increased in strength and number in attempts by the Japanese at outflanking manoeuvres.[25]

There was little time for any rest. At night the men snatched some sleep where they were, on a groundsheet if they were lucky enough to have one, without taking off their boots, rifles at their side and using their packs as pillows. Sheer exhaustion brought some sleep, uncaring of mosquitoes, other insects or snakes.[26]

On 10 January at 23.00 hours the Battalion reached Kuala Lumpur, but there was no intention to make any kind of stand in Malaya's mainland capital. After four days, orders were received to keep going further south to Labu and the Battalion was again given the task of blowing up a number of river bridges after all the division's retreating column had crossed. In the approach to some bridges, two vehicles and troops were lost to mines laid by Japanese patrols. But by 04.00 on 11 January the Battalion had destroyed the bridges and later reached Labu. From there they continued southwards towards Kluang. Gingell thought the retreat had become more controlled and organised.

> To maintain an orderly retreat, we employed rear-guard parties to keep in touch with Japanese forward units, and make them fight for every inch of ground. The overall objective was to gain time and delay the enemy at every opportunity. This went on day after day until 14 January when we reached the Kluang area, which was some forty-five miles north of Johore Bahru. We made camp in the Coronation Rubber Estate, and used the rubber tappers' huts for a planned stay of ten days, and were told that we were to act as the Division's reserve force.[27]

Intelligence reports came through that the Japanese had made new landings on the west coast. Every day brought changes of plan. On 17 January the Battalion withdrew south once more to Ayer Hitan. The retreat to the south continued in a series of stops and starts, rearguard actions, and attempted counter-attacks, which had little effect. Japanese forces were advancing south down the main road in increasing strength and on both flanks. On 25 January the inevitable decision was made. The division was to evacuate completely the Malayan mainland and all troops were to fall back to Singapore. The deadline for embarkation on boats at the port of Benut was set as 18.30pm on 27 January.[28]

Retreat to Singapore

It was not so simple to carry out such orders. Mid-morning of 26 January the Battalion and their brigade column were confronted by a series of roadblocks set up and manned by Japanese troops in concealed positions at Senggarang. Despite attempts, both direct and around the flanks, to break through the blockade the enemy could not be dislodged. With no time to spend trying to overcome the roadblock's defenders it was decided to detour around the roadblocks into the jungle to try to reach Benut by the deadline. Because the off-road detour would be on swampy ground, all vehicles and heavy guns had to be destroyed. At 16.30 the brigade's column set off on foot to trek cross-country to reach Benut. It was a desperate measure but it had become a race against time.

In the dark progress was slow and time was slipping away. On the morning of 27 January another gamble was taken. To alleviate an increasing logjam and confusion in the column's progress which had built up during the night, the British Battalion was given permission to try another route farther west. With recognition that the aim of reaching Benut by 18.30 that same day was now unattainable, they followed a river down to the coast. There they were gradually joined by remnants of the other two battalions of the brigade. The total number of men was down to around 1,500.

Some local villagers advised that at Ponggar, only five miles farther south on the coast, there would be a better place to embark onto a ship. A party of the Surreys sailed off in a Chinese fishing boat to contact the Royal Navy at Pontian Kechil some thirty miles away to inform them of the change of plan. Once a scouting party reported back that Ponggar was clear of the Japanese, the Battalion moved off. They had to believe that the Royal Navy would meet them at Ponggar.

Once they reached Ponggar it was a waiting game. Had the party on the fishing boat reached Pontian Kechil? Would the Navy be able to get some boats to Ponggar? Despite the Battalion being in an unknown coastal mangrove swamp, during the night the Royal Navy's gunboats HMSs *Dragonfly* and *Scorpion* somehow found them. Not without some considerable difficulty using small tenders, most of the Battalion embarked, while a small number of men were ferried away in local fishing boats. Corporal Clemens boarded a small tug, one of the last to leave.[29] Once they disembarked on Singapore Island the Battalion was transported by trucks to a military staging camp. 'We were dirty, bedraggled, unshaven, and generally demoralised,' in Clemens' view.

By nightfall on 30 January all Allied troops, nominally some 30,000, had retreated either by boat or across the causeway onto Singapore Island. Now the question on everyone's mind was, 'Would Singapore be a strong enough fortress?'

* * *

Author's Note:

The mystery letter was found among documents left by my late father-in-law, Harry Skilton, who served in 1st East Surrey Regiment, not the 2nd Battalion, nor was he in Malaya and Singapore. So, it remains a mystery as to how the letter came into his possession.

Notes

1. Gingell, Captain W., private letter, 8 April 1942; Veteran's Account, Harry Skilton
2. Evans, *Air Battle for Burma*, pp.11-14
3. Daniell, *The History of ESR*, Volume IV, pp.119-39
4. Veteran's Account, David Clemmens; *Clem*, pp.21-3
5. Gingell, Captain W., *The Malaya Campaign 1941-42* (The British Battalion, Reunion Meeting), Ref SHC ESR/3/8/3
6. Ibid.
7. Ibid.
8. Elphick, *The Pregnable Fortress*, p.97
9. Ibid., pp.219-21
10. Gingell, op.cit. (The British Battalion, Reunion Meeting), Ref SHC ESR/3/8/3
11. Ibid.
12. Elphick, op.cit., pp.219-21
13. Ibid., pp.215-17
14. Daniell, op. cit., pp 119-39
15. Gingell, op. cit. (The British Battalion, Reunion Meeting), Ref SHC ESR/3/8/3
16. Ibid.
17. Ibid.
18. Daniell, op. cit., pp.119-39
19. Gingell, op. cit., (The British Battalion, Reunion Meeting), Ref SHC ESR/3/8/3
20. Daniell, op. cit, pp.119-39
21. Gingell, op. cit., (The British Battalion, Reunion Meeting), Ref SHC ESR/3/8/3
22. Daniell, op. cit., pp.119-39
23. Gingell, op. cit., The British Battalion, Reunion Meeting), Ref SHC ESR/3/8/3
24. Daniell, op. cit., pp.119-39
25. Veteran's Account, David Clemmens; *Clem*, p.37
26. Gingell, op. cit., (The British Battalion, Reunion Meeting), Ref SHC ESR/3/8/3
27. Daniell, op. cit., pp.119-39
28. Veteran's Account, David Clemmens, op. cit., p.37
29. Ibid., p.38; Daniell, op. cit., pp.119-39

Chapter 10

No Refuge in the Fall of Singapore

In the first week of February, having crossed the Johore Strait from Malaya to Singapore and regrouping, the diminished remnants of the British Battalion had a brief respite from action. It was cut short when they were ordered to move urgently into the Bukit Timah area, about six to seven miles from Singapore city, and close to the Strait Causeway. The Japanese began crossing onto Singapore Island on 8 February, but Captain Gingell's spirits were re-energised by the arrival of reinforcements of about 100 men.

> Around 10 February, these reinforcements proved very useful, as we were drawn into a fight to repel a fierce attack by Japanese in the Bukit Timah village. The engagement was so close at times that we made a bayonet charge killing several enemy troops.[1]

Meanwhile, Corporal David Clemens was in a contingent of the British Battalion's Surreys troops which had taken up positions near the Royal Navy base. In the second week of February, to relieve another unit, they moved to different buildings and came upon a stash of tinned food. It seemed too good to be true and it was. Suddenly an uneasy calm came to an end.

> All hell broke loose, and automatic fire appeared to come from all directions. There were several casualties including myself. I was hit by a bullet in my right leg, just below the top of my femur. I only noticed it because of a warm sensation in that area, and put my hand down to my leg, and found I was bleeding.[2]

Clemens was able to walk back to their first aid post where they put on a dressing. After that he was ordered to get onto an ammunition truck that was taking casualties to the Alexandria Hospital.

> I struggled over boxes on the back of the truck, and settled down until we joined a long queue of ambulances waiting with their casualties. I suddenly remembered I had on the last pair of a number of women's knickers, which I had found in an abandoned house used as a billet at Ipoh.

Clemens panicked at the thought of what a nurse would think. Because there had been no opportunity for weeks to wash uniforms, underwear or any clothing, he had resorted to the wearing of the knickers. He decided to take them off as quickly as he could, which was not easy pulling his drill shorts and the knickers over his boots!

> I got them off and slung them hidden behind an ammunition box. I felt much happier, although it aggravated the bleeding of my leg. About an hour passed before I got into the hospital, where the bullet was easily removed, a dressing applied, then my uniform taken off and [I was] given pyjamas to put on. After a couple of hours I felt fine, and asked where I could get my uniform, and return to my unit.

Clemens was told he must leave in his pyjamas and socks, without his shoes, and report to the Ocean Building on Keppel Harbour.

> I spent a very uncomfortable night of 15/16 February in this office block, with three others. Next day about 11.00 hours someone came with a message to say that all weapons must be made unserviceable, ammunition dumped, and even any beer and spirits destroyed. As there was no sign of any Japs we ventured out.

Clemens was keen to try and find some clothes to replace his pyjamas. Abandoned vehicles were everywhere, as were the dead, both troops and civilians killed by the bombardments. In a car left with its doors open, he found some overalls and shoes, which he put on over his pyjamas. 'I continued to look for a vehicle with keys, and found a van. I started it up and drove into the city looking for any sign of British Battalion troops.'

Near Orchard Road he spoke with the driver of a stationary British truck and learned that a convoy of vehicles was leaving the Anzac Club at 5.00 p.m. to take troops to where the British Battalion was regrouping. But he had not forgotten those months in Singapore from September 1940 to February 1941, and those special times going out with Norah.

> As it was only 15.00 hours I decided to try and find what had happened to Norah. I had not heard from her ever since February 1941 when we had been deployed to northern Malaya. In a few minutes I was at the foot of the three flights of steps of the house where she used to live. I walked up those steps, and the main double doors were open. Most of the floor was missing.

Clemens heart sank. A bomb had clearly dropped straight through. He stepped inside tentatively and called out but there was no answer. 'I couldn't see any bodies, so I snatched a photo of one of Norah's sisters. And made my way out.'

As he walked down the house steps he saw a Japanese officer standing on the veranda of the neighbouring house. Clemens was shocked; he put his head down and half ran down the remaining steps to the van. There were no shouts from the enemy officer and, without a backward glance, he got into the van. Of course, in his overalls he must have looked like a civilian, he thought, started the engine, and took off.

> There were still over two hours before I had to join the convoy, and I knew where Norah's dressmaker lived who might know what had happened to her. I drove around, and found the house. I was quickly ushered inside, and told that the Japs were marking houses where there had been fraternising with the British. No one in the family knew what had happened to Norah and her family. They were Jewish and maybe had left before the Japanese invasion.

Clemens was given a meal and a shower and he gave them two boxes of tinned pineapple and herrings which he had found in the van.

> I joined the convoy and eventually found what was left of the British Battalion at Mt Echo, reported to my Company commander, and was told that I had been posted as missing believed killed. I learned that at 21.40 hours on 15 February Singapore had surrendered. Next day I was to use my van in convoys to transport all our stores and wounded to Changi, others would walk, where we would be imprisoned. On my twenty-seventh birthday I would become a PoW, with a very uncertain future.

* * *

Earlier on 13 February the surviving troops of the British Battalion, although having been in continuous resistance against incessant Japanese attacks and being forced to give ground, held positions in an area around Buona Vista and Holland Village. At about 10.00 p.m. Captain Gingell was ordered to report to the brigade commander.

> I was instructed to put together a group of men, with another officer and twenty-four other ranks, and including myself, to report at Singapore's Collier Pier by midnight. The object was to take this group by boat to Java,

> form a composite force with other troops sent there from other units, and strike at the Japanese from there. After selecting another officer and a few men to make up this party, I gave them all an opportunity to withdraw if they wished. No one would do so.[3]

Finding their way in the dark to Collier Pier in Singapore's docks amidst constant shelling was no easy task. Ironically, the light from the explosions, and blown-up vehicles on fire, did help them, and illuminated their way to the docks area.

> On arrival at the docks area the shelling became so heavy and intense, it was impossible to do anything but wait and hope for the best. The only cover we could find was to scramble into an open sewerage drain, to try and survive the barrage.

They were like skulking rats, hoping against hope that they would not be hit. The bombardment went on and on. Would they ever get out of this cesspit? Eventually, the shelling subsided and Gingell climbed out of the drain and searched around the vicinity for guidance on reaching Collier Pier. He found someone who advised that they head in the direction of a burning ship, which was about thirty minutes' walk away. He collected as many of his group as he could find in the chaotic darkness and set off towards the flames in the night sky.

The fires and destruction all around made their goal appear to be a forlorn mission, and Gingell was even unsure how many men were still with him. As they approached the burning ship, Gingell discerned the shapes of other vessels which appeared undamaged and his hopes rose. Two Royal Navy ships were readying to sail, and accepting military personnel who, like his group, were under orders to depart at once.

> We hurried aboard one of the Royal Navy ships in the dark, which I discovered was the *Dragonfly*, a gunboat of about 900 tons, which had previously carried us across the Strait to Singapore. We sailed at about 04.30 to get away while still dark, despite enemy aircraft which were still very active bombing and strafing the docks.

Once it was light and the men had eaten a ship's breakfast, Gingell carried out a roll call. Besides himself, there were just fourteen other ranks but he was aware that some men could have gone aboard other ships. Then, just before 11.00, the siren sounded for an air attack.

> Soon after a bomb hit us amidships, and inflicted devastating casualties, a large number being killed. Those of us who were able abandoned the *Dragonfly*, which sank in just a few minutes. In an instant, everyone had to take to the water. Unfortunately I was wearing only shorts.

When the *Dragonfly* was hit, despite the ship immediately listing and taking on water at an enormous rate, the crew, with their ingrained Royal Navy drill and discipline, managed to launch a small whaler into the sea.

> We swam or clung to anything afloat, and twice Japanese fighters machine-gunned us, inflicting more deaths and casualties. Somehow, we hauled and pushed those who were wounded into this small boat, but alas three or four died, and had to be given over to the sea's depths.
>
> For hours a few of us swam, floated, or clung to the small boat or other floating debris. I got very badly sunburnt, but it was the least of my worries. The day wore on, and the odds were heavily against our survival.

Death by drowning, lack of food and water, heatstroke, shark attack or Japanese fighters seemed to be the inevitable outcome for Gingell and the remaining men. As dusk began turning to night, luck was on their side. Land came into sight and the tide or current washed them ashore onto an island. They staggered up the beach and saw in the distance the shape of a shipwreck.

> We trudged towards it, and found that it was another Royal Navy ship, the *Grasshopper*, that had run aground after being hit. It was deserted but had not caught fire, so we were able to scavenge some food, water and other items from its stores. Its crew and passengers must have got ashore, and gone in search of help.

Luckily there was no rain during the night and they found some shelter under trees, passed the night with some of their scavenged food and water, and dried off.

> In the morning of 15 February we set off to try and make contact with the crew of the *Grasshopper*, and came across some of our men with Brigade Commander Coates. They were sheltering in a wood to avoid observation by Japanese aircraft.
>
> That evening under cover of darkness the Royal Navy moved us by a motor boat to Singkep where there was a good hospital. We stayed there until 23 February, when we went by hospital boat, the *Florence Nightingale*, to Rengat in Sumatra. From there we travelled by road transport across

> Sumatra, and arrived on 1 March at Sawah Weloente, where I saw several wounded men who had been bombed off other ships.
>
> We continued overnight by train from Sawah Weloente arriving early on 2 March at Padang. On the night of 2/3 March we embarked and left Padang on the Dutch ship SS *Weert*.

The SS *Weert* sailed westward across the Indian Ocean for seven days. For Gingell and the other surviving troops onboard, an uneventful voyage came with much relief and, on 9 March, they docked in Colombo, Ceylon. From Colombo, Gingell sailed to Bombay where he embarked on 29 March on another ship for the UK. He wrote the mysterious lost letter mid-voyage on 8 April, stating that he intended to post it as soon as he landed. Gingell did indeed reach the UK and disembarked safely. But did he post that letter, and if so did it reach Tommy? Who was Tommy, and were Gingell's kind thoughts conveyed to Mrs Thompson and Joyce?

Author's Note:

The mystery letter was found among documents left by my late father-in-law, who served in the 1st Battalion East Surrey Regiment, not the 2nd Battalion, nor in Malaya and Singapore. So it remains a mystery as to how the letter came into his possession and whether it did reach Tommy.

* * *

While British and Allied forces fought despairingly as they retreated to Singapore, on Wednesday 11 February 1942, the colony's governor, Sir Shenton Thomas, found that his official residence was within range of the Japanese artillery. After a night of very heavy shelling, Japanese air raids continued and shelling from the enemy's front lines just beyond the city's racecourse resumed. Next day, Governor Thomas, who was with his wife Daisy at 'Istana', Government House, wrote in his diary:

> Many air raids, and a battery of guns in the garden quite close to the House, which was shelled very badly, with appalling noise. One shell landed on the back verandah, under which many of our boys were sheltering. Twelve killed, including my own boy, three Gurkha soldiers and one amah. During a lull I crawled under the house with Dawson and Simson and found several bodies. The Gurkhas kneeling with rifles in their hands, the amah resting against the wall. No sign of wounds, and death must

> have been instantaneous from blast – all covered with yellow dust and almost unrecognisable.[4]

How had it come to this for Britain's pre-eminent colonial fortress in its Far Eastern Empire?

In the two decades after the First World War, Japan's essential problem was that it had a large population compressed into a few islands, with few raw materials of its own to support an industrial economy. After the horrors of the First World War there was international pressure to limit armaments. At a conference in Washington the Great Powers agreed the Washington Naval Treaty of 1922 to limit battleship construction on a ratio basis. With a lower limit than Britain and the USA, Japan felt cheated.

In 1931, on the pretext of an interest in the Manchurian railway, Japan invaded China and occupied Mukden, north of the Korean border. Following the global financial crisis of 1929, the USA introduced trade tariffs, known as 'Smoot-Hawley', and Britain introduced trade restrictions under the 'Imperial Preference', all trade barriers which led to Japan feeling that it had no option but to initiate a pre-emptive war with the USA. In 1937, Japanese troops occupied Nanking and the island of Hainan, a military interference in Chinese affairs totally opposed by the USA.

In 1941, Japan's aims were directed towards the so-called 'Greater East Asia Co-prosperity Sphere'. This 'New Order' envisaged the seizure of British, French and Dutch colonies. Countries such as Burma and Malaya would become 'independent' states under Japanese control. Australia, New Zealand and Ceylon would be absorbed into this Japanese Empire. Some proponents of the grand scheme even hoped to grab parts of North America, such as Alaska, western Canada and Washington State, USA.

When war broke out in Europe in September 1939, conflict in the Far East seemed unlikely to the British. However, Japan continued her war with China and towards realising the 'Co-prosperity Sphere'. By October 1941, the possibility of war with Japan was increasingly recognised in Britain and the USA. From occupied bases in southern Indo-China, Japan eyed the Malayan peninsula and Singapore.

Many Chinese in Singapore considered China their motherland and, when the Japanese invaded China, organised relief-fund activities to aid China's war effort. This anti-Japanese movement was closely monitored by Japanese agents. The Japanese began to plan their attack on Malaya long before December 1941. When Japanese aircraft bombed Singapore on 8 December 1941, the same day Japanese troops landed in southern Siam, and invaded Malaya, these actions had all been planned to be near simultaneous with the attack on Pearl Harbor.

Lieutenant General Tomoyuki Yamashita, C-in-C of the Japanese Twenty-fifth Army, used strategies developed specifically for the campaign's jungle warfare. Tanks were used in frontal assaults, while light infantry bypassed British defences using bicycles or boats. Malaya was largely covered by jungle, and only one railway and one road ran north-south. Japan's objective was to take the Malayan peninsula and Singapore before British reinforcements arrived. The British Army was ill-prepared for such an assault. In just seven weeks, the Japanese had captured Malaya and pushed the forces of Britain and its Allies back into the island of Singapore.

On 10 February Japanese troops reached the southern end of the Johore Causeway which linked Malaya with Singapore. The battle for Singapore Island began. Although British troops outnumbered the Japanese, the Japanese controlled the air. Air Vice Marshal Fulford of the RAF had only 158 aircraft to defend the whole of Malaya. Airfields scattered across Singapore and Malaya were really undefendable. At Singapore there was only one squadron of Brewster Buffaloes, which were obsolete, and inferior to Japanese fighters.

The Japanese used their advantage in the air to launch relentless bombing attacks on military and civilian targets. This prevented the British from setting up any effective defences and caused chaos in the city of Singapore, which had seen its population balloon as refugees poured in from the Malayan peninsula. As the defence perimeter shrank in and around the city, with civilian casualties mounting, water and vital supplies being cut off, Lieutenant General Percival informed London that the situation had become hopeless.[5]

By 12 February, the defensive perimeter of Singapore city had shrunk so much that the Japanese controlled about three quarters of the island. The battles for the vital reservoirs near Bukit Timah hill, only a few miles outside the city, were lost. The Japanese could cut off the water supplies any time they wished. The troops fought on, constantly bombed and shelled. Some lucky civilians, mainly Europeans, managed to escape on the last boats to leave. Abandoned cars were pushed into the docks so that they did not fall into the hands of the Japanese.

Singapore's capitulation was just days away. Journalist Noel Barber described the scene in Orchard Road. 'Half the buildings seemed to have been hit. Burnt out cars littered every corner. Here and there bodies lay waiting to be collected.'[6]

Governor Thomas' diary describes his last despairing days in Government House.

> Friday 13 February 1942:
> The rest of Government House staff have left, except Ah Ling, Daisy's Chinese boy. I urged him to go, but he burst into tears and said, 'I can't leave Lady'. What faithfulness. I found my boy's widow in the kitchen,

and sat down on the floor by her side and tried to comfort her. Gave her all the money I had.

Then we were deliberately bombed. One bomb fell in the parking place at the back, while I was in the pantry getting a drink for a despatch rider. He got under the table and I behind the refrigerator – bits flying about everywhere. On advice of all in the House we left in the evening for Singapore Club (at the Fullerton Building), where McKinnon has got two rooms for us. The garden is in a dreadful state, 15 great craters on the tennis courts.

Saturday 14 February 1942, Fullerton Building:
A much quieter night in the cool and comfortable rooms of the Singapore Club. More air raids and very noisy most of the day with heavy shelling all the afternoon, and a counter-barrage by our artillery close by. Percival came in and said position was no worse. Therefore we would carry on.

Sunday 15 February 1942, Fullerton Building:
Very heavy shelling by both sides. Fraser (Colonial Secretary) and Brigadier Newbigging went to contact Japanese for an armistice. Percival sent for.

Air raids are close to the Club. Water, food, ammunition are all finished.

The sky was filled with smoke from the shelling and air raids. On the river side of the Fullerton Building, solitary figures could be seen scurrying along the foreshore, half-bent over as if to escape the next explosion. It was clear the end was near.[7]

As the victorious Japanese advanced into Singapore's suburbs, it was obvious to Governor Thomas and Lieutenant General Percival that Singapore could hold out no longer. On the morning of 15 February, a British delegation bearing a white flag met the Japanese at Bukit Timah and arranged a ceasefire.[8]

Following the agreement of a ceasefire with the Japanese, on 15 February Percival and his aides met immediately with General Yamashita in the offices of the Ford Motor Company at Bukit Timah. Percival had received permission from London to seek surrender terms. General Yamashita was the last to enter the room, where the two delegations were seated either side of a long oblong table. He sat down directly opposite Percival. Yamashita was a stocky muscular man, his head and face reminiscent of a British bulldog. He leaned forward, his forearms on the table, and his piercing eyes stared into those of Percival.

The British general was a thin angular figure, his thin face drawn, with a hesitant look. Percival's translator spoke to Yamashita setting out the terms proposed in the British offer to surrender. Immediately these were conveyed to General Yamashita, he banged the table and poured forth a torrent of Japanese, clearly an outright rejection, and not once did he take his gaze off his beaten adversary.

Percival was stunned – and looked it. With perhaps the barest of a tremor on his lips, he half-turned to look at his aide, who was translating Yamashita's response. He had demanded a total unconditional surrender of Singapore and all Allied forces. Percival had no fallback option, and acquiesced to an immediate surrender.

The Japanese took control, imprisoning all Allied troops and personnel. They quickly renamed Singapore as 'Synon Lo' (Light of the South) and introduced a 'spring clean', which, to the Chinese in Singapore, became known as 'Sook Ching'. Any civilian, particularly in the Chinese population, who had been associated with or supporting the British colonial administration was arrested, imprisoned and, in many cases, executed. Estimates of those killed under the programme range between 50,000 and 100,000.

Sir Shenton Thomas, Lady Thomas, the Allied forces and many civilians were interned as prisoners of war for the next three and a half years. After nine months at Changi Prison, Governor Thomas was sent to Takao, a bleak cold prison island north of Japan. Lady Thomas was moved to the prison camp at Sime Road in Singapore.

Churchill described Japan as possessing a greater military machine than Hitler's Germany and that the loss of Singapore was 'The greatest disaster to British arms which our history records'.[9]

* * *

Author's Note:

Gunner Stan Durston, of the Royal Artillery, and his civilian wife Pat were two of those to be imprisoned at Changi's PoW camps. A summary of their personal experience follows, taken from a family memoir 'In Two Death Camps', recorded by their daughters Debra Brittingham and Carol Payne.

* * *

One of the men manning the Royal Artillery's massive 15-inch guns emplaced at Changi, known as the Johore Battery, which was aimed to deter any enemy from crossing the Johore Strait, was Gunner Stan 'Taffy' Durston of 7 Coast Battery, 9th Coast Regiment. Stan Durston was born on 3 September 1919 in Cumaman, South Wales and, like many at that time, left school at 14 and went to work in the coal mines. His wage was needed to support his mother and family after his father had died seven years earlier. He also volunteered in the St John Ambulance Brigade, played a number of sports and began to learn carpentry, before, at age 20, joining the Royal Artillery,

In 1939 he had been posted to 7 Coast Battery in Singapore where he met Ruth Bracken who was known as 'Pat'. Stan was of slim build, around 5-foot 10 with auburn hair, an extrovert, always smiling, who loved socialising with everyone. Like many Welsh, he loved singing and had a tenor voice. Pat Bracken was born in Malaya in 1925 of Dutch and Portuguese ancestry and moved to Singapore with her parents. After school, she worked as telephonist. Pat was only 4-foot 11 with dark hair, and olive skinned, an attractive but reserved teenager who loved her family.

She was a good match, a counterpoint to the outgoing Stan, a young man so far from home and family. Pat was still six months away from her 17th birthday when she and Stan married on 20 December 1941 at the Singapore Registry Office. It was as if they were openly defying the war and the Japanese bombing raids on Singapore. But they could not know how soon their wedding vows, their dreams and their lives would be so quickly and severely tested.

Stan and Pat Durston were able to begin their married life in married quarters on the large Changi military base, which had only been built six years before on the eastern tip of Singapore. It was very close to the Johore Battery, where Stan was one of those manning the 15-inch guns. Like everyone they were anxious about what was to come. The Japanese army was advancing through Malaya towards the Johore Strait, where a short causeway of only one kilometre crossed to Singapore.

During January 1942, Japanese air raids on Singapore were becoming increasingly frequent, ensuring no sleep for anyone. The wail of the sirens would be followed by the drone of the enemy bombers. Sometimes when Stan and Pat were unable to reach the air raid shelters in time they would huddle under their bed or kitchen table. It gave protection against falling debris or shrapnel, but not a direct hit.

The sound of anti-aircraft fire and the smell of acrid smoke would also assault the senses, so to grab a few hours of undisturbed sleep seemed to be a luxury. The days too were being broken apart by Japanese aerial attack. One morning, as Pat was pegging her washing on a line, an enemy fighter flew over very fast and low, strafing anyone who was in its line of fire – and she was. She threw herself to the ground thinking it was the end for her. When Stan heard the plane's cannon fire, he grabbed his rifle and ran out of the house, and fired despairingly at the fighter, its silhouette rapidly diminishing in the sky.

It left him feeling in a rage, and very afraid for Pat. Dropping his rifle, he rushed over to where Pat lay on the ground. He could not see any wounds and, as he turned her over, all he could say was, 'Pat! Pat!' She was alive, and in his arms. Pat sobbed with the shock mixed with relief that the fighter's fire had missed her. She had been very lucky.

With the war intensifying as the Japanese advanced towards the Johore Strait, all troops were ordered to return immediately to their units. The coast gun battery was being manned day and night, so Stan had little time to be with Pat. So, reluctantly, after only six weeks of marriage, in early February they decided that Pat should move back to her parents' house at Katong which should be safer. However, she refused to be evacuated out of Singapore. How could she leave when all that she had ever known was in Singapore, her parents, her brothers and, above all, her husband?

Her brother Ken was only 14 but changed his age to 16 and joined the Singapore Volunteer Force (SVF). Pat's cousin Sonny was 16 and in the Volunteer Field Ambulance, on duty all hours attending the wounded and dying. The war was finally being waged on Singapore Island, causing random death and destruction everywhere. The men in Pat's life were fighting for Singapore's, their families, and their own existence.

When Allied forces began to withdraw in the face of the Japanese attacks, Stan and the other men in the Johore Battery at Changi were ordered to put the 15-inch guns out of action by blowing up the muzzles with explosives and ensuring that other equipment was left inoperable. They then abandoned their positions at Changi to retreat to Singapore city. One of Stan's fellow gunners, George Keeling, was in the confusing withdrawal which left the troops to make their own way to find army staging posts in the city. Keeling was from Cheadle in Cheshire, 24-years-old, and had a similar upbringing as Stan Durston. After leaving high school, Keeling had worked in the coal mines before joining the Royal Artillery in 1937. He was 6-foot 4 of slim build, with black hair and an outgoing personality with those he knew.

Under fire with the constant pounding of shells exploding, Stan Durston ran, weaved and ducked to avoid the large shell craters in their path. In one shell hole lay the first Japanese soldier Stan had seen, an enemy corpse with his leg blown off. On reaching the outskirts of the city, Stan and his fellow troops found there were thousands of people milling in the streets. They had fled from surrounding areas looking for safety and protection. However, for many who tried to escape by the only way out of Singapore, by sea, and were able to board a ship, they never made it to safety.

Three cousins and an uncle of Stan's wife Pat were all drowned when their ship was sunk by enemy fire in Singapore harbour. Ships were sunk by Japanese naval and air attack during their evacuation voyages and even if passengers survived the sinking they often died at sea or on a deserted island. Those whom the Japanese rescued from sinking ships were taken into prison camps as slave labour to work until their death.

On Sunday 15 February, Allied forces surrendered. The invading Japanese had seized Singapore. The garrison city of young men lay down their arms, so sparing the civilian population from further hostilities, destruction and death. It came as a shock to everyone, civilians and military, and seemingly unthinkable even as the message of total defeat circulated.

There were around a million people concentrated within a few square miles. Food and water were in short supply. The tyranny of the Japanese occupiers was soon to be felt. Stories of atrocities, rape, murder and formal executions of troops and innocent civilians alike were increasingly heard, spreading fear everywhere.

In the chaotic withdrawal from Changi, Stan Durston had become very thirsty and hungry like everyone, and despondency threatened to overwhelm him. He sat down to rest at one point and wrote on a postcard to Pat of his feelings in this total surrender of Singapore to the enemy. Eventually, he found his way to a military staging post where an officer in charge, on hearing that Stan had a wife in Singapore, told him to take a bicycle and go quickly to see Pat. Japanese troops had begun a search of all homes and premises, frequently raping women and shooting innocent civilians. With those words ringing in his ears, his mind in turmoil, Stan grabbed the nearest bicycle and pedalled harder than he ever had before.[10]

* * *

Notes

1. Gingell, Captain W., *The Malaya Campaign 1941–42* (The British Battalion, Reunion Meeting), Ref SHC ESR/3/8/3,and Daniell, *The History of ESR Volume IV*, pp.119-39
2. Veteran's Account, David Clemens, *Clem*, pp.38-9, and private collection
3. Gingell, op.cit.
4. Shenton, *Diary 1942*, and Evans, *Air Battle for Burma*, pp.39-42
5. National Museum, Singapore, and Evans, op.cit.
6. Fort Siloso, Museum, Singapore, and Evans, op.cit.
7. Shenton, op.cit.
8. Fort Siloso, op.cit.
9. National Museum, op.cit.
10. Veteran's Account, Durston, *In Two Death Camps* (Brittingham and Payne)

Chapter 11

Escape from Corregidor – In the Air, Over and Under Water

Diane Capewell never knew her father. In her childhood her mother spoke of a relationship she had with her father, John Chamberlin, during the Second World War. He was a sailor in the US Navy stationed in Australia. She thinks that they may have met in late 1942 at a military ball in Melbourne.

Because of the demands of wartime service, their relationship was brief, and her mother believed that he must have been killed in the war. As Diane grew up, and for all her life, she assumed that her father had died without seeing her, or even knowing of her birth.

Then, a few years ago, Diane's daughter told one of her friends that her grandfather had been in the US Navy and had died during the war. This friend of her daughter, who had an interest in the history of the Second World War, undertook some research looking for any record of John Chamberlin's service in the US Navy. What she found was astounding.

John Chamberlin was born in New York, and at the age of 8 his mother, the only parent he knew, died. He, too, never knew his father. He joined the US Navy when he was 16, but he did not die in the war. Even more startling and bittersweet for Diane and her daughter, they learned that John Chamberlin played an invaluable part in the victory over Japan.

What follows are the stories of John Chamberlin's remarkable escape, and those of other US service personnel from Corregidor in the Philippines fleeing the Japanese invasion.[1]

* * *

During the 1930s Japan pursued an aggressive expansionist policy, invading and occupying parts of China, and exerting intimidatory pressure on Shanghai and Hong Kong. Relations between Japan and the USA deteriorated to an all-time low. It came to a head when the Japanese bombed Pearl Harbor on 7 December1941, invaded Hong Kong, bombed Shanghai, Singapore and the US Clark Field Air Force base in the Philippines. On 10 December 1941 the

Japanese Fourteenth Army, commanded by Lieutenant General Homma, invaded the Philippines. The 48th Yuitsu Tsuchihashi Division landed in Lingayen Gulf on the northern island of Luzon at three places, Vigan, Aparri and Gonzaga.[2]

The defence bases of the Philippines were situated around the capital of Manila on the island of Luzon. To the west of Manila Bay, on the Bataan Peninsula, there were 15,000 American troops and 65,000 Philippine military personnel under the command of US General MacArthur. However, the effectiveness of the Bataan stronghold was compromised by only 10,000 of the Philippines forces being fully-trained. Furthermore, while supplies of ammunition were plentiful, the influx of refugees into the Bataan Peninsula fleeing from the Japanese was exacerbating shortages of food, water and other basic supplies.[3] The Japanese landings were accompanied by overwhelming air raids, not only on Clark Field air base, but elsewhere, and especially on the US Navy docks at Cavite, destroying any credible capability for either air or naval defence of Luzon.[4]

In a Japanese air raid on the Cavite docks the submarine USS *Sealion* in the US Navy Yard was destroyed. Miraculously, the USS *Seadragon*, which was moored next to *Sealion*, was pulled clear, so escaping the fires and explosions on its sister submarine. US Admiral Hart, after learning early on 10 December of the loss of the Royal Navy's ships *Prince of Wales* and *Repulse*, ordered all surviving ships of the US Asiatic Fleet to abandon Manila. By nightfall of 10 December it was clear to many in the US Government that there could be no realistic defence of Manila, Luzon and the whole of the Philippines. More Japanese forces landed on the 12th at Lingayen Gulf. Over the remainder of December, in the face of the continuous and determined Japanese offensive, US forces fell back south towards the Bataan peninsula.[5]

The two divisions of the Philippines Army based in northern Luzon were no match for the highly-trained Japanese troops. On 24 December, General MacArthur accepted that the whole of Luzon could not be defended and ordered the evacuation of American military personnel and all Philippines Army forces from Manila to the Bataan peninsula.

MacArthur, who had retired from the US Army in 1937 to become the Defence Advisor to the Philippines government, was recalled by Washington in 1941, and given command of the US and Philippines Armies in the Far East. MacArthur now took his wife and son by boat across Manila Bay and moved into military quarters in the Malinta Tunnel on the island of Corregidor in Manila Bay. Corregidor, with its fortress complex, was considered to be part of the city of Cavite. The evacuation of all staff and troops from US HQ offices and other bases in Manila was largely completed by 31 December.[6]

Fortunately, the Japanese General Homma did not learn until the 30th that MacArthur had ordered a withdrawal to Bataan, too late for the Japanese to change their tactics. Even then, until 4 January units of the Philippine Army were able to keep open the road from San Fernando, some forty miles northwest of Manila, through the neck of the Bataan peninsula, so that forces in South Luzon were able to retreat into the Bataan area.

By early January 1942, the Japanese Fourteenth Army was readying to strike against US Army bases and positions on the Bataan peninsula. On 10 January, Homma sent a message to MacArthur:

> Sir, You are well aware that you are doomed. The end is near. The question is how long you will be able to resist. You have already cut rations by half ... you are advised to surrender.

Whether Homma expected MacArthur to comply is extremely doubtful. On the night of 11/12 January, the Japanese attacked by infiltrating through thinly-manned American lines in the foothills of Mount Natib, which MacArthur had been advised would be unsuitable terrain for any enemy breakthrough. The incursions forced US forces to withdraw to a second defensive line across the Bataan peninsula.[7]

* * *

It was not only regular US and Philippine forces that were at risk of being overwhelmed and captured by the Japanese. From 1929 until 1942 the US Navy had been conducting radio-intelligence activities from various sites in the Philippines, intercepting and deciphering Japanese military signals. Because the men who were conducting those operations in the Philippines when war broke out represented a significant portion of all naval personnel trained in this important intelligence function, they were designated for priority evacuation from Bataan.

In the intelligence units based in Corregidor, US Navy Chief Yeoman John Edward 'Vince' Chamberlin was one of the key members of the Fleet Radio Unit (FRU). It became critical, of the highest strategic importance, that Chamberlin and his FRU colleagues escape from the Philippines, so as to re-establish their signals' intelligence unit elsewhere. Their work to break the Japanese diplomatic cypher (*Purple*), would enable the reading of Japanese military planning, and associated force deployments. Such intelligence would be crucial for the US and its Allies to resist, and eventually turn back the Japanese onslaught.

Soon after the withdrawal of all American and Philippine forces to Bataan, the US Navy Chief of Naval Operations (CNO) directed that FRU be evacuated from Corregidor. While the FRU staff waited for orders to act on this evacuation direction, Chamberlin was involved in a programme of destruction of documents and equipment. The likelihood of the evacuation escape being by submarine, if possible, meant that space on board would be at a premium, and extremely limited.

> Our Diplomatic 'Red' and 'Purple' machines were disassembled and thrown into deep water and every sheet of classified paper or used carbon paper was burned. Ralph Cook had come to us from the IBM office in Manila. He spent his time disassembling our IBM equipment, crating it in boxes (boxes made from boards ripped from our houses and small enough to pass through the conning tower of a submarine) and piled these near the tunnel entrance.

Because the FRU was providing invaluable intelligence on Japanese plans and operations, Washington wished to keep the unit operational as long as possible and planned for its evacuation in three groups and staggered stages. Chamberlin was aware that some selective evacuations of individuals took place secretly under cover of darkness, without any announcement.

> During this period some of our people would disappear each time a submarine put into Corregidor. I do not know how the 'departees' were selected; I do know all departures occurred at night. Our first knowledge would be when, in the subsequent morning, someone would be missing. It would become our task to clean out desks, put abandoned clothing in an improvised 'Lucky Bag' maintained in the code room, and turn over all cigarettes to Pappy Lowery who was in charge of rationing of food and various other items. For quite some time we had been restricted to only two sparse meals a day, which were mainly plain spaghetti and soggy rice.

On this meagre daily diet Chamberlin had lost forty pounds in weight.

Then, during the night of 4 February, the USS *Seadragon* made it into Manila Bay undetected and docked at Corregidor. The first party of twenty-one FRU officers and men embarked, and before first light on the 5th *Seadragon* slipped away and set forth for Java. On 11 February *Seadragon* reached Surabaya in Java and disembarked the evacuees. A second FRU party of thirty-six officers and men were evacuated on 16 March, once again during the night aboard the submarine USS *Permit.*

The FRU work on interception and deciphering of enemy communications continued, but by late March 1942 the FRU strength had diminished to a final group of three officers and eighteen enlisted men. Chamberlin was uncertain whether the most valuable members were being evacuated first, or whether he and his remaining colleagues were being left until last to keep the critical FRU work going.

> Our workload had increased and we were working a minimum of 16-18 hours per day. Captain John Lietwiler detailed me to undertake the process of enciphering dummy messages on our enciphering machine. Putting our indicator on each, I must have typed well over a month's supply. These were turned over to Commander Callahan (OIC, NPO), who was to send out a certain number each day so as to confuse the Japanese once we had departed.
>
> The only enemy message traffic being translated was that for which we had a cipher key. One day, as a result of Rufe Taylor's translating, it was possible for Lietwiler to send a message to the Army advising that a Japanese convoy was at anchor in Subic Bay.
>
> At the time the only combat planes available were some P-40 fighters, based at Cabcaben, so General Wainwright, our overall commander on Bataan, requested a few more from the US air base at the Del Monte plantation on the island of Mindanao. When they arrived their belly tanks were removed and 500-pound bombs put in their place. They took off and made a surprise attack on the convoy. One pilot it was reported dropped a 500-pounder down the stack of, what he claimed was, a 15,000-ton ship. On his return he was so excited he forgot to lower his wheels and on landing scrubbed his P-40 aircraft.

At another time Chamberlin and his remaining colleagues intercepted a long series of messages for which much of the deciphering key had not been recovered. What was readable, however, seemed to indicate that a large invasion convoy was being readied by the Japanese.

> It appeared to be of such importance that Lietwiler sent off a 'priority' message to Washington requesting assistance to fully interpret the message. The response was negative, so Lietwiler himself became a 'cryptanalyst' for about thirty-six consecutive hours and as a result, we could translate the entire series of messages, which turned out to be a possible Japanese Invasion Plan for India. We immediately transmitted this to the British General Wavell. It was said that Wavell borrowed planes and pilots from the Middle East to augment his own forces and hit a Japanese supply

> convoy off the Nicobar Islands, with such force that the elements which remained limped back to Singapore.[8]

But hovering over Chamberlin and his colleagues in the final FRU group was the nagging worry that they might be left behind as expendable.

* * *

The Bataan peninsula had been cut off by Japanese forces and, in effect, was under siege during February and March although that had become something of a stalemate. To break the impasse, General Homma requested reinforcements from Tokyo. In stark contrast, Washington was unable to send any help to MacArthur who, on 11 February, informed the President that he and his family would remain in the Philippines with his troops, and fight to the end.[9]

The implications of MacArthur and his staff being captured by the Japanese, together with the political pressures from MacArthur's popularity with the American people, finally dawned on the US Administration. On 23 February, President Roosevelt ordered MacArthur to leave Bataan and to travel to Mindanao Island to the south, and from there to Australia to take command of all US forces in the region. MacArthur ignored this order but, on 10 March, he received another direct cable from Roosevelt: 'Proceed immediately to Melbourne (in Australia)' where he was to take command of all US Army troops in the Pacific Theatre.

He had no option but to comply. He decided to make his escape with his wife Jean, his 11-year-old son Arthur, and their Chinese *amah*, a child nanny, Ah Cheu, by means of one of the PT boats of Motor Torpedo Boat Squadron 3, commanded by Lieutenant John Bulkeley. It would be a 600-mile voyage at night, to try to avoid Japanese warships, submarines and aircraft, through uncharted seas, controlled by the Imperial Japanese Navy. Furthermore, because of engine wear and tear the PT boats were limited to a maximum speed of just twenty knots. It was a high risk choice. Although MacArthur was advised that using a submarine would be the safest means of evacuation, he argued that the Japanese would not expect him to be aboard a PT boat.

After handing overall command of the US Army and Philippine forces to General Wainwright at 7.45pm on 11 March, MacArthur left Corregidor with his family and a number of his close and key staff officers. MacArthur and his family embarked on PT-41 from Corregidor.[10] One of his staff was Colonel Charles Willoughby, his intelligence chief, who left in PT-35, one of the three other PT boats which left from Bataan.[11] The four boats joined together in formation at 8.00pm and set off into a severe storm. MacArthur described the hair-raising voyage that night through towering waves, as being like 'a trip in a concrete mixer'.

The four boats became separated during the night but only three, including PT-41 with MacArthur and PT-35 with Willoughby, met at the pre-arranged rendezvous, Tagauayan Island. In the daylight of 12 March, the three boats anchored there, hoping that they would not be spotted by any Japanese aircraft. When night came, the PT boats left their anchorage and headed into the wild open seas and the persisting storms. Lieutenant Robert Kelly, the squadron's Executive Officer, described waves up to twenty feet in height, which 'thundered over the cockpit drenching everybody'.

Among MacArthur's staff contingent was Admiral Francis W. Rockwell, who had never sailed in a PT boat, and clearly found their stability in the stormy seas as comparable with a cork. He was reported as saying, 'I wouldn't do duty on one of these boats for anything in the world – you can have them!'[12]

During that night a Japanese cruiser was sighted dimly. Lieutenant Bulkeley altered course and increased speed to their maximum of twenty knots. Although the Japanese ship appeared to be following them, the four PT boats were able to outrun it. To make up for lost time in the heavy seas, since aircraft were being sent from Melbourne to meet them in Mindanao, they continued during the day on 13 March across the Mindanao Sea. Tensions rose with the high chance in clear bright sunlight of being spotted by Japanese aircraft.

Their luck held and later that day MacArthur's boat, PT-41, first reached Cagayan on the north coast of Mindanao, and PT-35 with a relieved Willoughby a few hours later still in broad daylight.

> It was a clear dazzling day. Fortunately no Japanese planes cut across the blue sky, though the enemy was known to make regular mail flights from its forces on the south coast of Mindanao to Luzon. We were pretty conspicuous as the hours dragged.

On 12 March PT-32 had broken down with three engines out of action near Tagauayan, and was incredibly fortunate to be found on the 13th, and rescued by the USS *Permit*, a submarine, which having taken on board the crew and the evacuee codebreakers, destroyed PT-35. *Permit* was then ordered to take the codebreakers to Australia, where *Permit* and its invaluable passengers arrived on 7 April.[13]

* * *

Meanwhile, four B-17 bombers had taken off from Melbourne on 11 March,carrying supplies to Del Monte airfield on Mindanao, and with orders to return with MacArthur and his staff. After escaping from Java, the four aircraft were in a poor state of airworthiness, the aircrew heavily fatigued and, first, they had to fly to Batchelor Field air base about sixty miles south of Darwin in Australia's far north. They were scheduled to depart from Batchelor soon after noon on the 12th, so as to arrive at Del Monte during the night. One of the B-17s developed engine trouble and did not take off, while another lost an engine after take-off and returned to Batchelor. Captain Godman and Lieutenant Pease, pilots in the remaining two bombers from the 19th Bomb Group, flew on. Godman's aircraft began losing fuel during the flight, but they had passed the point of no return. On approach to Mindanao, an altimeter error caused Godman's aircraft to crash into the sea at 170mph. At Del Monte airfield their non-arrival was recorded as missing, and they were presumed dead.

Lieutenant Pease managed to find Mindanao's Del Monte airfield but, on landing, his B-17 had no brakes and was fortunate to come to a stop when going off the runway. When Pease was informed that MacArthur was not expected for twelve more hours, he was not prepared to expose the aircraft to standing on the runway in daylight, an easy target for Japanese fighters and bombers. He decided to depart with a number of evacuee groundcrew. Pease sent a message for another plane to be sent out to Mindanao. Consequently, MacArthur with his family and group of staff officers duly arrived at Mindanao, only to find no aircraft at Del Monte airfield waiting for them.

Having survived the hazardous, high-risk open sea crossing, one can only imagine MacArthur's reaction on hearing what had occurred with the four B-17s, and of Lieutenant Peases's decision to leave without him. No one could say how long it would be before Japanese troops arrived at Del Monte; precious time was slipping away. There were Japanese troops at Davao on the Mindanao south coast, only thirty miles away. An exasperated MacArthur sent a cable to Washington, demanding the best pilot, aircrew and aeroplane in the Pacific, be sent at once to Del Monte to rescue him, his wife and son, and his whole entourage.

In response, four more B-17s, newly arrived at Batchelor Field from the 14th Reconnaissance Squadron and in a better condition, were ordered to take off immediately for Del Monte. An experienced co-pilot from the 19th Group was included in the aircrew of each aircraft, to assist with the navigation to Mindanao. As if there was a jinx on the rescue attempt, once again two of the bombers suffered engine troubles, and did not take off. The other two planes did make it to Mindanao and landed safely. The two crews were overjoyed to meet Captain Godman, who had been reported missing and presumed dead. On crashing into the sea two gunners were killed, while Godman and the other crew were lucky to swim to land from a mile out in shark-infested waters. After struggling ashore, Godman and his surviving crew members had walked for two days through Mindanao's thick jungle, to reach Del Monte.

For the return flight the two B-17s intended to land at Darwin's airport. To carry all of MacArthur's family and contingent of staff officers, the two B-17s were so overcrowded, that no one was allowed to take any baggage with them. Once again, they took off at night, departing on 18 March at 2.30am, hoping to avoid any Japanese fighters. Mid-flight, a radio message was received that the Japanese had made a massive bombing attack on Darwin

Forced to divert to Batchelor Field, after refuelling the two aircraft then took off with some of the staff officers to fly another 1,000 miles to Alice Springs in central Australia. However, MacArthur's wife Jean could take no more of perilous open-sea voyages in small boats and flights in accident-prone aircraft and refused to fly with her son any further. Rather than the safety and re-establishment elsewhere of MacArthur and his staff officers, her priority was the survival of her son and *amah*. They drove in Australian supplied motor vehicles to Alice Springs, from where MacArthur and his family, with a few selected staff officers, went by a special train arranged by the Australian government to Melbourne.

The remaining officers later flew on two DC-3 planes to Melbourne. When, en route, MacArthur was changing trains in the state of South Australia, he spoke to some press reporters during which, in response to a question about his intentions, he made the promise 'I shall return', which became a famous quote. It was at the time a brave but outrageously optimistic promise, no doubt inspired by having survived a miraculous, improbable escape from the clutches of the Japanese.[14]

* * *

Unfortunately, MacArthur's departure sent a clear message to every American and Filipino soldier remaining on Bataan that, in the immediate future, there could be no US rescue force. Ammunition and food supplies continued to dwindle, but doctors and nursing staff in the field hospital in the Malinta Tunnel at Corregidor refused to be evacuated. Together with men's deteriorating health and physical condition, it brought the inevitable weakening of morale. In contrast, General Homma was able to reinforce his Fourteenth Army with an additional division and brigade.

On 1 April General Wainwright ignored another demand from Homma to surrender. As expected, on the 3rd, in combined frontal attacks and landings on Bataan in the rear of US positions, the Japanese attacked again. By the 6th the US defences were penetrated in a number of places. With the certainty of overwhelming defeat and enormous loss of life looming, General Wainwright opened negotiations with General Homma. The terms of the surrender were agreed on the 10th and 12,000 American and 64,000 Philippine troops would be taken prisoner.

Over the subsequent days and weeks the 76,000 troops, already in very poor physical condition, would be force-marched fifty miles from Bataan to San Fernando. It was estimated that more than 2,300 Americans and up to 10,000 Filipinos died on the Bataan Death March. Many of the survivors were later sent to Japan to work as slave labour.[15]

What would become of the last remaining group of FRU codebreakers? Two days before the secret negotiations and surrender terms were agreed, on the evening of 8/9 April it seemed unusually quiet and peaceful for the FRU men in the Malinta Tunnel. It was unusual because the normally constant roar of artillery had ceased for a while. However, Chamberlin and a few others were beginning to think it was ominous and that they were to be left behind, and left to their fate.

> There was little to do in the Tunnel. We stood around talking. About 19.30 hours the telephone in the code room rang and one of NPO's coding officers called to Lieutenant Lietwiler. Ed Gaghen, who had made Chief so recently he didn't yet have a hat, and I edged close enough to hear Lietwiler's telephone conversation.
>
> Apparently he was being directed to repeat back everything said, so we could hear the entire conversation. When we heard 'only the clothes on the men's bodies, be ready to leave in five minutes, a truck is coming', our spirits lifted, and we started preparing.

The last remaining personnel of the FRU, feeling stranded and forgotten in the Malinta Tunnel, included three officers, Lieutenants J.M. Lietwiler, R. L. Taylor, and R.E. Cook, with eighteen enlisted men who included Chief Yeoman Chamberlin. At that time no one in the group of FRU evacuees, or in the Navy boats and submarine they were about to board, knew that Bataan had fallen and surrender negotiations with the Japanese had commenced.[16]

On hearing that they were finally to be evacuated Chamberlin felt as though he had been injected with a shot of adrenalin.

> I changed to a clean suit of khaki, stuck a second suit under my shirt, filled my pockets with tooth brushes and tooth paste and put on the best two

> caps. Saying to Gaghen, 'I can only wear one', I tossed him the other. We were ready to leave the Tunnel.

The other FRU men had also thrown themselves into a similar flurry of preparations in the few minutes given them.

> A telephone call was made to Sid Burnett who was manning the D/F site. As Sid recounted later, when he hurriedly left the D/F he was wearing a WWI tin hat, carrying an Enfield rifle and wearing an ammunition belt with bayonet and scabbard attached. As he ran to the Tunnel he threw it all away. He arrived in time, but out of breath. Commander Callahan was given last minute instructions by Lietwiler who then joined us in the stake-bodied truck and we headed for the dock at North Bottomside.

At the dock they climbed into a motorboat, in which the governor mechanism in its engine had been removed, to allow it to reach maximum speed. The orders were to rendezvous with an unnamed submarine somewhere in the open water.

> We sped off, and it seemed to fly through the water. Scarcely a minute or so later Cabcaben Bay was lit up by a massive explosion. It must have been the detonation of aviation gas, bombs and other ammunition stored there, but strangely we did not hear the sound. As we started to pass a minesweeper its gunner sewed a seam of .45 slugs from a 'tommy' gun across our bow. I didn't know a boat could stop so suddenly. The skipper of our boat called out the first name of the captain of the minesweeper, identified himself and explained what he was doing. He was given a 'go-ahead' as the Minesweeper Skipper shouted, 'I am stopping everything going through tonight. I guess you know why!'

They cruised on along the Bataan shoreline towards Mariveles, eyes peeled searching for a low dark hull of a submarine in the water.

> The minesweeper skipper said he thought it would be the USS *Seadragon*. Coming back to mid-channel we stopped near a Minesweeper, and were told that yet another Minesweeper was further out in the minefield tied up to a submarine, which was unloading stores.

After narrowly escaping being hit in a Japanese air raid at the Cavite docks, the *Seadragon* had already evaded further enemy detection to evacuate an earlier group of FRU men. Chamberlin prayed that its luck would hold.

> We headed into the minefield and passed under an unbelievable bower of fireworks. It seemed that every gun and mortar on the Rock was firing at Bataan and firing as fast as loading would permit. Flames from these weapons leaped 100 or more feet in the air. We found the minesweeper we sought, and went alongside. We boarded and crossed its deck to a submarine. Sure enough it was the *Seadragon.*
>
> No sooner than we had cleared the conning tower did we hear the Acting Commandant give us our sailing orders: 'Get the Hell out of here.' He was so afraid a combat ship might be lost that he had stopped the unloading of tons of food stores still in the *Seadragon*, and badly needed by the thousands of starving troops and civilians on Corregidor and the Bataan peninsula.

At 9.20pm on 8 April, the USS *Seadragon* eased away from its moorings with the minesweeper and slowly probed its way through the minefield. Soon after, Chamberlin heard that General Wainwright had surrendered to the Japanese. He sighed with relief that they were getting away with perhaps only minutes to spare. 'We were a working team of code-breakers heading for a haven called Australia!'

Knowing that the next depth-charge explosion could destroy them, for *Seadragon*'s crew and passengers time passed excruciatingly slowly. But, finally, the sonar indicated that the Japanese ships had moved away. For the evacuation voyage, the USS *Seadragon* was ordered to resume regular patrol operations, because of the threats from the Japanese Navy. Into the night, *Seadragon* dived quickly to periscope depth in the darkened sea. Despite being dangerously overloaded with its evacuees in flight from the Japanese, the USS *Seadragon* was soon forced to dive to an extreme depth to evade attack from Japanese depth charges and enemy aircraft. The die was cast, *Seadragon* must deliver its invaluable cargo of the final group of FRU code-breakers to an Australian port or, if they were captured, the intelligence war in the Pacific could pivot in favour of Japan.[17]

On 11 April, in accordance with its orders to conduct regular patrol operations, *Seadragon* attacked a Japanese destroyer in waters to the west of the Philippines. When the spread of torpedoes it had launched all missed the target, the destroyer counter-attacked *Seadragon*. To survive the repeated depth-charge attacks by the destroyers and other Japanese warships called to support the hunt for the US submarine, *Seadragon* dived to an extreme depth and stayed there for twenty-four hours to survive. As the batteries and air quality degraded with all unnecessary equipment shut down to save power and silence any noise, the air became so rancid many men became very ill.

Once the depth-charge attacks had ceased for a lengthy period, *Seadragon* slipped away as quietly as possible. From there on it sailed uneventfully via the Madrassa and Lombok Straits and finally arrived in Fremantle, Western Australia on 26 April. Soon after, the evacuees of the FRU transferred to another US Navy ship and docked on 6 May in Melbourne.[18]

* * *

After joining his other staff in Melbourne who had flown ahead of him, General MacArthur moved his HQ to Brisbane in Queensland where he established his US Command for all US Army forces in the Pacific and Far East theatre. From there, he commanded the fight back in the Pacific and eventual victory over Japan. With hindsight, if MacArthur and his HQ staff had been killed or captured by the Japanese, or not survived their gruelling and hair-raising escape to Australia, it would have been an enormous setback to the Allies' Pacific War with the consequences for its outcome unknowable.

In particular, if MacArthur's Intelligence Chief, Major General Willoughby had similarly been lost or, perhaps worse, if he had fallen into the hands of the Japanese, the consequences would have been disastrous for Allied codebreaking and intelligence in the Pacific and Far East. In 1987, for his service and work in the Second World War, Willoughby was inducted into the US Military Intelligence Hall of Fame.

John Chamberlin and his fellow FRU evacuees from the Philippines were integrated in Melbourne with staff of the Australian Signals Directorate and other Allies, and the combined entity renamed as FRUMEL In their daily work FRUMEL had to deal with the delay in the messages, sent out by OP-20-G in Washington, USA, which provided the daily cipher key for the Japanese *Purple* code.

Despite repeated requests for daily keys to be sent more promptly, OP-20-G did not improve the speed at which they disseminated the key. Finally, in an example of the ingenuity and expertise of the personnel at FRUMEL, Chamberlin got around OP-20-G's slowness by having the first two Japanese diplomatic messages from Shanghai intercepted and forwarded to him. This allowed him to break out the key from the first message, and confirm it as correct in the second.[19]

Chamberlin was later promoted to lieutenant and made a significant contribution in intelligence services to win the war in the Pacific. He had an eminent post-war career, reaching a senior position in the Foreign Office of the US Government in Washington. Clearly, if he and his FRU colleagues had not been evacuated safely, the intelligence work would have been damaged severely with a major negative impact on the US and Allies' war effort in the Far East.

Diane Capewell never knew her father, or anything about him, until recent years. She now knew that her father's life and career had made a significant contribution to winning the war against Japan and also for freedom, peace and prosperity in the world.

The evacuation and perilous journey to Australia of General MacArthur, his staff, Chamberlin and the other FRU members was one of the most incredible escapes and survival stories of the Second World War. Failure would have been a major strategic setback with catastrophic effects.

Notes

1. Capewell, Diane, Private Collection (Chamberlin)
2. Cleaver, T.M., *I Will Run Wild*, p.85
3. Bauer, Lt Col E., *The History of World War II*, pp.274-5
4. Cleaver, op.cit., pp.90-5
5. Ibid.
6. Cleaver, op.cit., p.98
7. Cleaver, op.cit., pp.101-4
8. Veteran's Account, Chamberlin, Lieutenant J.E. 'Vince', *Corregidor, The Final Days*, The US Naval Cryptologic Veterans' Association, PO Box 16009, Pensacola, Florida, USA, and Capewell, Diane, Private Collection (Chamberlin)
9. Cleaver, op.cit., p.157
10. Cleaver, op.cit., pp.158-9
11. King, and Lubianski, *The Military Service of Major General Willoughby*(monogram)
12. Wikipedia.org/wiki/Douglas_MacArthur
13. Cleaver, op.cit., pp.158-9
14. Cleaver, op.cit., p.160, and The MacArthur Museum, Brisbane
15. Bauer, op.cit., p.275
16. Pearson, US Naval Cryptologic Veterans' Assn
17. Veteran's Account, Chamberlin, Lieutenant J.E. 'Vince', *Corregidor, The Final Days*, The US Naval Cryptologic Veterans Association, PO Box 16009, Pensacola, Florida, USA, and Capewell, Diane, Private Collection (Chamberlin)
18. Pfennigwerth, *A Man of Intelligence*, pp.280-1, and Capewell, Diane, Private Collection (Chamberlin)
19. Fahey, *The Factory*, p.115

Chapter 12

In a Battle Against the Japanese at Milne Bay, it is a Battle for Australia

On the first Wednesday in September each year, the Australian Defence Force, the various veterans' associations and other government and allied countries' representatives commemorate in cities and towns across Australia the 'Battle for Australia'. This anniversary and commemoration dates back to a battle against the Japanese at Milne Bay in New Guinea in September 1942 when the Australian Government and public feared that they may be invaded and occupied by the Japanese. After the Battle of Milne Bay, the Australian Government announced the commemoration to be *The Battle for Australia*. The Battle for Milne Bay has largely been unknown or forgotten around the world and, even in Australia, is little recognised outside of the Australian Defence community.

In August and September 1942 at Milne Bay in eastern New Guinea, an invading force of Imperial Japanese Navy marines threatened to overrun the Australian 7 and 15 Infantry Brigades. The Japanese aimed to occupy New Guinea before considering any possible plans to invade Australia. The Japanese landed a large force on the north shore of Milne Bay, including tanks and their elite marine troops, before surging inland with the aim of taking possession of the Australian airstrips.

Milne Bay is at the extreme south-eastern tip of New Guinea, very hot, wet, muddy and rife with crocodiles and various tropical diseases. Malaria, which was endemic in the area, the rain and mud were additional debilitating and lethal enemies for the Australian troops facing the Japanese. Since Pearl Harbor, Japanese troops on land had been unstoppable everywhere in Asia and the Pacific. Although Australian troops were still holding back the Japanese with some success on the Kokoda Track, some Allied soldiers at Milne Bay in their hearts must have had grave misgivings on the battle to come.

* * *

In late August 1942, a large Japanese fleet sailed from their naval base at Rabaul in Papua New Guinea (PNG), carrying a Special Naval Landing Force (SNLF) of elite marines and support troops. The objective of the SNLF, protected by the Imperial Japanese Navy's 18th Naval Cruiser Squadron, was to go ashore on the far eastern promontory of PNG at Milne Bay and capture the Allies' recently constructed airfields. The SNLF orders from their Commander, Hayashi Shojiro, culminated with the words, 'smash to pieces the enemy lines and take the aerodrome by storm'. Milne Bay was considered by the Japanese to be a crucial air base for air raids on Port Moresby and planned advances along the south coast of New Guinea.[1]

Rain-clad mountains surround the deep water of Milne Bay, the shores of which stretched for about thirty miles to the open sea, and were some seven miles wide. With an annual rainfall of over 300 inches, there was rarely any clear sky, and regular sea mists. Milne Bay had attracted General MacArthur's attention and he required the establishing of airstrips and bases there to patrol the sea approaches to Port Moresby. With its deep water anchorage, it was seen as a future fleet support base. The first Allied troops arrived at Milne Bay in late June.[2]

In mid-July, General MacArthur at his relocated HQ in Brisbane, Queensland Australia, received intelligence from the FRUMEL codebreaker unit in Melbourne that indicated the Japanese had plans to attack and occupy Milne Bay towards the end of August. MacArthur's Chief of Staff for Intelligence, Brigadier Charles Willoughby, in his interpretation predicted that a Japanese attack was imminent. The FRUMEL codebreakers also provided intelligence on the composition of the Japanese landing force and its ships. This interception of the enemy's plans was a clear illustration of how fortunate the Allies were, that MacArthur, Willoughby, other staff officers, and the American FRU codebreakers, had survived their incredible evacuation and escape from Corregidor in the Philippines.[3]

One airstrip on Milne Bay's Goodenough Island, Gurney airfield, was operational, and two others were under urgent construction. The Gurney airfield allowed fighters of Nos 75 and 76 Squadrons RAAF to give protective cover to American bombers based at Port Moresby for raids on Japanese forces on the New Britain and Solomons islands. More important was the critical strategic need to prevent Japanese capture of the Gurney airfield. From Milne Bay the Japanese would be able to mount a major assault on Port Moresby, attack and disrupt shipping to and from northern Australia and isolate Australian troops in their momentous battles on the Kokoda Track. In the jungle of the Kokoda Track at this time Australian troops had been pushed back, and everywhere in south-east Asia and the Pacific Japanese forces were overcoming all opposition.[4] Japanese aircraft were bombing Darwin in northern Australia and Japanese submarines were making exploratory attacks against Sydney harbour and other ports on Australia's east coast.

In the last week of July, the Curtiss P-40 Kittyhawk fighters of Nos 75 and 76 Squadrons RAAF had transferred from Port Moresby to Milne Bay. In No.75 Squadron, Sergeant Roy Riddel's first and lasting impression of Milne Bay and its airstrips was of the dreadful living conditions with mud and rain everywhere. The Americans brought in jeeps which immediately became bogged down. The airstrips were just mud with matting overlaid, which did not prevent the mud oozing up and spraying into wheel wells, flaps and wings when aircraft were landing. The constant rain and mud brought mosquitoes, malaria and dysentery.[5]

At age 20, Roy Riddel had enlisted in the Australian Army in July 1939 as war threatened. At the time, Riddel was a student at Queensland University and had also worked in a bank. Becoming disenchanted with army life in August 1940, he and a few others were able to transfer to the RAAF. Flying training followed in Australia and the UK where he saw service flying Spitfires with No.66 Squadron RAF. In June 1942, Riddel and other Australian pilots were transferred back to serve with the RAAF in Australia.

During his time based at Port Moresby, Riddel and other P-40 Kittyhawk pilots had learned the hard way in combat with the Japanese Mitsubishi A6M *Reisen* fighters, known as the 'Zero' by Allied pilots, that the P-40 had some serious disadvantages against the Zero. The Zero was far superior in a dogfight, far more nimble and manoeuvrable, and able to easily outturn a Kittyhawk. However, the P-40 Kittyhawk had a greater maximum speed, which could be exploited during an attack from a height advantage and, if possible, speeding away from whirling dogfights.

On 11 August, at about 2.30 p.m., the siren sounded, and Riddel scrambled with twelve other 75 Squadron pilots. The initial warning was that two Japanese bombers with three escort fighters were approaching. It soon became clear that there were many more Zero fighters in the enemy attack, thirteen or more, to be intercepted.

The engagement quickly became a confusion of individual dogfights, kill or be killed. Flying Officer Mark Sheldon and Sergeant Francis Shelley were shot down and lost. Two Japanese fighters were claimed as destroyed by 75 Squadron and six damaged, although many Kittyhawks also sustained damage. There were similar engagements every day, sometimes on patrols twice a day.[6]

The Japanese may have been unaware that, in late July, Nos 75 and 76 Squadrons had relocated from Port Moresby to Gurney Field, but it did not deter them. Soon after first light on 26 August, a patrol of Kittyhawks sighted Japanese invasion barges and other craft, which were about one and a half miles offshore from the small mission settlement known as KB Mission. The

Kittyhawks dived into a strafing attack before returning to base to refuel and re-arm. Four more attacks during the rest of the day left a number of barges on fire or sunk near the shoreline.[7]

Scrambling once more on the 27th, Riddel took off with five other Kittyhawks in response to a warning of an approaching air raid. He was flying with his close friend Sergeant Stu Munroe when they found themselves heavily outnumbered. They were confronting twelve Zeros and eight Type 99 dive-bombers attacking Gurney Field. To make it worse, the enemy fighters' markings showed that they were from the elite and very experienced *Tainu Kokutai* Squadron. While they tried to climb and jockey for position to take on the Zeros, Riddel could only look on in dismay as a Zero swept in behind Munroe and, with a burst of fire, sent his smoking Kittyhawk crashing into the jungle. He did not see Munroe bale out before it was enveloped in an explosion of flame and black smoke.

The same Zero then turned and came head on at Riddel, who avoided being drawn into a turning dogfight. After a number of head-on attacks and passes, Riddel got in a burst of fire on the Zero's starboard wing. It went down in a rolling dive, leaking oil and Riddel saw the explosion as it smashed into the ground's lush foliage. He climbed away seeking height and found company with his squadron leader, Les Jackson. Soon after, they swooped on two Zeros which were trying to destroy with their machine guns another Zero that had ditched in the sea. Later, Riddel would describe their fire on the two unsuspecting Zeros as like shooting clay pigeons. It brought the squadron's score in the engagement to five Zeros destroyed.

Although Riddel was credited with two Zeros destroyed in the engagement, he had lost another close friend in Stu Munroe with whom he had shared a tent. It was a hammer blow to Riddel. He had lost four close friends in operations in UK and just two weeks earlier it was Sheldon and Shelley gone, and now Munroe.

Day after day, interspersed between intercepting Japanese air raids, the two squadrons carried out air-to-ground attacks on enemy infantry positions. The repetitive strafing stripped the palm trees of their foliage, sending the Japanese troops scurrying to find other cover.[8] Because of the very real threat of the Japanese capturing Gurney Field, on 26 August the RAAF squadrons had been withdrawn to Port Moresby. Yet, despite the flying time to reach Milne Bay, rotating flights of Kittyhawk fighters maintained air support over the battlefield through the daylight hours to strafe and bomb Japanese positions continuously. This meant that during the day the Japanese marines spent most of their time back from the shoreline, taking cover in the jungle to hide from air attack.[9]

* * *

During the night of 25/26 August the Japanese invasion fleet had sailed into Milne Bay and, despite losing some shipping and men to attacks by the Kittyhawk fighters, the SNLF began landing its marines on the eastern shore. However, although the Japanese found that on land there was no immediate opposition, they had made a critical mistake which would have severe consequences. They were many miles away from their planned landing point. To attack and capture the Gurney airfield, the Japanese marine troops were faced with trudging through dense and swampy jungle. It was not long before advance scouting patrols of Australian troops engaged the Japanese in hit-and-run skirmishes and alerted Allied commanders to the invading force.

For the initial landings, Commander Hayashi put ashore some 1,200 troops of the SNLF. However, as with Allied commanders, he was almost certainly not fully aware of the difficulties his men would face. The tropical vegetation of the jungle, an absence of roads, rain, mud, humidity and heat would all sap men's energy and morale. In those last few days of August, despite the loss of supplies from Allied air attacks on their ships and having to find a way through the dense jungle, the Japanese SNLF marines pressed on towards the Gurney airstrips. They even found a route for two tanks to keep up with their advance. By the evening of the 30th the marines could see their first objective, the No.3 airstrip.[10]

Two Australian infantry brigades under command of Major General Cyril Clowes, the 9th, 25th and 61st Battalions of 7 Militia Brigade, and the 9th, 10th and 12th of the AIF Brigade, together with artillery and anti-aircraft units, confronted the invading Japanese forces. On the night of 25 August and subsequent days on Milne Bay's northern coast, the Japanese marines had been held up and slowed by a fighting withdrawal by 61st Battalion back to the KB Mission.[11]

Having largely overcome the three militia battalions of 7 Militia Brigade, the Japanese advanced towards No.3 airstrip, which they had assumed was operational. On 30 August, Corporal Allan Gardner was in the battle-hardened 2/12th Battalion which had been in action in North Africa in 1941. It went forward towards No.3 airstrip, meeting very strong resistance from Japanese troops, who at 3.00 a.m. on the 31st, attacked across the airstrip's open ground.[12]

Allan Gardner, who had been born on 2 September 1914 in Atherton, North Queensland, Australia, was just three days away from his twenty-eighth birthday. In the rich farming area of the Atherton Tablelands, he left school at age 13, like so many other children in the farming community in those times, to begin work on a farm. By the time he enlisted in the Australian Army in February 1941 and was sent to join 2/12th Battalion in the Middle East, he was six feet tall and weighed around twelve stones, dark hair, slim, tanned and fit from the farm work.

Within six weeks of enlisting and very little training, Gardner and his 2/12th Battalion were in Tobruk, Libya and in the war. Despite Gardner's curtailed school education, he was outgoing and energetic, very much a team player, which had contributed to his promotion to corporal. He was moving along a muddy and thick jungle track near to No.3 airstrip when the battalion began to take fire from Japanese positions, and casualties.

> As I went forward Ted Stagg was some way in front of me, and was hit. When I found him lying on the ground, I tried to help him, but I was told to keep advancing as stretcher bearers were close by, and coming. When I saw Jocky Small further along that muddy jungle track he was dead, and hardly recognisable, lifeless with a massive head wound. Jocky Small and Ted Stagg were among our first casualties.[13]

A small consolation was that only seconds after Small had been hit in the head, Captain Bill Kirk spotted the sniper responsible and shot him. It was a bitter revenge, for Small had been Kirk's batman. Nothing could be done for Stagg or Small. Gardner went on in the advance.

> As we got a short distance past No.3 airstrip I noticed a soldier of the 61st Battalion slumped on the ground, his hands tied behind his back with signal wire, and he had been bayoneted a number of times. Seeing the atrocities meted out to some of our 61st Battalion troops, and also on the native men and women of New Guinea, made us even more determined to overcome the Japs.
>
> After battling all day along a terrible jungle track of mud, it was getting towards sundown when we halted and began to dig in for the night. On one side we had the beach and the ocean, and on the three other sides of our camp perimeter we beat down and brushed the jungle to give us a better view of any Japanese attack. Men of C Company were dug in parallel facing the track. B Company were deployed along the Gamma river perimeter, while HQ Company held the line from the track back to the beach.

With dusk turning to dark, a lone lugger craft appeared. It had sailed from Gili Gili near the mouth of the Gamma river, carrying ammunition and food for Gardner's 2/12th Battalion. The lugger could only anchor offshore, so that the ammunition and boxes of hot food had to be ferried by rowing boat to the beach where Gardner and others were helping in the unloading.

> It was at this moment, as we were unloading the supplies, that all hell broke loose. More than 100 Japanese marine troops emerged on the muddy track up against our all round defensive perimeter.

Unbeknown to both Gardner's 2/12th Battalion and the main force of Japanese marines, earlier that day some 2/12th troops of a forward listening and observation post had shot and killed at least one leading scout of the marines' party. It may have prevented the Japanese from learning of the strength of the Australian overall force and positions. During the night of 30/31 August, Gardner and his 2/12th troops faced a number of fanatical attacks by the Japanese marines to capture No.3 airstrip.[14]

> Well, they attacked all night from different directions, each time turned back by the fire of our three rifle companies. Except one Jap marine did break through the line of our company.

Somehow not stopped by the fusillade of rifle fire, the Japanese soldier ran at the Australian line with a fixed bayonet. To Gardner. it seemed that he was suicidal, and intent on a hand-to-hand fight.

> Tom Macauley blocked his path and tried to avoid the thrust of his bayonet. Tom grabbed him and throttled the life out him, but the Jap had already ripped Tom right up his back. Another of our men, George Lucas, was also badly wounded, among a number of our casualties.
>
> Just after daylight Ken Burton and Mike Steady went on a patrol out from our perimeter, to see how many Jap marines were killed. A sniper shot Ken through the shoulder which almost blew his arm off. Mike got him back inside the perimeter, then Sid Griffiths carried him to the beach, where he was laid out amongst our casualties waiting to be evacuated by boat.

The following night, 31 August/1 September, more than ninety Japanese were killed in their attacks on the 2/12th Battalion camp by the Gamma river. It effectively destroyed that particular group of SNLF marines who had failed to find their way around No.3 airstrip. Without their leading scouts' reconnaissance to warn them, the Japanese column perhaps did not realise that they were making their way through such strongly held Allied positions. Gardner concluded that they did not know what they had encountered.

> In effect they had run into an ambush by a superior force dug into prepared defensive positions. While our three companies fought it out at our

> overnight camp by the Gamma river, our A and B companies had advanced as far as the KB Mission across the No.3 airstrip. They suffered some casualties as they approached the KB Misson. On that first night they had a hectic time holding their position there at the KB Mission, and against a Japanese marines contingent with a couple of tanks.

The KB Mission consisted of a few native huts and a jetty to handle small craft such as the luggers *Laurabada* and *Lakiotis*, which were crucial for re-supplying the Australian troops and evacuating casualties. In the battle around the KB Mission, both Japanese tanks were in action, although only briefly. One was put out of action when a crew member stood up out of its hatch and was shot through the head. The other tank became bogged down and was abandoned. About sixty Japanese troops were killed in their attempt to take the KB Mission, and some with bayonets.

On 1 September, Gardner went forward from the Gamma river with three companies of 2/12th Battalion, to join their two other companies at the KB Mission.

> On 1/2 September the reunited full Battalion spent their first night together at KB Mission – but what a night! It never stopped raining and we had already been wet through for days. We set up an all round Battalion defence in a coconut plantation, where it fringed the jungle and rigged up a trip wire with a few tins of small stones. Each time those tins rattled, then moments later the Vickers gun would open up with a cone of fire along the trip wire.
>
> That night Bill Wylie and I were on the second line of defence when a runner with a message from Battalion HQ to the front line, came out and warned us of his mission. His was a risky job. Later that night we let him pass without challenge as he again came from HQ with a message for C Company on the front perimeter. After leaving us when challenged for the password by another of our men, he was inexplicably shot in the leg, but a stretcher bearer was able to evacuate him.

Worse friendly fire casualties were to come on that same night. In case the Japanese advanced with more tanks, eight men were sent out to mine the track. They crossed the battalion's perimeter into no man's land without incident but, on returning, were seen by Japanese troops and fired upon.

> The gunshots caused our men on the front perimeter to open up, and most of the eight men were killed by our own fire. After some native tribesmen

> informed us of some Japanese using one of their huts, an officer took a small patrol to investigate. When this officer kicked the door open, a Japanese machine gun opened up, killing him instantly. The rest of the patrol killed some of the Japs, although one or two got away.

While at KB Mission, Gardner was in a party ordered to take food supplies, ammunition and abandoned Japanese equipment, in a rowing boat to an anchored lugger near the shore.

> The sea was pretty rough at the time, and we had trouble getting on board. An officer wanted everyone in the party, the meal boxes for C Company, and all the ammunition loaded. Not surprisingly, halfway to the shore the overloaded boat was swamped by a wave, and down we went. Two men, Youl and Morrison, were drowned, while the rest of us struggled through the currents and surf and swam to the shore.
>
> Near sundown we were informed that the Battalion was moving back to Gili Gili. We half-drowned survivors were told that we could return that evening to our platoon, if we wanted to, by jungle track. Since anything at all moving after dark was shot at by the enemy or even our own troops, all but Don Senescall and myself decided to stay with C Company.
>
> Then Don and I decided to risk a return on the lugger that evening, and we rowed a dinghy out to it. The crew were trying to tie a Jap barge to the launch to be towed back to Gili Gili. It was not long after we departed that the Jap Navy opened up its guns on C Company, whom we had left on the shore.

On the lugger's arrival at Gili Gili, a transport ship of some 8,000-10,000 tons, the *Anshon*, was being unloaded. Troops were disembarking and cargo being unloaded. In the melee of men and equipment, Senescall and Gardner found themselves taking shelter for the rest of the night in a thatched hut with some gunners.

> Just after we were settling down in the hut, a Jap Navy cruiser lit up our hospital ship in the bay, the *Munder*, with a searchlight. I thought, they are going to sink her, with all our wounded soldiers aboard. For once, the big Red Cross on its side saved them, and the Japs held their fire and ordered it straight out of the bay at once.
>
> Then the Jap Navy put their searchlights on the *Anshon*, which was tied up at the Gili Gili wharf. At the first explosion I thought it was a bomb, and shot out of the hut into a trench.I found some of the other blokes

beat me there. The first naval shell blew the back off an officers' hut near where we had been. With a powerful searchlight illuminating the area like daylight, the Jap Navy were shelling the *Anshon*, intent on sinking it. Then the Jap cruiser swung his gun and landed some shells onto No.1 airstrip, and for good measure more shells onto C Company's camp, from where we had left on the lugger. The shelling killed a number of our C Company troops, whom we had left there.

The overall casualties of that night in 2/12th Battalion were 43 dead and 26 wounded. With the Jap searchlight seeking the troops out they had one hell of a night.

On 2 September the 2/9th Battalion arrived and, on 3 September, began to relieve 2/12th Battalion, taking over the advance against the Japanese. On the afternoon of 4 September, attempts to attack Japanese positions by two companies of 2/9th Battalion were foundering with increasing casualties. They were being repeatedly repelled by the deadly fire from three Japanese machine-gun posts. Corporal John French decided that something had to be done differently. He must have thought that one man might get close to the machine-gun emplacements without being seen. On his own initiative, he ordered his section of men to take cover, while he went forward alone to attempt a hand grenade attack on the enemy machine gunners.

Armed with a sub-machine gun and some grenades, French darted towards the machine-gun pits. Using whatever cover he could, he threw grenades precisely into two of the machine-gun pits, putting them out of action. Any element of surprise was now gone. He was then seen running at the third position, firing his sub-machine gun at the Japanese troops, despite being under fire and hit himself. The enemy machine gun went silent, and French could no longer be seen. His men later found him dead in front of the third machine-gun pit. All of the three Japanese gun crews were also found to be dead.

Corporal John French was posthumously awarded the Victoria Cross for this selfless act which undoubtedly saved an unknown but considerable number of lives of his fellow soldiers and created a substantial incursion into the Japanese lines. With hindsight, it has been speculated that this setback, coming on top of a number of heavy losses and forced pullbacks, was the last straw for the Japanese command. On the night of 4/5 September, the Japanese began pulling back their troops. By 5 September, the Japanese command had to accept that the invasion at Milne Bay had failed and ordered a formal withdrawal of the surviving SNLF marines by sea.[15] Their usual tactics of massed frontal attacks had not worked.

In his report on the battle, Major General Clowes estimated that, out of an attacking force of more than 2,000 SNLF marines, the Japanese had lost at least 1,000 men killed and many more wounded.[16] Later figures have estimated from various sources, including Japanese authorities, that out of 2,599 Japanese troops landed, only 1,318 re-embarked.[17] Allied casualties recorded were 172Australians killed or missing and fourteen Americans killed.[18] The fighting was so brutal and unforgiving that no prisoners were taken on either side.

* * *

On the night of 5 September, it was the first Wednesday in the month and Japanese motorboats were ferrying their remaining troops to their ships waiting in the bay. By 6 September, the Japanese command had evacuated their forces, except for a few isolated remnants cut off in the jungle.[19] This day was declared by the Australian Government to be commemorated as the Battle for Australia, to be held each year on the first Wednesday in September. The Battle of Milne Bay was the first major defeat on land of Japanese troops.

Until Milne Bay there had grown up a thought that the Imperial Japanese Army was invincible. Now, in newspapers and radio around the world, the word spread that the Japanese had been beaten at Milne Bay in New Guinea and pushed back into the sea. The idea and belief that Japanese soldiers could be defeated took hold. While it was a relatively small battle, though with terrible deaths and casualties, it had a huge psychologically positive effect among Allied peoples around the world. After the Battle of Milne Bay, the military and civilians alike knew that the Japanese Army could be beaten – Milne Bay was a beacon of hope.

Allan Gardner survived the Battle of Milne Bay although he contacted malaria along with a vast number of other troops on both sides but recovered to survive the war in the Pacific. Post-war he trained as a carpenter and worked all his life in housing and other construction projects. With his first wife Veronica, Allan had three children, two sons Adrian and Ross, and a daughter Rhyll.

Roy Riddel's good fortune in surviving air combat in the UK and at Milne Bay did not last. While on a training flight with his squadron relocated back in Australia, he was badly injured and left paralysed after a crash landing. Despite being in hospital for three months, he recovered, resumed flying, and at the end of the war took up his studies again at Queensland University. Riddel qualified as a dentist and then practised dentistry for more than thirty years.

Roy Riddel and Allan Gardner are two fine examples of so many millions of people in Allied countries, military and civilian, who did not ask what their government or country could do for them. They gave more than was asked of them, and 'did their bit' to win the worldwide struggle for freedom.

Notes

1. Casey, *The RAAF at Milne Bay, Wartime,* p.23, and Boettcher, *Eleven Bloody Days, The Battle for Milne Bay*, pp.60-2.
2. Casey, op. cit., p.23, and Royal Aust Artillery Assn, 80th Anniversary Commemoration, *Battle of Milne Bay*
3. Wikipedia, en.wikipedia.org/wiki/Battle_of_Milne Bay pp.7-8
4. Casey, op. cit., p.23
5. RAAFA, Sitrep Issue No.25, p.12, *Roy Riddel – RAAF*
6. RAAFA, Sitrep Issue No.24, pp.24-5, *Roy Riddel – RAAF,* and Sitrep Issue No.25, pp.11-16, *Roy Riddel – RAAF*
7. Casey, op. cit., p.24
8. RAAFA, Sitrep Issue No.25, pp.13-16, *Roy Riddel – RAAF*
9. Casey, op. cit., p.25
10. Casey, op. cit., p.24, and Boettcher, op. cit., pp.60-2.
11. Clowes, *The Clowes Report on the Battle for Milne Bay*, p.12
12. Veteran's account, Gardner, Allan, Private Collection, Rhyll Hansen.
13. Veteran's account, Gardner, Allan, Private Collection, Rhyll Hansen (and all subsequent direct quotes).
14. Clowes, op. cit., p.17
15. Casey, op. cit., p.25, and Boettcher, Op. Cit., pp.119-20
16. Clowes, op. cit., p.29
17. Boettcher, op. cit., p.122
18. Clowes, op. cit., p.44
19. Casey, op. cit., p.25, and Boettcher, op. cit., p.124

Chapter 13

Under the Japanese Jackboot in Singapore

There have been many books and accounts written of the ordeals suffered by prisoners of war, and civilians at the hands of the Japanese military. Every individual's experience was unique. Their stories show us the evil and horror of war, and the inhumanity and brutality of totalitarian regimes like those of the German and Japanese Axis in the Second World War.

To defend the Strait of Johore between Singapore and Malaya the British authorities had built a formidable fortress base at Changi where the Royal Artillery erected coast gun batteries, including some massive 15-inch guns. The famous British fortress was now a prison for thousands of PoWs and civilian internees, all facing a future of pain, deprivation, drudgery, hunger, disease and, for many, death.

Very quickly after all Allied forces had retreated across the Johore Strait from Malaya, Japanese infantry began landing on Singapore island. On 8 February Allied commanders ordered a fight to the last man, yet only a week later, on 15 February, there was a formal surrender to the Japanese. The fall of Singapore had come in a chaotic rush.[1]

British and Allied troops, like the British Government and the rest of the world, were shocked and astounded at the rapid collapse and surrender. 'To hear that we had capitulated left us dumbfounded', said one soldier.[2]

In the confusion and devastation, amidst the shelling and bombing in those final days, troops and civilians found themselves in an existential struggle to survive. For every individual, military or civilian, the challenges were different. Death, uncertainty and random fate dominated, and tomorrow seemed a long way off.

* * *

For Stan Durston riding madly through the chaos on his bicycle, the only thought was to reach his wife Pat. By the time Stan arrived at Pat's house in Karong, a Japanese sergeant was just leaving with two other soldiers. What terror Pat and her family must have undergone when these Japanese troops, with rifles and fixed bayonets pointing at them, had burst into their home? Although Pat's father was still shocked from the soldiers' intrusion, when he saw Stan he reacted quickly. He shouted to Stan to stand fast and not do anything to obstruct the Japanese troops, which would further endanger their lives. Already Pat's parents knew of many young women, some of them neighbours, who had been raped and then murdered in their own homes.[2]

Stan walked over to Pat who was crying uncontrollably. He grabbed her left hand and, pointing to her wedding ring shouted, 'Wife! Wife!' The Japanese sergeant arrogantly pushed Stan aside and walked out of the gate. The other two soldiers followed him, passing Pat's pet dog Judy who lay in the gutter, writhing in pain with a broken leg. Judy had been brutally beaten down when she had tried to protect Pat.

Pat continued to sob and was hysterical but Stan knew he had to let go of her. He had only a few moments before he must leave to return to his unit's assembly area. Despite the trauma of what had occurred, once everyone calmed down a little he would have to go. Pat had suffered a violation, a crime of war, and would very rarely speak of this incident again. It would be a secret that she would keep to herself and share only with a trusted few about what took place that day.

On leaving the house, Stan jumped on his bicycle and turned away from the Japanese sergeant and his two men who were standing at the end of the street. His anger welled up inside. He was incensed and willing himself to cycle back and try to kill the Japanese NCO for what he had done. Somehow, he summoned up reason, and self-control he did not know he had, to contain his anger for fear of further reprisals which would probably have meant the execution of Pat and her family.

As he rode away reluctantly, a Chinese man signalled to him to stop and look behind. Stan stopped, put a foot down on the ground and twisted around. The two Japanese soldiers had raised their rifles and were aiming at him to shoot him in the back. With that, he got off his bike, turned around and walked slowly back towards the three Japanese, perhaps towards his death.

Stan walked towards the enemy troops, hands in the air, until he stopped a few yards from them. All the time their rifles remained pointing at his heart. One word from the sergeant and he was dead. It was not to be. He was then marched, with a gun repeatedly jabbing him in the back, to an old colonial building which was being used to assemble surrendered Allied troops.[3] Thousands of them were about to be marched in the searing heat to the Changi base which the Japanese were setting up as a PoW and civilian prison camp.

After the surrender of British and Allied forces on 15 February 1942, all military personnel and European civilians – men, women and children of all ages – were, over a three-week period, forced to march to the former British military fortress and base. The only possessions they were allowed to take were those they were able to carry. At Changi, a distance of about twelve miles from Singapore Cty, they were all imprisoned.

The straggling line of PoWs and internees appeared endless and, in the heat, on dirt roads and scrubby terrain, hunger, thirst and exhaustion set in quickly. February is the hottest month in Singapore with daytime temperatures in the low 30sC and only dropping to around 27C overnight, with very high humidity. The ordeal was a harbinger of what was to come. For those who would survive the march and the years of imprisonment at Changi, it was also a psychological shock that would be a lasting memory.

* * *

Pat Durston's brother Ken, who had enlisted in the Singapore Volunteer Force only months earlier, was also a PoW. The Japanese military command issued an edict for all British and Eurasian civilians to be registered and to assemble at certain places in Singapore. Later, all those civilians would be humiliated by being forced to walk, with only the possessions they could carry, through Singapore's streets to the Changi prison. They were all prisoners now.

Fortunately, Pat's family were regarded as Singapore locals and exempt. That enabled them to remain in their house although, like everyone, they were forced to wear an armband or star on their clothing when going out and were not permitted to speak to anyone except family. The Japanese implemented an evening curfew and anyone caught out of their house after 6.00pm would be shot on sight. It was enforced ruthlessly by Japanese military patrols.

After a long hot march with other PoWs from a staging point, Stan arrived at an assembly camp at Changi where thousands of men were all milling around. No one knew what was to become of them and certainly not the suffering to be endured in the years ahead. It would soon be transformed into an endless daily life of hunger and thirst, disease and illness, barbed wire, hard labour and injuries, beatings from brutal Japanese guards and, for an increasing number, an early death.

While the Changi prison arrangements were at first chaotic, Stan was asked by a Lieutenant Bevan in his artillery battery, if he would help him find a working truck. He was to go with the lieutenant into Singapore City to pick up some wounded men who had been turned out of hospitals and bring them back to Changi to be cared for by British military doctors and nurses who were also PoWs.

On finding a driveable truck, Stan and Bevan managed to siphon petrol from other damaged or broken-down vehicles. Each time they made a trip to pick up wounded men, Stan was able to call in and see Pat on the pretext that he needed water for the radiator. After a few weeks, the Japanese halted their ambulance trips to Singapore and back to Changi. Their Japanese captors had become more organised: all men were put into small groups or working parties.

During the first few months of captivity, Stan went blind without any apparent cause. It lasted for three weeks before returning to normal. According to Stan, his recovery came after eating raw carrots, peanuts and a teaspoon of marmite, as recommended by a camp doctor! Despite this alarming episode, Stan continued to arrange for notes to be smuggled out to Pat, telling her that he was well.

In one note sent back by Pat, she told Stan that she was pregnant. In view of their situation, Stan advised Pat to get rid of the baby since he felt it was not the time to be bringing new life into the world. He did not know if he would survive being a prisoner and, even if he did, there was no way of knowing how many years it would be before possible release.

It was a huge worry for Pat and her family as it should have been a happy occasion, not a time of fear and despair. Although Pat and Stan had only shared seven weeks of married life together, and it was uncertain whether they would live to be reunited, Pat had hopes for the future and decided not to abort the baby.

Some weeks later, Pat's cousin, Sonny, who had enlisted in the Singapore Volunteer Field Ambulance Service, was forcibly taken from his parents' home by Japanese troops against his will and, like many others, drafted into the Japanese Army. Consequently, as soon as an opportunity presented itself, Sonny managed to escape. He was taking a huge risk of being caught; if he was found, torture and death would have followed.

Sonny's fear of being recaptured and, as a consequence of Japanese reprisals that would be taken against his family, kept him from sending a message to tell them of his escape or where he was hiding. Japanese troops did go to the family home to look for him but his father said that he had not seen Sonny since the day they had forcibly taken him from their home. After a lengthy interrogation and threats to him and his family, the Japanese soldiers finally believed him and left. The family now knew that Sonny had escaped and feared for his life. They also dreaded that the Japanese troops would be back.

Sonny's parents did not know it but, while on the run as an escaped PoW, he posed as a Singapore local and bizarrely managed to find work on a Japanese-manned fishing boat. It went out daily on the seas not far outside the Malacca Strait. While at sea, Sonny saw evidence of the executions of his fellow countrymen, their bodies having been dumped at sea to become food for sharks, which were numerous and scavenging the decaying corpses.[4]

* * *

As time went on under the Japanese occupation, starvation, malaria and various diseases began to affect many people still allowed to live in Singapore. To survive was an everyday struggle to obtain food and medicines, essential for life itself. Malaria was rampant, with mosquitos thriving in the pools of water in the many bomb craters, continually refilled by the frequent rains. Because medicines, when available, became too expensive for most people to buy, it was becoming harder and harder to stay healthy. The rigour and restrictions of the Japanese occupation were making it increasingly difficult for Pat and Stan to get messages to each other. They could only rely on people they knew well, and trusted, to smuggle a message between them.

In one message, Stan asked Pat if she could walk past a compound where he was working in a forced labour group. He just wished to see her, if only at a distance, and know that she was well and healthy. When he saw Pat walk by, he got the shock of his life. She was so big with her pregnancy. Pat came closer to the compound's fence while Stan kept his eye on the guards. At a moment when they moved out of sight, he threw two tins of condensed milk over the fence and a silver spoon. He had retained the spoon from a time before coming a PoW. Pat would later sell the spoon for food for her baby.

After the baby's birth Pat was able to send a note to Stan telling him of the address where she was staying with her parents and that, if possible, she would love to see him and show him the baby. The next day he was in a working party going to a site not far away from Pat's address. When close to the location, Stan slipped off the back of the truck when the guards were looking the other way and ran between the two large houses that Pat mentioned in her note as being close to her house.

When Stan arrived at Pat's house for a moment it was an overwhelming emotional reunion. He was at once given a glass of milk, but he knew he had to be quick and gulped it straight down. His visit was dicing with death, his and theirs. He embraced Pat who was now so thin, and her long black hair was cut short. Taking their baby in his arms for the first time, he could see that she was so like him with her blue eyes, ginger hair and fair skin. Only a minute or so had passed when, through the doorway, he saw three Japanese work-group guards walking down the street.

Saying good-bye to his in-laws in an instant, and then handing their baby back to Pat he said to her, 'I'll be all right, they won't catch me.' Unknown to Stan, it would be the last time he would see Pat's parents. There was no time for a bittersweet farewell as he dashed out of the back of the house. He ran, ducked and jumped over garden hedges and walls, hoping the Japanese would not see him. He felt like an animal being hunted and expected a bullet in his back at any time. He had no idea where he was going.

When he at last stopped to catch his breath, Stan found himself on the edge of a road. He looked up and down and froze. Coming down the road was the truck with his work group. He hesitated, then reluctantly stepped out in front of the truck. He waved his hands in the air signalling it to stop. Fear gripped him; he had to think fast. With gestures and odd words in English and Japanese, he tried to make the guards understand that he had fallen out of the work truck.

At first, they stared with rifles ready, then, after a few words among themselves, they bundled him into the back of the truck. No doubt it was easier than explaining to a superior how they had lost a prisoner, then re-captured and shot him. In the back of the truck, Stan reflected on his outrageously good fortune. Next time he might not be so lucky.

If caught, escaping prisoners were not tolerated. Earlier, three of Stan's artillery friends had tried to escape. They had asked him to join them but, because of Pat living in Singapore with his baby and her family, he decided against it. All three escapees had been re-captured outside the Changi perimeter fencing for which the Japanese showed them no mercy. All three were made to dig their own graves and then shot. Once again fate had favoured him.

This momentary meeting with Pat would be the last time they would see each other for three years. Neither would know whether the other was dead or alive. While on daily working parties in many areas of Singapore, Stan was put to work on a variety of manual labour, such as repairs to buildings, the docks, digging ditches and in gardens. In the prison camp there was one particular Japanese guard who picked on Stan, and would shout at Stan to call him 'master'. Stan would always say nothing.

On one very warm night Stan was sleeping outside in the open. Some instinct woke him suddenly. The same Japanese guard was standing over him with his bayonet fixed and pointing it directly at his throat. Stan just stared in shock; his eyes wide in fright. Nervously, he smiled back at the guard. He lay there in silence, but he could hear the sound of his heart pounding rapidly in his ears. If he were to make any sudden move the bayonet would be plunged into his neck.

Stan forced a nervous smile, more a taught grimace. The guard then simply stepped back, turned and walked away. Had he been foolhardy to sleep out in the open? One thing was certain, fate had favoured him again. From time-to-time, Stan was beaten by the guard, but he knew that if he cried out in pain, it would be harsher. So, he kept his silence and, eventually, it seemed he earned the respect of the guard. Later he told Stan he was 'Number one prisoner' and ceased bothering him.

Besides the exhausting forced labour and beatings by guards, hunger and cravings for food were ever present. On one day an old decaying shark was obtained by the prisoners' cookhouse. It was tough to eat and had a taste of ammonia. The PoWs were so desperately hungry they would eat anything, but the rotten shark meat made many sick. On another occasion, a sheep was obtained, although amongst thousands of PoWs there was little meat for each man.

While Stan was out of Changi on working parties around Singapore, he and others did much bartering when they had the chance for food if possible, and any other items of any kind that were in demand by the PoWs. Sometimes, it was possible to buy small cigars for 50 cents each and then smuggle them back into Changi and sell them for as much as a dollar. Smuggling anything into Changi, however, was an offence and, if caught, the punishment would be brutal, possibly fatal.[5]

* * *

After the surrender of Singapore, David Clemens of the Surreys and British Battalions was instructed to transport the wounded and others unable to walk to Changi and he made a number of journeys driving the van he had commandeered earlier. After this work, as with Stan Durston and many others, he was taken out of Changi by the Japanese guards in working parties each day around Singapore and the island. In this work the guards soon began to use Clemens as a driver.[6]

David Clemens was born in 1915 in East London with a twin sister, Dorothy, and eleven other siblings. At sixteen he left school and enrolled in the London School of Nautical Cookery. Following a number of jobs on ships and in hotels, and being rejected by the Royal Navy, he joined the Army. Despite the Royal Navy rejection because of a 'hammer toe' condition, he took up running in the East Surrey Regiment and won a number of notable Army races. While in Shanghai with the Surreys, he won a ten-mile race against competitors from other military and local Chinese teams.

One day, while Clemens was in a PoW working party travelling out to the Ford factory on the Bukit Timah Road, a medieval horror confronted them. Near a local shopping area, stuck on top of four tall posts, were four human heads. Four local thieves from the Malay, Chinese and Indian communities had been executed and decapitated. Their heads had been put on display as a warning and left there to rot.

On another day, Clemens tried to protect a young Chinese boy who, on bringing some beans to sell to Clemens, was being beaten by a Japanese guard. Such an intervention and disobedience by a PoW brought the death penalty. Clemens had reacted instinctively but now faced the ultimate punishment meted out so frequently by the Japanese. A Japanese officer ordered him to kneel down and drew his lethal Samurai sword.

As he dropped to the ground, Clemens noticed the morose silent faces of the other PoWs who were watching in horror. He was going to be decapitated; his head would also soon be on top of a pole.

Within a second or two, he was hammered into the ground and his face rammed into the dirt. Then Clemens heard laughing by the Japanese guards. He must still be alive. He was pulled to his feet, dragged over to a tree and tied to it. What now? his mind raced. But he was left for some time like that before being untied and taken back to Changi. Clemens had been extraordinarily lucky.[7]

Another PoW being used in working parties like Clemens, in effect as forced or slave labour, was George Keeling, a fellow gunner of Stan Durston in the Johore Battery at Changi. Keeling was twenty-four years old, six feet four tall, fit and strong from his work as a gunner, and so clearly was a good PoW specimen to be allocated as a slave labourer to a work party.[8]

Sadistic beatings, torture and execution of PoWs by the Japanese, for their own ends, apparent pleasure, and to keep control, were arbitrary and frequent. Guy Sebastian was an aircraftsman in the RAF at the time of the surrender and, with the other thousands, marched to the Changi prison. Because of Sebastian's ancestry, Sri Lankan, Portuguese and Indian, the Japanese authorities tried to coerce him to join the Indian National Army (INA), which was fighting for India's independence from Britain. Sebastian refused to do so and, although tortured by the Japanese to force him to join the INA, he held out. Because he would not comply, he was branded with a hot iron to mark his intransigence and subjugate his spirit.[9]

From the middle of 1942 the Japanese began shipping male prisoners to Japan and other countries in South East Asia and the Pacific to work as slave labour in mines, construction and other heavy industrial projects. It is not known how the Japanese selected the prisoners to be transported, though no doubt strength, general fitness and physique were factors. Clemens, Keeling, and Sebastian, with tens of thousands of other PoWs, would soon feel the Japanese jackboot press harder on their necks. They would be shipped by sea, or transported overland by their slave-masters, like cattle to work until they died at some unknown location.

* * *

For Pat and her family living in the community under the Japanese regime in Singapore, the restrictions and increasing food shortages were becoming worse day by day. The Japanese authorities began encouraging people to move to undeveloped areas of Malaya to establish new settlements. Pat's father was in favour of moving and discussed the two options with the family members: leave for unknown territory or stay in Singapore and possibly die of malaria or starve to death. They had previously lived in Malaya and, in the end, Pat's father made the decision that they should go.

They and many others were to be transported to Bahau to a new settlement named by the Japanese as Fuji-go, in the Pahang jungles of Negri-Sembilan.

The Japanese authorities painted an attractive image of land which would be made available for each family to settle and develop under the stipulation that they must be prepared to work hard in the harsh conditions. The settlers were told they would have first to clear the land of jungle vegetation, plough the soil and grow crops not only to feed themselves but also to send food back to Singapore where people were starving. They were given to think that, under this arrangement, they would be free of restrictions by the Japanese and would be self-sufficient and independent.

After much preparation and things to do when moving, Pat's family said their farewells and lined up at the railway station for their long journey, unsure as to what was to happen on their arrival at Bahau. Before they left, one of their relatives offered to adopt Barbara, to spare her the hardships which lay ahead. Pat would have none of it; she naturally wished to care for her daughter herself and stay in Singapore.

Whether the Japanese authorities knew that Pat was married to a British soldier is not known. She had stated on Barbara's birth certificate that her husband was a mechanical engineer and away, and that she lived with a friend. Nevertheless, she had to wear a red star on her clothing in public at all times, which indicated that she was a civilian enemy but not yet interned,

Pat's parents left on the journey to Bahau in Malaya, travelling in a hot uncomfortable goods wagon with very few short stops along the way. Pat intended to follow later when baby Barbara was old enough to walk. When Pat's parents and the other settlers arrived at Bahau, all they could see was a railway siding with a long hut next to the line. Hungry and tired from their journey in goods wagons, they alighted with all their worldly goods. They were told that they would have to carry all of their belongings and walk on foot further inland for several miles on rain-soaked tracks. With thick jungle forest towering above them, hundreds of people, with their bags and animals, struggled to keep moving slowly on gravel muddy roads.

When the straggling column finally arrived at Fuji-go, they found that there was not much there other than a couple of long timber huts for living in and a partially-cleared area of jungle of about four square miles. This was supposedly the Japanese propaganda version of utopia, a promised land, a Shangri-La. It had been a lie. The jungle was often a mass of vegetation, its canopy blocking out the sun. The settlers anguished over what they had left behind.

Each family had to build their own rudimentary hut while trying to clear the land for planting. While they worked and ploughed the soil, they had to survive on what little food they had brought with them and some grain supplied occasionally by the Japanese authorities. Some settlers had brought their own seeds to grow crops while some had a few animals with them, such as ducks, chickens, goats, cats and dogs. Nevertheless, the unavoidable fact was that everyone had to grow crops to survive, and to meet Japanese demands.

Pat's parents and other Eurasians from Singapore City environs found it extremely difficult to farm the land. They knew very little of how to sow and grow crops and much had to be learned from Chinese settlers about cultivation. Pat's parents had deliberately travelled with Chinese settlers for that reason. The soil at Fuji-go was poor quality, composed mainly of clay and sand. Water was also scarce and had to be drawn from wells by hand, hauled in buckets from a stream if not too far away, or pumped from bores which had first to be dug.

The tropical downpours, humidity, mosquitos and insects of many kinds added to their misery. The Japanese made all internee settlers work long hours every day whatever the weather. Very soon the infestation of mosquitos spread malaria amongst many of the settlers. In December 1943, Pat's father won an award for his cultivated plot, one of only a few settlers' successes, but there were many failures.

Around this time Pat's mother cut her leg while walking on a sharp-edged tropical plant. Her leg became infected and ulcerated and, because of a lack of medicines and hospital care, gangrene took hold. Her condition became life threatening, and she was taken to a local hospital, but her leg was amputated. It was too late; her kidneys finally failed, and, after much pain and suffering, she died.

This left Pat's father devastated and heartbroken. Sometime later in 1944 in grief he suffered a heart attack and also died. Both Pat's parents were only in their mid- to late-forties. Then, following their deaths, Pat's younger brother Duncan, now an orphan at fourteen, contracted Blackwater fever and died. Meanwhile, in Singapore Pat had not heard anything from her parents and was unaware of their and her brother's deaths. She continued to live in hope that they had found a better life and an unwavering belief that Stan was still alive in Changi prison.[10]

* * *

In the Changi prison the Japanese guards left the daily running to the British officers. Daily tasks were allocated to prisoners such as cooking, cleaning and disposal of human and other waste. Little time was left before evening curfew. The outlook was grim but a determination to endure soon sprang up. It was a daily struggle to survive with minimal healthcare where the risk of incidents causing injury, and the impact of diseases, increased rapidly. The lack of food, clean water and poor sanitation, combined with hard slave labour, took its toll.[11]

In response to the extreme adversity, some prisoners turned to their own inventiveness and improvisation. Professional expertise and specialist knowledge of some inmates, such as medical, dentistry, engineering, gardening, carpentry and other skills, were pursued, so as to subsist as best they could. Work parties of prisoners deployed around Singapore by the Japanese guards were paid a mere 10 cents per day, but it was something. The work outside the prison compound also gave them an opportunity to steal food or buy medicines and other useful items.

Before the transportation of PoWs to overseas countries as slave labour began, the Changi prison population had swollen to around 10,000. Changi had been built to house around 600 prisoners. PoWs slept side by side, with no room to move, and with some out in the open. For all prisoners, PoWs or civilian, hunger was a constant torment. 'When you're really ravenously hungry, you'll eat anything, even bits of army blanket, because the very fact of swallowing something was relieving,' was the opinion of Sergeant David Griffin.[12]

Prisoners were allowed some personal possessions but items such as radios, cameras, compasses etc. were banned. However, some radios and cameras were kept hidden and used only when the guards were not around.

In the former Robertson Barracks, now housing prisoners, one of the rooms was used for church services and named as St Luke's Chapel. One of the PoWs, Bombardier Stanley Warren, painted the wall with exquisite murals of scenes in colour from St Luke's Gospel. Just as inspirational as his paintings was his ingenuity in adapting various materials, such as chalk, to mix hues of paint and the use of human hair collected from prisoners to create paint brushes.[13]

Many PoWs and civilian internees became creative to fend off despair and fill empty hours with meaning. A library was set up with books which prisoners had brought with them. They threw themselves into numerous pursuits, such as embroidery, drawing, painting, acting in a play with other prisoners, writing, music and singing, patient care of other prisoners, teaching and learning. To find some normality in their imprisonment, they turned to creativity and innovation. Any kind of material or discarded items were used for various purposes to make clothes; bits of old pipe, and fragments of old shell cases were made into musical instruments such as a flute. Improvised music and singing lifted their spirits.

The realisation that he had to find a way to survive within himself dawned quickly on Alfred Williams of the Royal Corps of Signals:

> from the start in February 1942, it would be a long time before I became a free man again, with this in mind and the wish to survive the days, weeks, months, and perhaps years, I knew I must make each day useful and interesting.[14]

Sergeant David Griffin of 8th Australian Division summed up what each PoW must do:

> Each man created for himself a microcosm in which he could crawl – flowers, hobbies, poetry, painting, writing, what you will. And the most contented prisoner was the one who could build the most perfect microcosm, and disappear most effectively in it.[15]

David Griffin was one of those PoWs who established a Literary Society in Changi, which provided an escape from the brutality, despair and disease of the Changi prison. Before the war, Griffin was a lawyer, having graduated from Sydney University. Not long after men and women became prisoners, waves of dysentery and depression surged through Changi from which hundreds died, and thousands were left weak and exhausted.[16] The Literary Society offered prisoners an escape, a world of learning, short stories, poetry and plays. It encouraged inmates, many who had never written before, to enter a sanctuary of the mind, by writing and reading their work to other prisoners.[17]

Griffin was like most PoWs in trying to blot out the ignominious surrender to the Japanese. He realised that all one's diminished energy and mental focus must be concentrated on how to survive. Those who could achieve this kind of resilience settled into a meagre day-to-day existence. The Literary Society was one way to live in the past and dream a fantasy life.[18]

Although photography in the prison was banned, some prisoners had smuggled cameras inside. Anyone found with a camera suffered severe punishment. However, the guards tolerated drawing and painting, writing and newsletters, so that such work by inmates has provided a glimpse into that ordeal of prison life under the Japanese regime.

A 'black market' was established in various items in demand for everyday life in prison. Some daring prisoners found ways to get out at night through the prison's barbed-wire fencing, to bring back food, cigarettes and anything useful. Since the Japanese distributed very meagre meal rations, prisoners continually sought alternative sources of food. In October 1942, the prison authority set aside a plot of land to allow prisoners to grow some crops themselves.

Civilian internees and PoWs were distributed across various locations within the former military garrison buildings at Changi. Families of civilians were ruthlessly separated, women and children in one block and men in separate blocks of the original military jail. PoWs were held in other places with British and Australian troops in different compounds, while the former Robertson Barracks housed a shared hospital. As prisoners were selected and sent away by the Japanese as slave labour on work projects overseas, by the end of 1943 the Changi prison population had shrunk to only around 5,000.

Day by day, the toll of injuries, disease and the effects of malnutrition mounted. The lack of food, clean water and other essentials, together with the impact of hard labour, struck down many inmates. Each day, to get through the adversity, the prisoners turned their attention to innovation and to improvise with whatever materials they had to meet their daily needs. Those from pre-war professions, such as engineering, dentistry, medicine, surgery and other medical specialties, and trades and skills such as carpentry, gardening etc., came up with ideas to use anything useful for the prisoners to survive. Even so, by 1944 death by starvation and disease had become rampant.[19] Incarceration seemed to be a life sentence, or until death ended it.

David Griffin wrote a number of poems and read them to other PoWs in the Literary Society. His poem 'Changi Days' was evocative of their living hell, with its final four lines showing the prisoners' despairing dreams:

> These Changi days, Appearing endlessly,
> Squandering the treasures our world has to give,
> Great god, power, being, force, or destiny
> Uproot these strangling wires and let me live.[20]

* * *

Notes

1. Changi Prison Museum, Changi, Singapore.
2. Ibid.; John Nevell, 2/10th Field Regiment, 8th Division, AIF.
3. Veteran's Account, Durston, *In Two Death Camps* (Brittingham, and Payne).
4. Ibid.
5. Ibid.
6. Veteran's account, Clemens, *Clem*, pp.43-4; and private collection
7. Veteran's account, Clemens, op. cit., pp.45-6
8. Veteran's account, Keeling, George; private collection, Keeling, David.
9. Veteran's account, Sebastian, Guy; private collection, Sebastian, Ivan.
10. Changi Prison Museum, op. cit.
11. Ibid.
12. Ibid.; Griffin, David.
13. Changi Prison Museum, op. cit.
14. Ibid.; Williams, Alfred.
15. Changi Prison Museum, op. cit.; Griffin, David.
16. Griffin, *Changi Days*, p.21
17. Changi Prison Museum, op. cit.
18. Griffin, *Changi Days*, pp.50-1.
19. Changi Prison Museum, op. cit.
20. Griffin, *Changi Days*, p.53; Changi Prison Museum, op. cit.

Chapter 14

Slaves of the Emperor – Until you Die!

The use of enemy captives taken prisoner during a war as slaves for forced labour, whether defeated troops or civilians of a conquered country, and working them until they die is a despicable practice as old as the human race. Like its Axis ally, Nazi Germany, the Japanese regime had no hesitation in also exploiting its PoWs and subjugated peoples as forced labour. Such slaves were taken and put to work wherever there was a need to support the Japanese economy and war machine.

Very soon after completing the imprisonment of all captured Allied troops in Changi, many male prisoners were quickly commandeered as forced or slave labour to work on various projects on Singapore Island and mainland Malaya. In the second half of 1942, from Singapore and Japanese-occupied countries throughout South East Asia and the Pacific, thousands were shipped overseas as slave labour for such as the Siam (Thailand)-Burma railway construction and to many other mining and infrastructure worksites in Japanese occupied countries and in Japan itself.

* * *

In one of the train's enclosed stinking cattle trucks David Clemens stood, crammed in shoulder to shoulder with fellow PoWs, and swayed with the train's motion. The heat and humidity were stifling and unbearable. For two days the train trundled north from Singapore through Malaya to Banpong in Siam. The hundreds of PoWs in the cattle trucks had no alternative but to urinate and defecate on the floors of the trucks. Only one meal, a small cupful of rice, was given each day at a station stop. It was September 1942 and Clemens was in a group of PoWs being taken as slave labour to a destination and fate unknown. Like the others being transported he thought they were on a journey to hell, or were already in it. 'It was a nightmare made worse by the fact we were travelling into the unknown.'[1]

On arrival in Banpong, Clemens was put into No.6 working party, in which he and others drew some morale boost from the elan and spirit of fellow brothers-in-arms. No.6 working party consisted mainly of East Surreys and their sister regiment, the Royal Marines. In the Siege of Gibraltar in 1704 Colonel Villier's Marines took part; they later became the East Surrey Regiment. From Banpong, their working party was transported to Kanburi where their first task was to complete the building of a bamboo hut to house about 120 PoWs.

Each hut was 120 feet by 10 feet wide, in which one long continuous bamboo bed stretched the whole length, and on which sixty men slept crammed together side by side. It meant that each man had a bed space two-feet wide and six-feet in length. An open corridor walkway was four-feet wide for the hut's length. At one end of each hut were the external latrines, seven-feet deep, two-feet wide, and fourteen-feet in length, with a number of raised footrests for crouching. Like others, Clemens experienced the distaste encountered if you were not able to use the front trench. It meant that he sat facing the backside of someone in front, as he moved his bowels and flies swarmed around. 'One made a very careful approach for fear of falling into this cesspit, that after initial use became a mass of writhing maggots.'[2]

Once their bamboo hut was complete, Clemens and his group were put to work building the embankments for the railway line, which was to run some 415 kilometres from Banpong in Siam (now Thailand) to Moulmein in Burma. In backbreaking work, they dug out the earth, filled a basket with two handles, carried it to a railway line site, dumped it, then repeated the work continually. Each day, work commenced at 6.00am, with a short break at midday for some rice and cooked vegetables, and lasted until late in the evening under lights.

Illness and death were common. Combined with overwork in tropical heat, the main causes were malnutrition, malaria, dysentery, and tropical ulcers, which hardly any PoW escaped. In bad cases, ulcers could cover a whole leg or arm and amputation was common. In the worst cases, some men were glad the surgeon decided to amputate. Clemens and those who could stomach it were able to watch. 'Amputations became so common that we were encouraged to witness them from outside a mosquito net.'[3]

Clemens was not immune from illness, being struck down by a severe bout of malaria, which put him in the prison hospital to save his life. Once he was discharged, the guards marched him on foot to Kinsayok to work in a railway marshalling yard. After that came a move to Tamarkan to work on the building of the infamous bridge on the river Kwai.

On 24 October, George Keeling, a fellow gunner of Stan Durston, was in another group of PoWs transported by road truck and rail from Singapore through Malaya to Siam. Like Clemens, he was just slave labour and arrived at Tamarkan to be put to work on the Siam-Burma and its river Kwai bridge. Keeling was placed in working group No.10, so probably did not have any contact with Clemens in No.6 Group.[4]

Again and again, Clemens was stunned by the brutality of the guards who, apart from officers and senior ranks, were Korean. They would beat any man who was sick, slow or unable to work. 'I think as they were literally also prisoners of the Japanese they tended to treat PoWs even worse.'[5]

To comprehend, although not to understand, the logic of the Japanese indifference to brutality and the ever-increasing death rate of PoWs, it is necessary to recognise their view that PoWs were a plentiful supply of expendable slaves. To complete the Siam-Burma rail alone, it is estimated that the Japanese used more than 60,000 Allied PoWs and around 250,000 local men as slave labourers. The numbers of prisoners of all nationalities made casualties insignificant. The line was completed in just eighteen months, and the bridge on the river Kwai is still in operation today – a legacy of the obscene human cost. It is estimated that 16,000 Allied PoWs and 90,000 locals died while working on the line's construction.

In addition, in the Japanese way of thinking, to be taken prisoner was dishonourable and to be wounded or become sick was not much better. Clemens saw how they treated their own wounded soldiers at the Kinsayok rail yards.

> In trains arriving in the yards from the Burma front, wounded Japanese troops were dumped in stationary steel trucks, without medical treatment or food, probably en route to Bangkok. It was appalling, we were moved to give them some of our water, and when a train arrived during our meal break we shared our rice with some of them.[6]

In early 1944, Allied air raids on the Japanese in Siam gave Clemens and the other PoWs some hope of surviving their tormented life. On one occasion, they rejoiced on witnessing one such air raid which hit and blew up a nearby ammunition dump.[7]

* * *

Pat Durston's brother Ken who, at 14, had joined the Volunteer Force just before the fall of Singapore, was also a prisoner in Changi. In April 1943, Ken was allocated by the Japanese to a new work group, F-Force. The Japanese spread a cover story that it would be a rest camp with plenty of food. Ken and thousands of PoWs and civilian internees were to be sent to Siam as a labour force. Stan Durston was initially among the men selected but exchanged his place with another man who was not well and who firmly believed the rest camp story, whereas Stan was motivated more to stay in Singapore to be close to Pat and his daughter Barbara. The day came when Ken with the other chosen men were transported in trucks to the Singapore railway station.

They were all boarded onto a train, packed like cattle into steel wagons with little ventilation and those men who had clung to the hope of going to a rest camp quickly faced a grim reality. After several days of the train trundling northwards towards Thailand, in these hot cramped conditions, lacking food, water and toilet facilities men were falling sick. The only chance of a wash was at the occasional places where the train stopped for water for the engine.

The train's final stop was at Bangpong in Thailand from where they walked to Kanchanburi, then on again to work camps at Kami-Sonkuri in the Pagoda Pass, in total more than 100 miles. Although they marched mainly at night, the heat hardly varied and the daily tropical rains meant they were wet nearly all the time. Malaria and dysentery were rife and each day men succumbed to the ordeal. Those who were unwell, like the man who had taken Stan's place, were the first to die. Many developed severe skin complaints but, regardless of the PoWs' condition, the Japanese marched them onward through thick jungle terrain. Dense bamboo covered some tracks and men were constantly bitten by flies, mosquitoes and other insects. Ken felt that he went into a kind of trance.

> I never knew what day it was, or how far we had walked. My family would not know whether I was alive or dead, and their memory was dream-like, very distant. I detached my mind from the past to be able to survive each day.[8]

Ken was placed into camp No.2 at Kami-Sonkurai; all around was the untamed jungle, always damp and intimidating despite the harsh sun. Where the trees were taller and entangled with twisted vines the canopy would filter the sunlight. Brutal punishments, bashings and beatings were carried out daily by Korean guards. Those would regularly result in death for an unfortunate victim. Every day it seemed someone would die.

The railway line had to be built no matter how many men died. All the prisoners were expendable. The Japanese aim was to build a supply route north into Burma and, eventually, to India which they planned to invade next. Using very basic tools, Ken and other prisoners were employed for twelve hours or more each day to smash and crush large rocks into small rocks as ballast which was laid between the sleepers on the railway line.

The building of the railway became a chain of human misery, degradation and death. There was huge loss of life for thousands, a march into hell for all prisoners, who were truly slave labourers. Under atrocious conditions many, probably in the thousands, succumbed to cholera and died. After many months of backbreaking work, Ken also became seriously sick and was lucky to be taken back to a camp at Tambaya where he recovered sufficiently to be transported back to Changi. There he spent the rest of the war, barely surviving on an increasingly meagre food ration, effectively a starvation diet, until the Japanese surrender in August 1945. Despite their deteriorating health, both Ken and Stan, and the other prisoners, were employed on the construction of the runways which after the war would become the basis for Changi airport.[9]

* * *

When the Japanese captured Singapore, Guy Sebastian was 19 years old, an RAF aircraftsman, and among the thousands taken prisoner and marched to Changi. Because of Sebastian's Sri Lankan/Indian heritage, the Japanese authorities tried to coerce him to join the Indian Resistance Army (IRA), which was fighting with Japan for India's independence from the UK. Sebastian was faced with an awful choice: betray his unit and comrades, join the IRA and likely die in battles against the Allies; succumb to torture and possibly die from its effects; or, if he survived the torture, be transported as a slave labourer and worked to death. Sebastian refused to join the IRA and, with seven other PoWs, was tortured by the Japanese to comply. He held out, because of which he was branded with a hot iron to mark his intransigence and subjugate his spirit. It left him with a branding scar the size of a 20c coin on his back.

In the prison accommodation, which comprised buildings of the former British base such as troops' barracks, warehouses and a prison, there was a shortage of everything – clothing, chairs, bedding, food, water and other everyday utensils and equipment. The lack of clean water and proper toilets led to dysentery and many other diseases. Food rations distributed by the Japanese prison guards were meagre, amounting to a typical one to three ounces of weevil-infested meat and rice per person each day. Many prisoners spent much of their time confined in a bare concrete cell with up to eight in a cell that had originally been built for one prisoner.

Sebastian was not held in Changi for long before he was transported with others to work in Java which had also been captured and occupied by the Japanese. From there, he was subsequently shipped to work on the island of Okinawa and then to mainland Japan. Sebastian was in a group of eighty British PoWs who arrived on 14 August 1944 at the Hitachi No.8-B work camp, situated ten kilometres west of the town of Hitachi near Tokyo on the east coast of Honshu. There were about 150 Dutch and 180 American PoWs in the camp. Prisoners worked in the coal and copper mines of the Nippon Mining Company.

In forced labour Sebastian was in effect a slave, working much of the time in a coal or copper mine with no discernible future, only a daily routine. An early death was a probability, perhaps the only certainty. But Sebastian had an aptitude for foreign languages, began to pick up the meaning of the guards' commands and gradually learnt to speak Japanese. This enabled him to act as an interpreter between the Japanese guards, the camp's PoW officers, and his fellow work-group prisoners. It meant that he was seen as very useful to the Japanese authorities and allowed him to communicate on behalf of his fellow prisoners, and help avoid misunderstandings.[10]

* * *

Thousands of PoWs were shipped as slave labour back to the Japanese mainland. Most of the PoW camps were built close to mines and factories in industrial areas between Tokyo and Nagasaki in the south-east of Honshu, while a few stretched farther north on Hokkaido Island. When PoWs came ashore from their prison ships, they were very uncertain what was to become of them. Very quickly, it became apparent that they were mere commodities. Standing on a port's docks or quayside, the men were bedraggled, gaunt and in ragged clothes as they were lined up for inspection. Passing Japanese civilians looked away as businessmen assessed the PoWs as slaves for their company's worksites.

Once they arrived at a work camp their sense of worth, of being a human being was degraded further. Short haircuts, that were shaven nearly bald, plus drab, numbered Japanese uniforms enforced by the camp guards, undermined the men's sense of being a military prisoner. The winter of 1943-44 in Japan was severe, the coldest for seventy years. In conjunction with the hard labour, little food of poor nutrition, freezing temperatures, no heating, the lethal impact of respiratory diseases such as pneumonia hit hard and the death toll increased rapidly.

As the war progressed during 1944-45 and the Allies advanced across South East Asia and the Pacific, imports of raw materials such as coal into Japan were being restricted. Shortages forced the Japanese to re-open old coal mines on their mainland. For the PoWs working in the mines, that made their jobs even more dangerous. A lack of equipment and vehicles meant that work was manually very intensive. In addition, in some mines, once men were underground, they could walk up to two hours to reach the coal face, then work for eight hours or more, then walk back for two hours to the mineshaft.[11]

The Japanese military authorities must have taken a particular dislike to Sir Shenton Thomas, the Governor of Singapore. For some opaque reason, the Japanese only kept Thomas in Changi for nine months. Rather than leave him there, they then transported him to Takao, a bleak cold prison island in the north of Japan. His wife Daisy remained an inmate of the Sime Road prison block at Changi.[12] Like Stan and Pat Durston, their separation and each not knowing if the other was alive or dead, would have been heartbreaking – an anguish impossible to imagine.

Notes

1. Veteran's account, Clemens, *Clem*, p.57, and private collection.
2. Veteran's account, Clemens, op.cit., p.58
3. Ibid., p.59
4. Veteran's account, Keeling, George; private collection, Keeling, David.
5. Veteran's account, Clemens, op.cit., p.58
6. Ibid., p.59
7. Ibid., pp.57-61
8. Veteran's account, Durston, *In Two Death Camps*, (Brittingham, and Payne)
9. Ibid.
10. Veteran's account, Sebastian, Guy
11. Nelson, *Prisoners of War*, pp.177-87
12. Shenton, *Diary 1942*; Evans, *Air Battle for Burma*, pp.39-42

Chapter 15

Liberation – and the Ultimate Triumph

The days, weeks and months passed and, in PoW camps, turned into years of endless drudgery and ever-debilitating health. For PoWs who continued to survive, and civilians under the Japanese yoke wherever they were, there was no dependable news of the war and no sense of whether their purgatory would ever end.

During 1944, Pat Durston and her daughter Barbara in Singapore were able to travel on a goods train to Bahau in Malaya to see her parents and brother, only to find on arrival that all three had died without them knowing. Once again, Pat's life had changed in the most tragic way. Any thought of staying in Bahau and living with her parents was extinguished. She returned to Singapore to find a way for the survival of herself and her daughter. It was two years since she had seen or had word from Stan and she had no idea whether he was still alive. She was alone, not knowing what was to happen to her next.

Along with many others who had to wear a star on their clothing, on 28 March 1945 Pat and Barbara were imprisoned in the Sime Road Internment Camp in Singapore. Her family were now all lost and left behind in Bahau. Being thrown into prison was another blow and further heartbreak for Pat. She was young, still in her teens, and vulnerable, having everyone she had loved taken from her slowly one by one. Still not knowing what had happened to her husband Stan, all she had was Barbara.

Pat never found out what had happened to her family's bodies in Bahau. They may have ended up in a communal grave or in the jungle swamps; there are no known records of the people who were transported there to be forgotten as the incidental deaths of the war. Pat believed that her parents and younger brother were just three of some 300 people who had died of poor health and disease at Bahau. She could only make the best of the time she was now given. She began to feel some relief to be entering Sime Road Camp, hoping for a degree of protection and to feel settled in one place. Her hopes were to be short-lived.

Sime Road Internment Camp was situated opposite the Singapore Golf Club near McRichie Reservoir. The camp, which had been previously the Malay Military Command and damaged in the Japanese invasion had been rebuilt by PoWs during the years since 1941. Unlike Changi, which enclosed PoWs behind a barbed-wire fence, Sime Road was only surrounded by natural fencing, known as a Kajang fence, to keep the internees inside the camp, although there was a constant watch by guards. Any attempt to escape was pointless as there was nowhere to go for sanctuary. To get off the island was nearly impossible. If it was tried, on recapture a severe beating or death would be the punishment.

Mistreatment was inflicted by the Japanese guards on men, women and children alike. Day-to-day living was such a huge effort that, by early 1945, many people were too weak or sick to try to do anything but survive from one day to the next. Over the years, the Japanese had been holding on to and storing the Red Cross parcels for their own use instead of distributing them to PoWs and internees. Only on special occasions were a few parcels distributed, and in those all the food rations had been pilfered. In the daily rationing of food and rice, maggots were a big part of the internees' diet.

In Sime Road Camp more than 5,000 internees co-existed in cramped flea-bitten, bug-infested conditions. The women and children were segregated from the men, and work was allocated according to age and wellbeing. But everyone was expected to do something to survive. After years of barbaric Japanese repression and captivity, many prisoners were dying daily in both Sime Road and Changi. Pat had not heard a word from Stan in Changi over the years, although she harboured a hope that he was still alive. Devoid of any news, no one could see an end to the war and their plight.

Pat was now 19 years old, with a Sime Road Camp number 4318, and an ID number 1355; her daughter Barbara's number was 1354. Her arrival at Sime Road was recorded by a Captain Nelson, who noted everyone who entered the camp. Those records are held in the Imperial War Museum in London. Pat spoke very little of the camp's conditions, but said:

> Some women's hair turned white as if overnight. And some women even became very friendly with the guards to seek their favours. You could not be too judgemental, as each person had an agenda to stay alive the best way that they could.

When the guards came looking for young women, the women who were openly prostitutes would try to hide Pat so that she could not be seen. Barbara saw two guards dragging her mother Pat away, as she tried to resist and kick them. So as to be not seen alone, and as an easy target for the guards, women walked around in pairs as much as possible.

Clean water was always in short supply in the camp as were food and medical supplies. Many internees died from malnutrition and all were very thin and fading away. Some became too sick to go on and just gave up living. Malaria, beri-beri, dysentery, body lice, skin ulcers and malnutrition were common.

Pat would save some of her daily rice ration, go without herself, so that there was extra nourishment for Barbara who, like many others, was suffering from rickets, worms, lice and malaria and was lacking the necessary calorie intake so important for a child. Many times Pat thought that Barbara would not make it through the night. Luckily, the internees at Sime Road had a doctor amongst them, on whom Pat was able to call. Despite Pat's inexperience, with her maternal instinct and care she was able to sustain Barbara.[1]

* * *

While Pat and Barbara in Sime Road and Stan and Ken in Changi were struggling to just survive, Pat's cousin Sonny was still evading capture by continuing to work as a fisherman. On 30 January 1945, while fishing in the strait, his fishing boat came under fire from a British submarine. The boat was hit, burst into flames and began to sink. In the confusion, Sonny saw his chance, dived into the sea and swam towards the submarine, frantically calling for help.

The submarine came around and plucked Sonny and a Japanese fisherman out of the water. After spending some weeks on board the submarine, he was handed over to the authorities in the port of Fremantle in Western Australia. Because of the risk of Sonny and the Japanese fisherman being spies, they were both imprisoned. Once the authorities were able to verify that he was a citizen of Singapore and not a threat, he was released with new papers and sent by train across Australia to an internment camp in Queensland. How lucky this outcome was for Sonny as in his previous circumstances he might not have survived. Back in Singapore, however, Sonny's family was notified by the Japanese authorities that he had drowned at sea with the rest of the crew.

During Stan Durston's time as a PoW in Changi he always kept a photograph of Pat and himself on their wedding day in 1941. One of the PoWs was Leo Rawlings, a sketch artist. Stan asked him to sketch two copies of himself and Pat from their wedding photograph. After the war, Leo Rawlings became famous for his wartime sketches depicting the daily lives of PoWs.

By the end of 1944 Stan had worked nearly everywhere in Singapore – the cookhouse, the vegetable gardens, the barracks, the docks, many buildings across Singapore and digging tunnels under what is now Changi airport. When working on the docks, at one time a PoW with only one leg steered a truck without an engine while other PoWs had to pull it with a rope. The Japanese guards made the PoWs work twelve hours a day under a boiling hot sun. The language barrier and culture clash with the guards could at times make things even worse.

However, Stan had some ability to converse with the Japanese. Because of his love of languages, he could speak his native Welsh and English and also a little Tamil, Malay and Japanese. Sometimes his ability to understand a few Japanese words could bring a favour for him and his fellow PoWs. A Japanese sergeant would say to Stan that if he got the men to work a little faster, he would then get them some extra food, such as tapioca or sweet potatoes. The sergeant would then receive praise from his senior officers.

Most of the time, the men would steal vegetables and fruit from gardens and farming plots to obtain extra food if they had an opportunity while out on working parties and smuggle them back into the camp. They did this to stay alive but if caught beatings would be inflicted on a whole group, not just one man. As a result, many PoWs suffered and some died from their injuries. For some transgressions those caught were sent to Outram Road jail, where they were beaten and tortured, then sent back dead to Changi. In this time of misery and captivity, death was an adversary which you could meet on any day.

Finding any way to supplement the meagre ration of rice was an existential need. One day, while Stan was working in a party on a railway line, someone spotted a local man with a young calf. After some lengthy bartering for the calf, they managed to smuggle it back into the camp. The PoW cook was a butcher by trade, so he quickly dealt with the calf. It was then cooked, shared out and eaten by the men before the Japanese guards could find it and take it for themselves.

Snakes, rats, anything that crawled and could be caught was added to their cooking pots as protein and then added to their daily quota of four ounces of rice per man per day. As for those who were sick, each healthy man would donate one ounce of rice out of his own food to help the sick survive. It was a case of no work, no food according to the Japanese rules. Sadly, most of the sick died anyway. Because of the lack of vitamin B in their daily diet, Stan was always aware of losing his eyesight as had happened before for three weeks. When cooking the daily rice rations, the maggots were left in because of a belief that they added some protein, and even some flavour.

Co-operation amongst the prisoners was essential to help each other and stay alive. Stan always tried to keep his brain alert and his body active to keep himself going, so he could lose patience with anyone who had a defeatist attitude. On one occasion, a Scottish soldier told him that he could not go on any longer and that he wanted to give up and die. Stan was immediately so riled that he said that he ought to be ashamed to call himself a Scotsman. The soldier jumped from his seat, clenched his fists and threatened to hit Stan. He told the Scot this had brought out his fighting spirit and, hopefully, would enable him to survive.

One of the PoWs, who had been best man at Stan and Pat's wedding, was allocated by the Japanese with many others to be shipped to Java and then on to Japan as slave labour. The men were embarked and crowded into stuffy ships' holds with no light and little ventilation. At sea, en route from Java to Japan, some of those prison ships were sunk by Allied submarines and aircraft unaware that they were full of PoWs, most of whom stood little chance of surviving and therefore drowned.

By 1945, in the humidity of tropical conditions the clothing and footwear of prisoners in Changi was either threadbare or non-existent. Stan had become accustomed to going barefoot and swore that he could walk on barbed wire and not feel it since his feet had become so calloused and hardened over the years. Many men had succumbed to diseases such as cholera, dysentery, beri-beri, malaria and others endemic to the tropics. Out of Stan's artillery unit, of an original ninety-eight men only twenty remained alive.

Around this time Stan contracted beri-beri in his groin where his testicles were peeling and enlarged, and in his tongue which was also peeling. As a result, he became jaundiced and very sick but was still beaten by the guards for working too slowly. The Japanese guards would shout 'kurra speedo'. Although some men gave up on living, that was mainly in those severely weakened by sickness and disease. The boreholes dug to be used as toilets were a death trap for the weak and frail. At night, many a sick man would fall into one of the holes and be unable to crawl out. They then died from the gases and fumes.

There were also many tunnels and trenches dug around Singapore. Stan and other surviving PoWs feared that, before the Allies could reach Singapore and liberate them, the Japanese were likely to execute the remaining prisoners and dispose of the bodies in the tunnels and trenches. It was an understandable fear. After three and a half years of the most degrading and brutal captivity, men were just shadows of their once strong youth. With hope of rescue all but gone, many were both physically and mentally broken.[2]

* * *

From working on the Siam-Burma railway at Tamarkand, David Clemens was moved to a new work camp at Takuli, near to the border with China. The work was building a jungle airstrip for the Japanese air force. In Clemens' view, because the air force guards were more lenient, the work was more productive, without the constant screaming of 'Speedo!' and frequent beatings.

When, in mid-1945, the guards re-allocated Clemens and his fellow PoWs away from work on the airstrip and put them to work on digging defensive trenches, rumours spread that the Allies were making major gains in the war. In addition, the Japanese separated all PoW officers from other ranks. If the war was turning in the Allies' favour, were the guards worried that there might be a rebellion by PoWs organised by the officers? Clemens began to think that the rumours were more believable than so many others in the past. 'After over three years in captivity without real news, we just had to cling to and believe in what little rays of hope there were on offer.'[3]

Then one morning in the middle of August 1945 Clemens lined up with the other PoWs in the normal routine and waited for the guards to march them to the day's work at the airstrip. It was nearly finished, apart from some tidying up. For nearly four hours, they stood around waiting until they were told to stand down as work was halted. Gossip and speculation soared. Were Allied troops approaching? Could the war soon be over?

Time passed slowly into the afternoon and Clemens felt the uncertainty arising in some 300 PoWs. Would the guards shoot them all before Allied troops arrived?: 'the Japs were still in charge and we were still confined to the camp area, there was no word from them of the war being over, but what else could it be?'[4]

As there were no guards to be seen, Clemens and three other PoWs decided to walk to the nearest local village to see if they had any news. As they emerged into a clearing, they were confronted by the sight of three British paratrooper officers walking in their direction. They had been dropped by parachute near various PoW camps to arrange for the Japanese to hand over their arms and organise the evacuation of PoWs.

The paratroopers brought news that, on 16 August, the Japanese Emperor had announced Japan's surrender – it was all over. A few days later a Dakota aircraft landed and took out the first group of PoWs. However, it was unauthorised and further flights were delayed because of cholera breaking out at a nearby camp. Not until 20 September did Clemens get his flight out. He and some thirty other men huddled on the plane's bare deck, which had previously been used for carrying freight. They did not care, they had no luggage, no clothes but the rags on their backs – but they were alive, free, and going home.[5]

* * *

The last few months in Changi, April to August in 1945, were very difficult. Food had just about been exhausted, not only for the prisoners, but also for the Japanese and people of Singapore. Rumours were circulating that the war was tipping very strongly in favour of the Allies. This was reinforced by the Japanese more frequently releasing their hoarded Red Cross parcels to the PoWs.

As word-of-mouth rumours spread of the war nearing its end and circulated amongst PoWs, internees and Japanese guards, conditions were slowly changing for the better. Letters and postcards to family members were now being allowed.

Stan and Pat were able to send messages to each other. When the first Allied planes flew over Changi, Stan's excitement was so hard to contain. Leaflets were dropped telling the prisoners and Japanese that the war was over. After the Japanese cities of Hiroshima and Nagasaki had been destroyed by atomic bombs, the Emperor had ordered a surrender. Japanese troops must surrender everywhere, and all hostilities had to stop.

For Stan Durston this news stirred an emotion that had lain dormant for three and half years. His dream was no longer just to survive, but of a new life with Pat and his daughter Barbara. He had an unbreakable belief that they were still alive somewhere. Yet, when the first Allied troops and medical staff arrived at Changi, they were horrified at the squalid living conditions in the camp and the emaciated state of the PoWs and internees. When cigarettes were handed out, although he did not smoke, Stan took one in the excitement.

Then when Stan and Pat each learned through messages that they had survived, and Barbara too, they were so overjoyed – impossible for anyone else to describe. What elation they all felt at liberation, a wonderful time for everyone in the camps. Very soon it was the Japanese who had to remain behind barbed wire. All prisoners were instructed to remain where they were as medical supplies, food and help would be arriving soon. The occupation and captivity that had lasted for three and half years had finally come to an end.

Sadly though, for some men it was too late, since at first their emaciated bodies could not digest the solid foods being distributed. For many, this intolerance to normal food contributed to their deaths, so tragic after struggling to stay alive for so long. Some foods were recalled and dietary content modified. For a while Stan kept to Nestle's condensed milk, until his body could tolerate solid foods. In time things began to improve.

From what Stan had saved from the daily 10 cents pay and his canny loans and trades, he was able to send Pat $4 whenever he could, within the new regulations, to help with her needs and Barbara's. His ability to survive had been a combination of good luck, determination and ability to adapt to any situation and so, coming out of those dark years, he found so much hope.

For Stan, Pat, their daughter Barababara and brother Ken, it had been three and half years of hell and separation, yet they were alive and reasonably healthy. In a heart-wrenching reunion the tears flowed. All four were very thin and malnourished but very excited that this day had finally come. For Pat, her thoughts sadly were also for her father and mother and youngest brother who had not survived.

The conditions in the camps for internees and PoWs alike had been appalling with meagre food rations and hardly any medicines available for the sick. It had meant that those who were ill either suffered through their sickness and recovered, or simply died. Some went out of their minds in fear of the daily reprisals that often took place.

Barbara was 3 years old and, having only known the camp life, was shy and bewildered. At first, she felt quite uncertain of these two men, Stan her father and Ken her uncle. It did not take long, however, before the four of them with other internees and PoWs were living in a new routine with improved food, clothes and healthcare. The fit and well were placed in a selection programme in which arrangements were made to evacuate soldiers and their families to their own countries as soon as passenger ships were ready to take them.

After clean clothes were issued, showers, medical examinations and treatments completed satisfactorily, the day came. Stan, Pat, Barbara and Ken were issued with passes to leave Singapore to travel by ship for England. After several days of waiting, all four set sail in September 1945, destination Liverpool, on the SS *Monawai*. What thoughts went through their minds as they sailed away? They had spent three and a half years in a living hell, on a once thriving Singapore island which had been left ravished by war and destruction.

Every liberated internee and PoW had in effect been given a life sentence of memories of their days as prisoners, of what they endured to survive, and of so many people who had suffered and perished under the flag of the Rising Sun. For those lucky to be alive and leaving, they never wanted to speak of Singapore, Changi or the camps again. It was time to bury the past and to look forward to a brighter future without the constant threat of death each day.

The ship called at Colombo in Ceylon (now Sri Lanka) for further health checks and more clean clothes for the ex-prisoners. While in port, a photograph was taken of Pat, Stan and Barbara, which was published in a London newspaper, entitled 'Three came back'. It was a picture of Pat holding Barbara, and Stan in khaki uniform, standing at the ship's rail.

It is impossible to imagine the impact of the war and being imprisoned on Stan and Pat's early years of marriage. They had been apart far longer than the few months they had known each other before the Japanese invasion. For three and a half years, the daily fear of death and finding the courage to keep on going to survive must have penetrated deep into their souls. It seemed to them that fate spared so many people while others were not so fortunate.

Maybe destiny played a part. Unknown to them, they had all played a part in the shaping and outcome of the Second World War. A time of cruelty, savagery and barbarity was thrust upon Stan and Pat and their generation, and they came through it.[6]

* * *

While Stan and Pat Durston were en route to Britain, news of their survival was reported in a London newspaper of late 1945:

> Gunner Stanley Durston the son of Mrs B. Williams and the late Mr Durston of Wembley, London, has been a prisoner of war (PoW) of the Japanese since the fall of Singapore in February 1942. After being liberated, Stanley Durston has recently met his wife Pat, who had been interned by the Japanese, and his three-year-old daughter, Barbara, whom he had never seen. They are now on their way by ship to England.
>
> While serving in the Regular Army, Durston married Pat before the Japanese invasion. While a PoW he was unable to see his wife, who gave birth to their daughter Barbara while Durston was in prison. Mrs Williams has not seen her son since his marriage and will meet his wife Pat for the first time when they arrive in England.
>
> For more than two years Durston was reported as 'Missing', until his mother received a card from him saying that he was alive. Nor had she heard from Pat until she [had] recently received a letter with a photograph of Stan and Pat re-united, and holding their daughter Barbara.

Stan and Pat Durston with their daughter Barbara duly re-united with Stan's mother. In due course, Stan gained an appointment as assistant manager with Pearl Assurance Company in Harrow, London. Later, in 1958, with two more children, Alan and Carol, they emigrated to Australia where two more daughters, Debbie and Cheryl, were born. Stan and Pat's initiative and spirit to live life to the full was undiminished, and their special bond unbroken by the suffering endured during the war.

Stan loved socialising, always a smile on his face, and, from his Welsh upbringing, possessed a rich tenor voice, with which he played the leading man in a production of the famous musical 'The Student Prince'. Pat also enjoyed the social life which came with Stan's work but, first and foremost, loved her family of five children and fourteen grandchildren.

Pat's family remember her as a caring, wonderful mother who provided them with a spotless and welcoming home. She never complained, got on with life which, as a survivor of the war, her ordeals had taught her. In 1982, at only 57, Pat died from cancer. Stan died in 2001. Their descendants, who now include twenty-seven great grandchildren, will always remember them as an inspiration to them all.[7]

* * *

David Clemens returned to his hometown of Colchester in Essex, UK. He weighed only seven stones and, compared with his former self, his body was just skin and bone. Clemens was confronted with an unimaginable family tragedy. In the final months of the war his twin sister Dorothy had been killed in a German V2 rocket attack and another sister had died when her home was hit in a Luftwaffe bombing raid. Yet he had survived more than three years in a Japanese PoW camp and his brother had been a PoW in a German camp where, despite a horrendous march in winter through Poland when many froze to death, he had also lived through it. Clemens vowed to always count his blessings and make every day a happy one.

In Colchester, he met Irene Mercer and their relationship blossomed. He signed up in November 1945 for another twenty-two years in the Army and, in January 1946, he and Irene married. Clemens did not forget his talent for running. At age 67 he took it up again, competing in such as the London and Glasgow marathons, and internationally in Canada and Australia. Slaving for the Emperor had not broken David Clemens.[8]

* * *

On the completion of the Siam-Burma rail line, George Keeling and his working group were moved to another worksite. When the Japanese surrender came, he was in a camp in Saigon, Vietnam, from where he was evacuated in September 1945 to the UK. Back in his hometown of Cheadle in 1949, George married Mary Smith and, having left the army, moved back into the civilian workforce. George gained an appointment as manager of Maunders paint and wallpaper store, first in Gloucester for fourteen years, then in Shrewsbury for twenty years.

While living in Shrewsbury he also served for twenty years in the Royal Observer Corps. George and Mary had three children, Jane in 1950, David in 1952 and Helen in 1957. Although like so many, probably the majority of veterans, the war and PoW experience left George with the effects of PTSD, he retained an engaging outgoing personality with those he got to know. He had found a way to overcome everything that the slavemasters of the PoW camps had thrown at him.[9]

* * *

At Tokyo PoW Camp No. 8-B at Hitachi after the Japanese surrender on 15 August 1945, Guy Sebastian was given two letters of recommendation by two American officers of the camp's PoW HQ, Major Earl P. Short and Captain Charles Underwood, both of the US Army. In the letters he was commended for discharging his duties, often in charge of working groups:

> Guy Sebastian, a member of this command, has been an outstanding soldier and individual during most trying times at this prisoner of war camp. His loyalty and energy are recognised by the men and officers here (Captain Charles Underwood).
>
> His knowledge of and efforts with the Japanese language were a great help to the prisoners on many occasions (Major Earl P. Short).

Sebastian returned to Kuala Lumpur in Malaya and took up an appointment as a hospital assistant in a dental hospital. He also founded a branch of St John Ambulance, served as its area staff officer and had a successful career in the dental and health services industry. The years of PoW slave labour had failed to diminish or weaken Guy Sebastian.

Sebastian was very well liked by everyone and was awarded an honorary medal by the local sultan for his services to the community. Guy married and had two children, a son Ivan and daughter Nellie. Ivan emigrated to Australia and named his son, Guy, after his grandfather. Guy Sebastian, with the same name as his grandfather who survived more than three years as a Japanese prisoner of war, is a very popular and successful singer, entertainer and presenter on TV and in other media in Australia.[10]

* * *

In 2002, Sir David Griffin put together and published a selected collection of some of the poems written by PoWs of the Changi Literary Society. In his introduction in this book of poems by himself and other PoWs in Changi PoW camp, Griffin tells of how sometimes people ask how PoWs of the Japanese were eventually freed. His answer is:

> We were saved by the atomic bomb.
>
> We were ... due for execution the day after any invader set foot on the sacred soil of Japan, ... or of Singapore. Later we learnt that our execution had been in fact imminent ... .[11]

The atomic bomb providentially saved the lives of PoWs in the many Japanese camps throughout South-East Asia, the Pacific and Japan. The Japanese military had issued orders to execute and dispose of all PoWs if Allied forces invaded Japan.

David Griffin returned home to Sydney where he practised law, became chairman of Nabalco, a major alumina producer, served as alderman and later as

Lord Mayor of Sydney. In 1972, he was appointed CBE and, in 1974, knighted for public services.[12]

The former Governor of Singapore, Sir Shenton Thomas, survived his captivity in the bleak winters of northern Japan while his wife, Lady Daisy Thomas, also lived through her time in the Sime Road prison camp in Singapore. Like Stan and Pat Durston, they endured the constant anguish of separation and the mental desolation of not knowing the plight of the other. They only had the hope that their partner was alive and that they themselves would survive. But they did and were duly re-united on liberation.

* * *

On 22 January 1946, Major Bill Gingell attended a Reunion Dinner of the British Battalion. In his speech at the dinner, Lieutenant Colonel C.E. Morrison, who commanded the British Battalion in the Malaya campaign, thanked Major Gingell for making the arrangements for the Reunion Dinner and for keeping the Battalion well fed during the campaign.

To those present who had been PoWs like himself, he stated how lucky they were, as after the war a document had been found at the Japanese HQ in Bangkok ordering a local commander to 'dispose of the prisoners as thought fit'. Morrison also emphasised to everyone that the Battalion had done everything expected of it: 'The British Battalion never gave up any ground throughout the campaign without definite orders from Brigade HQ.'

Nearly three months after his remarkable escape from Singapore, on 9 May 1942 Bill Gingell had disembarked at Liverpool. Just three weeks later, on 1 June, he finalised his account of his experience of the Malaya campaign. But did he post that letter, which he had written on 8 April onboard ship? This collection of stories has come full circle. Did Mrs Thompson receive Gingell's letter? Perhaps a relative or friend of Gingell or Mrs Thompson may read this book and be able to solve this mystery.[13]

* * *

It has been estimated that in the Second World War there were 50-55 million civilian deaths, 20-25 million military deaths and five million deaths in PoW camps.

The survivors, a few of whose stories have been told in this book, like millions of others, stared down the forces of evil and, with a combination of resilience, stoicism, belief and some good fortune, returned to a new life and so achieved their personal and ultimate triumph over man's inhumanity to man.

Notes

1. Veteran's Account, Durston, Private collection; *In Two Death Camps* (Brittingham, and Payne).
2. Ibid.
3. Veteran's account, Clemens, *Clem*, pp.65-6; private collection (H. Skilton, and B Evans.)
4. Ibid.
5. Ibid.
6. Veteran's Account, Durston, op. cit.
7. Ibid.
8. Veteran's account, Clemens, *Clem*, pp.68-80, op.cit.
9. Veteran's account, Keeling, George; private collection, Keeling, David.
10. Veteran's account, Sebastian, Guy; private collection, Sebastian, Ivan.
11. Griffin, *Changi Days*, p.27; Changi Prison Museum, op. cit.
12. Griffin, op. cit., p.12.
13. Gingell, Captain W., *The Malaya Campaign 1941-42* (The British Battalion, Reunion Meeting), Ref SHC ESR/3/8/3.

Postscript

Survival, an Obsession

After the Kempei-Tai guards had pushed the bleeding McCormac back into the Singapore compound he knew that the next time the Japanese took him for interrogation, they would torture him to death. The next torture session came soon enough. A Kempei-Tai officer, Teruchi, pulled his Samurai sword out of its scabbard and, with two hands, waved the blade inches from McCormac's eyes.

> Teruchi jabbed but McCormac, tensed and waiting, managed to jerk his head aside in time to save his eye. The point speared through the fold of skin at the corner of his eye, grated on the bone and tore through and out.[1]

Very few prisoners in Singapore managed to escape. In his book *Escape or Die*, the celebrated author Paul Brickhill wrote the enthralling title story of how McCormac escaped the clutches of his Japanese captors in Singapore. With others from a slave labour work-gang, he escaped from Singapore by way of a small boat to Java and, after five months on the run, was eventually rescued by an RAAF Catalina flying boat.

Paul Brickhill was a fighter pilot who made his own incredibly fortunate escape. On 17 March 1943, flying a Spitfire in No.92 Squadron RAF against Axis forces in Tunisia, he was shot down by an enemy fighter. Brickhill's parachute opened only seconds before landfall and despite being dragged by the parachute across a minefield and suffering serious injuries and wounds, he survived.

He was captured and sent to Stalag Luft III PoW camp south of Berlin, where he helped organise an escape plan for a large number of the PoWs. Secretly he documented what in 1950 would become a worldwide bestseller book, *The Great Escape*, and subsequently a similarly very successful film of the same name. He also wrote two anthologies of escape stories, *Escape to Danger* and *Escape or Die*.

Millions of men and women, military and civilian, knew the all-consuming fever to escape from the enemy or survive as a prisoner. Brickhill was one of the most accomplished in putting such experiences into words. He himself had known and endured the struggle to survive, the fear, the self-doubt, the physical pain and mental demons to be overcome. In a German PoW camp, and then post-war, Brickhill had an insatiable drive to tell the stories of survivors' ordeals. In addition to his books, he wrote stand-alone articles on incredible escape and survival stories.

In *Seconds to Live* by Brickhill, Harry Wheeler was flying an RAF Typhoon fighter in August 1944, strafing German troops with rocket and cannon fire. On 8 August he was shot down but crash-landed behind Allied lines. The next day he was not so lucky and, when shot down and captured, felt that he had little chance of survival as a PoW. But like so many he found a way, the strength to never give up and, with good fortune, survive.

It is said that every participant in a battle has a differing, unique and personal perspective of its engagements and course. We all apply some coherence in telling or recording the many chaotic and random experiences of our lives. Inevitably in survivors' stories there will be some subliminal influence of relief in the telling. Yet Paul Brickhill knew only too well the adrenaline surge and trauma of escape and survival. He narrated his escape stories as any writer must do, to both inform and engage the reader's interest. While Brickhill's skill as a storyteller is self-evident, the essence of his work retains the authenticity of the survivors' eyewitness accounts, and he clearly became somewhat obsessed with telling their stories.

The concept for this book, its stories of escape and survival by both military troops and civilians, was born in the depths of the pandemic. To write the stories in this book, and hopefully for its readers, has been inspirational. It became for me an obsessive challenge.

* * *

On 28 January 1742 thirty emaciated Royal Navy sailors staggered ashore on the Brazilian coast from a battered small boat, which was waterlogged and close to sinking. Some nine months earlier those men and fellow crew had been shipwrecked nearly 3,000 miles to the south on a desolate uninhabited island off the coast of Patagonia. They claimed that they were the only surviving crew from HMS *Wager*, although they were accused of being mutineers. In one of the longest voyages by castaways ever recorded, they had named their patched together boat, '*Speedwell*'.

While writing this Postscript I happened to be reading *The Wager* by David Grann,[2] a tale of shipwreck, mutiny and murder in which I found an uncanny coincidence or happenstance. In Chapter 1 of *Escape, Survive – or Die*, 'The miraculous evacuation at Dunkirk – but is there still time for a French romance?' Bill and Augusta Hersey were able to escape across the Channel in the Royal Navy minesweeper HMS *Speedwell*.

Perhaps it was karma telling me the book was now complete.

Notes

1. Brickhill, *Escape or Die*, pp.12 & 21
2. Grann, *The Wager*, p.163

Bibliography and Sources

Bauer, Lieutenant Colonel E., *The History of World War II*, Lifetime Distributers, Sydney, Australia, and Amber Books Ltd, London 2009.

Beevor, Anthony, *The Second World War*, Back Bay Books, Hachette Group, New York, USA 2012.

Boettcher, Brian, *Eleven Bloody Days, The Battle for Milne Bay*, Alan Emery Hyland Printing, Sydney, Australia.

Brickhill, Paul. *Escape or Die*, Book Club Ass., Bell & Hyman Ltd, London 1985.

Brotherton, Joyce M., *Press on Regardless* (unpublished), Imperial War Museum (Cat. No. 6649 97/25/1)

Burn, Alan, *The Fighting Captain*, Pen & Sword Books Ltd, UK, 2022.

Chant, Chris, *Aircraft of World War II*, Amber Books Ltd, London 1999.

Cheshire, Group Capt. Leonard, VC DSO DFC, *Bomber Pilot*, Hutchinson & Co, Ltd, 1954.

Clarke, Hugh, *Prisoners of War*, Time Life Books, Sydney, Australia, 1988.

Cleaver, TM, *I Will Run Wild – The Pacific War from Pearl Harbor to Midway,* Osprey Publishing Ltd, UK. 2020.

Clemens, David, *Clem*, Horseshoe Press, Colchester UK, 1990.

Collier, Richard, *The Sands of Dunkirk*, Collins, London, 1961.

——, *War in the Desert*, Time Life Books, Caxton Publishing Group, London, 2004

Cooper, Anthony, and Perl, Thorsten, *Dispatch from Berlin*, New South Publishing, Sydney Australia 2023

Corfield, Justin, *The Fall of Singapore*, Talisman Publishing Pte Ltd, Singapore, 2019.

Crosby, Francis, *A Handbook of Fighter Aircraft*, Imperial War Museum, Hermes House.

Daniell, David Scott, *The History of the East Surrey Regiment – Volume IV*, Ernest Benn Ltd, London, 1957

Doherty, Richard, *Churchill's Greatest Fear, The Battle of the Atlantic*, Pen & Sword Books Ltd, UK, 2015.

Elphick, Peter, *The Pregnable Fortress*, Hodder & Stoughton, London, 1995

Evans, Bryn, *The Decisive Campaigns of the Desert Air Force 1942-1945*, Pen & Sword Books Ltd, UK, 2014.

Evans, Bryn, *Air Battle for Burma*, Pen & Sword Books Ltd, UK, 2016.

——, *Airmen's Incredible Escapes*, Pen & Sword Books Ltd, UK, 2020.

Fahey, *The Factory,* Vol.1 1947-1972, Allen & Unwin, Sydney, Australia 2023.

Gibbs, Patrick, Wing Commander, *Torpedo Leader on Malta*, Grub Street, London, 2002.

Grann, David, *The Wager*, Simon & Schuster Ltd, UK, 2024.

Griffin, *Changi Days,* Simon and Schuster Pty Ltd, Australia, 2002.

Hall, Timothy, *The Fall of Singapore* 1942, Methuen Australia Pty. Ltd., 1983.

Herington, John, *Air War Against Germany and Italy 1939 -1943*, Australian War Memorial, Halstead Press, Sydney 1954.

Holland, James, *Big Week*, Bantam Press, Penguin, UK 2018.

Kennedy, *Menace*, Book Club Associates, UK 1979.

Konstam, *The Battle of North Cape*, Pen & Sword Books Ltd, UK, 2014.
Korda, Michael, *Alone*, Liveright Publishing Corporation, New York, 2017.
Larson, Erik, *The Splendid and the Vile*, Crown/Random House, New York, 2022.
Loosely, Stephen, *Wartime Charter a handy blueprint for the Indo-Pacific*, US Studies Centre, University of Sydney, Australia, 2023.
Mackersey, Ian, *Into the Silk*, Granada Publishing Ltd, London, 1978.
Mann, Leslie, *And Some Fell on Stony Ground*, Icon Books Ltd, London, 2014.
Masters, David, *So Few*, Eyre & Spottiswood Ltd, London 1945.
Meyerowitz, Seth, *The Lost Airman,* Atlantic Books, London, 2016.
Middlebrook, Martin, *The Nuremberg Raid*, Cassell & Co, London, 2000.
——, *The Berlin Raids*, Cassell & Co, London, 2002.
——, *The Battle of Hamburg*, Cassell & Co, London 2000.
——, and Everitt, Chris, *The Bomber Command War Diaries: An Operational Reference Book 1939-1945*, Midland Publishing, UK 1998.
Morton, H.V., *Atlantic Meeting*, Methuen & Co.Ltd., London, 1943.
Nelson, Hank, *Prisoners of War*, ABC Enterprises, Sydney, Australia, 1985.
Odd Bods UK Ass, *ODD Bods at War 1939-45*, Veritage Press Pty Ltd, Gosford, NSW 2250, Australia
Pfennigwerth, *A Man of Intelligence,* Rosenberg Publishing Pty Ltd, Australia. 2006.
Pitchfork, *Shot Down and in the Drink*, Osprey/Bloomsbury Publishing Plc, UK 2005.
Saunders, Hilary St George, *RAF 1939-45 Vol III The Fight is Won*, HMSO, London 1954.
Terraine, John, *The Right of the Line*, Pen & Sword Books Ltd, Barnsley, UK, 2010.
Time-Life, *Rising Sun*, Time-Life Books, Inc., 1977.

National Archives, Kew, London, UK

AIR 27-149-10 ORB June 1940, No.10 Squadron RAF
AIR 27-1234-15/16 ORB August 1943, No.207 Squadron RAF
AIR 27-678-35/36 ORB September 1943, No.207 Squadron RAF
AIR 27-1928-13 ORB July 1944, No.466 Squadron RAF

Veterans' Accounts

Campbell, Flight Sergeant Keith, OAM.
Chamberlin, Lieutenant J.E. 'Vince'.
Clemens, David.
Craig, Peter.
Durston, Stan, *In Two Death Camps* (Brittingham, and Payne)
Gardner, Allan.
Gingell, Captain W., *The Malaya Campaign 1941-42* (The British Battalion, Reunion Meeting), Ref SHC ESR/3/8/3
Good, Flying Officer Bryan, DFC.
Griffin, David.
Hollings, Wing Commander Albert, DFC.
Keeling, George.
McRae, W.W. 'Bill', DFC AFC, Ld'H
Penny, Group Captain Herert A., OBE.
Sebastian, Guy.
Sommerville, Flying Officer R. 'Bob'.
Wiggins, Wing Commander Lloyd, DSO DFC, No.38 Squadron RAF.

Private Collections

Campbell, Flight Sergeant Keith, OAM.
Chamberlin, Lieutenant J.E. 'Vince' (Diane Capewell)
Clemens, David, and *Clem*, Horseshoe Press, Colchester UK, 1990 (Skilton, Harry).
Craig, Peter, (Tom Ireland).
Davidson, Ian, and Green, Bill, *Escapers All, The Tank Journal*, London, February 1995.
Durston, Stan, *In Two Death Camps* (Brittingham, and Payne, née Durston).
Gardner, Allan, (Rhyll Hansen, née Gardner).
Good, Flying Officer Bryan, DFC (Suellyn Everett).
Hollings, Wing Commander Albert, DFC (Geoff Hollings).
Keeling, George, (Keeling, David, Dist. Professor of Cultural Geography Emeritus, Western Kentucky University).
McRae, W.W. 'Bill', DFC AFC Ld'H. (Sue Templeman, née McRae).
Penny, Group Captain Herbert A., OBE (Nick Penny).
Sebastian, Ivan.
Sommerville, Flying Officer R.'Bob' and French, Squadron Leader John 'Frank' (Lesly Sommerville).

Miscellaneous Sources

Casey, Shane, *'The RAAF at Milne Bay, Wartime'*, Australian War Memorial (jounal), Issue 93 Summer 21.
Changi Prison Museum, Changi, Singapore.
Changi Prison Museum – John Nevell, 2/10th Field Regiment, 8th Division, AIF.
Clowes, Major General Cyril, *The Clowes Report on the Battle for Milne Bay*, Australian Military History Publications, Loftus, NSW, Australia.
Fort Siloso Museum, Singapore.
Gingell, Captain W., private letter, 8 April 1942.
King, and Lubianski, *The Military Service of Major General Willoughby* (monogram).
MacArthur Museum, Brisbane, Australia.
National Museum, Singapore.
National War Museum, Malta.
North Cape Memorial, *'The 1943 Sea Battle by North Cape'*, Nordkapp, Norway.
Pearson, US Naval Cryptologic Veterans Ass.
RAAFA, Sitrep Issue No.25, Australia, June 2023.
Royal Aust Artillery Ass, 80th Anniversary Commemoration, *Battle of Milne Bay.*
Second World War Experience Centre (SWWEC) – https:/war-experience.org
The Final Days, The US Naval Cryptologic Veterans Association, PO Box 16009, Pensacola, Florida, USA.
The Sydney Morning Herald, Obituary *Keith Campbell OAM*, 20 July 2019.
The Wartime Memories Project, https://wartimememoriesproject.com/ww2/view).
Thomas, Governor Sir Shenton, *Diary 1942*, (Fullerton Hotel, Singapore)).
Wikipedia, en.wikipedia.org/wiki/Battle_of_Milne_Bay.
Wikipedia.org/wiki/Douglas_MacArthur.

Note

Every effort has been taken to attribute the final rank obtained to each of the above veterans, their awards and other decorations.

Index

Notes:

1. Every effort has been taken to attribute the appropriate rank as the last known and used in the text, which however, may not be the final rank attained of those mentioned in the index, and to state individuals' awards where known.
2. It has not been possible to research the rank or full name of some participants.

Part 1: Military, Air and Naval Forces

Part 2: General